Between two worlds: science, the environmental
movement, and policy choice

CAMBRIDGE STUDIES IN ENVIRONMENTAL POLICY

The objective of this series is to explore the policy implications arising from our existing scientific knowledge of global problems in environmental management. The books in the series will critically examine the science, and then in the context of political and socio-economic realities, explore how this information can best be used for rational policies of environmental management.

BETWEEN TWO WORLDS

Science, the Environmental Movement, and Policy Choice

LYNTON KEITH CALDWELL
Department of Political Science and
School of Public and Environmental Affairs
Indiana University

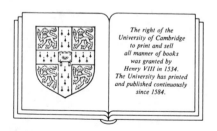

The right of the
University of Cambridge
to print and sell
all manner of books
was granted by
Henry VIII in 1534.
The University has printed
and published continuously
since 1584.

CAMBRIDGE UNIVERSITY PRESS
CAMBRIDGE
NEW YORK   PORT CHESTER   MELBOURNE   SYDNEY

Published by the Press Syndicate of the University of Cambridge
The Pitt Building, Trumpington Street, Cambridge CB2 IRP
40 West 20th Street, New York, NY 10011–4211, USA
10 Stamford Road, Oakleigh, Victoria 3166, Australia

First published 1990
First paperback edition (with corrections) 1992

Printed in Great Britain at the University Press, Cambridge

British Library cataloguing in publication data

Caldwell, Lynton Keith, 1913–
Between two worlds: science, the environmental movement and
political change
1. Environment. Conservation. Implications of
economic development
I. Title
333.7′2

Library of Congress cataloguing in publication data

Caldwell, Lynton Keith, 1913–
Between two worlds: science, the environmental movement, and
political change/Lynton Keith Caldwell.
p. cm.
Includes bibliographical references.
ISBN 0 521 33152 8
1. Environmental policy   2. Man–Influence on nature.   I. Title.
HC79.E5C33   1990
333.7–dc20   89–22313 CIP

ISBN 0 521 33152 8 hardback
ISBN 0 521 33743 7 paperback

CUP

To Helen

Contents

Preface

OUR CHANGING RELATIONSHIP TO EARTH

Although the primary question posed in this book can be answered only in the future, that answer will be forecast by action in the present. Stated simply, the question is: will humans adapt their ways of life to conserve the natural systems upon which their future and the living world depend? Allowing for natural forces beyond human control, today's answer will determine the quality of life that will be possible in tomorrow's world.

Yet the question does not imply a simple answer. Yes or no answers would be indefensible. Inadequate information limits the possibilities of response; unenumerated variables and unforeseeable events make uncertainty inevitable. Even so, choices made today can narrow or expand future options. A critical task for human society today is to reverse trends that narrow those options. In this task science plays a role – essential but sometimes ambivalent. Whatever the intentions of scientists, the understandings made possible through scientific inquiry are altering assumptions and attitudes regarding the effects of human action on the planetary environment. It should be apparent that effective interaction of scientific inquiry with informed citizenry is a condition necessary to an optimal future for life on earth.

From another perspective, this book examines the concept of 'sustainable development,' a phrase which threatens to become a thought-stopping cliché. The intent behind the phrase is rational and necessary to guide the realization of human potential without detriment to the biosphere. It is the dominant theme of *Our Common Future*, a report of the World Commission on Environment and Development (1987). But the expression is very general and is susceptible to a range of interpretations, some of which would allow for a stable but ecologically impoverished world. As with our primary question, the phrase 'sustainable development' is inadequate if read only as a simple proposition. It cannot become a reliable guide to policy until a number of subsidiary questions have been answered. The more important of these questions will be addressed in the following chapters, but basic among them are the following:

(a) What kind of development is consistent with what kind of environment; and how can science clarify the options?

(b) How can science advance human welfare in ways compatible with the integrity, diversity, and continuity of the biosphere?

(c) What beliefs must be abandoned, which values revised, and which institutions changed for man-earth relationships to be sustainable at high levels of economic and environmental quality?

(d) What new attitudes and behaviors must people and their governments be persuaded to adopt that will sustain a world of high economic and environmental quality?

(e) What strategies may be necessary to achieve a human society that will enlarge rather than diminish future options and the quality of life on Earth?

This book does not attempt to answer these questions. Its purpose is to help the reader see their importance for the future of mankind and the biosphere. Answers will require a dedicated and concerted effort by many people – a challenge posed by the World Commission on Environment and Development.

The book attempts an integrated analysis of the interrelationships between science, the environmental movement, and public policy. The focus is on policy – the decisions, agreements, and behaviors of peoples, governments, and international organizations relating to human inter-actions with the biogeochemical systems of the planet. In the human perspective these systems constitute 'the environment' when they are interactive with humans. Environmental policy deals with these interactive relationships only when they arouse popular concern leading toward action. Objects in themselves are not environmental until related to other objects, living or inanimate, that are 'environing' or 'environed'. Understandings of the significance of human-environmental relationships continue to be enlarged by advances in the sciences and their applications, which alter the assumptions, beliefs, options, and ethics of people and ultimately their political behaviors. In this growth lies our best hope for the future.

The word 'policy', which in this book links science with the environmental movement and politics, is not self-defining. It describes a course of action taken, or professed, by governments, groups, or individuals. Derived from the Greek term *polis*, meaning city in a generic sense, policy extends to personal as well as public affairs. The identification of 'a policy' may be ambiguous to the extent that what is professed and what is done, or not done, may be different. An older meaning, implicit in some usages today, is that of 'strategy'. This usage carried a suggestion of purposeful manipulation. Thus strategy may signify a direct and open course of policy or it may serve purposes indirect and opaque, although not necessarily deceptive. Both aspects of strategy may be found in environmental policy.

The term 'polity' has been used to indicate a social arrangement or system for cooperation and decisionmaking. A 'planetary polity' identifies a system for limited governance over mankind's relationship with the biosphere, but it does not imply a world government. The distinction is important; elements of a planetary polity are already in place, whereas world government remains a theoretical and disputed proposition. Limited governance through a planetary policy need not lead to world government. On the contrary, cooperation among people and states in protecting their common life-support base makes safer their pursuit of their separate cultures and values. These political propositions in no way depreciate concern for non-human life, but its future, as never before, depends upon human behavior guided by belief about man's changing relationship to the living earth.

Only in recent decades has social concern for environmental relationships assumed the character of a political 'movement' – a concept that will require clarification later in this book. The relationship of the environmental movement to public policy and to science is complex, sometimes paradoxical, and, in general, poorly understood. The social phenomenon called 'environmentalism' is treated here as an accentuated aspect of a larger and broadly diversified public concern, the focus and degree of which varies widely among groups and individuals. It should be distinguished from the use of this term to categorize theories of geographical determinism that were influential a half-century ago. There is, nevertheless, a conceptual linkage between those earlier theories and contemporary interpretations of man-environment relationships. Environmental activism sometimes appears to be also an indirect manifestation of other discontents. To understand the response of governments to environmental issues it is therefore necessary to comprehend the various and often contradictory aspects of the environmental movement, and to appreciate the role of science in changing perceptions of mankind's relationship with the planet Earth.

The environmental movement, broadly conceived, breaks with many assumptions and values that have dominated modern history. With due recognition of its paradoxes and contradictions and the often ambiguous role of science in its advancement, the aggregate character of the environmental movement is that of a social force attempting to shape the world future. A major influence in this progression is the growth in scope and depth of scientific knowledge regarding the planet and its natural systems. Nearly every science contributes to this growth of knowledge which, when related to human experience, values, and ethics, may lead to fundamental changes in perceptions of humanity's circumstances and possible futures. Such changes have influenced the course of national politics and international relations, and have been evident in inter-relationships between science and religion.

The objective of this book implies an effort toward synthesis. To integrate seemingly disparate but actually related bodies of data, and to attain a coherent focused outcome, careful structuring of the text is required. To these ends the book is divided into three major divisions in which the organizing themes are: I Comprehending the planet Earth, II Developing a planetary paradigm and III An emerging planetary polity. Attention is given especially to the interactions of environmentalism and science in generating public and international environmental policies. Three chapters within each section approximate a quasi-dialectic sequence of *cause – effect –* and *policy consequence*. The book concludes with a postscript, which summarizes the place of environmentalism in the modern world in relation to future prospects.

Nearly twenty years have passed since, in an essay for the Scientists' Institute for Public Information (New York), I wrote that the confrontation of modern society with the limitations of its environment had created a 'A Crisis of Will and Rationality'. That crisis has not passed and appears to have deepened. But an important distinction should be drawn between a crisis of mentality and morality, induced by recognition of conflict between human behavior and planetary realities, and the climacteric which characterizes the present relationship between modern society and the natural world. This relationship has come about independently of human perception or intention; it is manifest in the environmental problems of resource depletion, pollution and overpopulation. The crisis lies not in the changing circumstances of mankind's planetary relationships, but in human responses.

Reconciliation of man with nature and the achievement of a sustainable economy within the biosphere now appears more difficult and more necessary today than it did two decades ago. Resistance to 'environ-mentalism' has grown with growing realization that safeguarding the biosphere and humanity's future will require far-reaching changes in personal and institutional behavior – in expectations and priorities. Recognition that this is a world of limits as well as opportunities strikes at the cherished belief that whatever mankind can imagine, mankind can do.

In response to changing and differing perceptions of man's place on Earth, the environmental movement has proceeded along more than one course of action. One choice has been to accept the political and economic realities of the times and work for mediation and compromise with the techno-economic forces engaged in environmental transformation and resource development. Many of the large-membership environmental organizations, or at least their leaderships, have taken this option, especially in the United States. Accommodation and persuasion are the strategies pursued. Another option has been guerrilla warfare against ecologically destructive forces within the economic system and even against the system itself as incurably destructive. A third option, and perhaps the most promising, is to enlarge, refine, and extend public understanding of environmental issues and their significance. The goal of this option is a new view or paradigm of life on Earth leading to implied changes in human behavior and public policies. Its strategy is to transcend the now dominant ethos, replacing it with one more valid and hence more sustainable. Psychologically, this may be the more difficult route to pursue, but is the one most likely to have a lasting, value-shaping influence on political choice. The advancement of international environmental education promoted through UNEP, UNESCO, IUCN, WWF, and the International Environmental Education Association, among many other organized efforts, is fundamental to this purpose and may be our best cause for hope.

In summation, *Between two worlds* addresses the changing relationship of mankind's world to nature's Earth. The change is a consequence of interactions between population growth, technological advancement, scientific discovery, and a rising consciousness throughout society that the world of the historical past cannot persist into the changing conditions of the future. We are today in a historical discontinuity – in effect – wandering between the modern world of the past half-millenium and a different world which must be created if civilization, and perhaps humanity, is to survive. Our transition is marked by confusion and paradox, for we have no road-map to guide us into the future.

At issue is the possibility of attaining the ideal of a harmonious, productive, and sustainable society of man-in-biosphere. The issue is fundamentally one of an informed ethics and morality. It is also an issue of rationality. Differing versions of what is reasonable are presently in conflict. In this contention the role of science is crucial, for through tested knowledge it may be possible to ascertain more nearly the approximate truth regarding the consequences of human behavior in the biosphere, and this knowledge may affect beliefs in what is necessary and reasonable. There are few if any certainties in this confrontation, but *if* humanity does surmount this crisis of will and rationality and attain a new and higher level of behavior in relation to the biosphere, a higher level of civilization will also have been achieved.

Acknowledgements

A book of this character is obviously indebted to hundreds of scholars without whose ideas and investigations it could never have been written. The work of some is acknowledged, both in the references and throughout the text, many more remain unacknowledged, but not unappreciated. Appreciation is also owed to the many agencies and individuals who provided information and materials in response to my requests.

In the actual production of the book specific indebtedness should be acknowledged: to my wife Helen who endured my preoccupation with its preparation, and was a sympathetic but discerning critic, to Nicholas Polunin who conceived the idea of the book and the associated series, to the editorial committee who reviewed my initial proposal, to Thomas Malone and to William C. Clark for helpful suggestions, and to Robert V. Bartlett who critiqued the initial draft of the manuscript.

Appreciation is also due to the Department of Political Science and the School of Public Affairs at Indiana University for logistical assistance, and to Carol Fischer and Jennifer Mitchner for producing the typescript. The professional competence and dedication of the libraries at Indiana University were indispensable to the preparation of the work, and very special thanks belong to the Reference Department, the Government Publications Department, and to the Library of the School of Public and Environmental Affairs.

PART I

Comprehending the planet Earth

The planet is not yet a center of rational loyalty for all mankind.
René Dubos and Barbara Ward (1972) *Only one Earth*. New York: Norton, 220

Until early modern times, in mid-seventeenth century, human perceptions of the Earth and mankind's environmental relationships were largely intuitive. Empirical observation could go no further than experience and the available methods, instruments, and modes of inquiry permitted. Experience had been limited by restricted human mobility and by the shortness of human life in relation to changes wrought by human impact upon the environment. The growth of science, slow at first, accelerating in the nineteenth and twentieth centuries, increasingly revealed hitherto unperceived relationships among humans and their environments. Evidence of adverse consequences of human action, joined with scientific explanation, led to recognition of the human predicament and to the gradual emergence of a new view of mankind's role on earth. Astronautic venture into outer space provided the first views of the whole planet Earth in the infinity of the cosmos. This vision became a powerful catalyst of environmental consciousness and a symbol for the environmental movement.

The United Nations Conference on the Human Environment (1972) was a watershed event in human relationships with the Earth. The conference epigram 'Only One Earth' symbolized a change in human perceptions that would become a new factor in the development of ethics and in the evaluation of alternatives in policies affecting the environment. That process of attitudinal change, although visible, has not yet become a compelling force in political choice. Even so, a planetary perspective is growing throughout the world and has already induced at least rhetorical commitment from governments in the United Nations World Charter for Nature (Burhenne & Irwin, 1983).

Throughout this process science has played a critical role. At least in

I

modern Western society, traditional assumptions have been undercut by scientific findings respecting many aspects of life. But science is providing a new though partial view of life on Earth and the place of humanity within it. The emerging concept of the biosphere as a self-organizing, self-maintaining, life-giving system reaffirms the intuition of ancient people who, without science, lived intimately with nature and whose brains, it seems were as fully developed as our own. Far beyond our present science remains the ultimate mystery of life and cosmos. We begin to see the immaturity of our boasted 'conquest of nature', and to understand that our very survival as a species depends upon a profound respect for the creation to which we belong.

I
Science and environment

Readers of this book may be helped by an explanation at the outset of how its thesis progresses. The book serves two related purposes which have influenced its structure. It introduces a series of books on the sciences of the environment, and it offers an interpretation of the roles of science and the environmental movement in the historical transition now changing the world. To lay a foundation for these purposes, a consideration of basic concepts is needed. The following three chapters address this need, interpreting the meanings of *science, environment, policy,* and *biosphere* to enable readers more easily to follow the argument developed in the subsequent chapters. Persons familiar with the environmental sciences may move rapidly through Part I to the development of the historical thesis, beginning with Part II. To have moved directly to the heart of this thesis at the outset would have left many readers unprepared to benefit fully from this and subsequent volumes in the series.

We begin, therefore, with three basic questions. First, why has mankind's environmental future become a question of policy? Second, why must this question be answered through politics? And third, how has science influenced the environmental choices and alternatives that confront humanity?

The cultural aspect of human behavior is pertinent to all three questions. Beyond basic biological factors, collective human behavior is organized and directed through culture, which is developed through social learning and which determines social response to the challenges and opportunities of the environment. Science, as an aspect of culture, has greatly expanded the scope of human possibilities and the ability to estimate probable consequences. Nearly all aspects of applied science now have world-wide implications and, to obtain their benefits without

3

liabilities, deliberate and informed choices must be made. Human decisions with respect to energy utilization, population dynamics, natural resources and powerful new technologies are inherently collective in their applications and effects. The choices are ultimately social, often political, and may be more than the sum of individual preferences. Only through processes of governance (in a generic sense, which includes more than political government), are people able to guide or control their collective environmental behaviors. Transactions between humans and the natural world are unlike those between people. Social consensus, implicit or explicit, governs what individuals may do, but the possibilities inherent in nature determine what may be done. Not all human preferences are realizable in the real world; possibilities are not infinite, and basic relationships between man and nature are not negotiable. Nature does not bargain, and the biosphere is not a marketplace.

Science has become a major manageable factor in the human environment. Its role is too important to be left to inadvertence, and clearly it is not being left to chance. How science is developed and applied will be a major determining factor in mankind's environmental future. The environmental impacts of human behavior, increasingly impelled by developments in science, are now seen to have planetary implications. Their effects are expressed in changes in the air, water, soil, biota, and ecosystems, some of which benefit but some endanger the environmental future. To safeguard that future and to realize beneficial options, governance in some form, transnational in reach, has become a necessary instrument of policy. Thus, although the unpredictable is always latent in human affairs, the growth of scientific knowledge appears to have made the future of mankind on earth in large measure a matter of deliberate political choice.

Human attitudes and beliefs about the relationship between man and earth form paradigms within which environmental policies are developed. Since the seventeenth century, and especially during the twentieth century, science has altered beliefs and caused changes in mankind's cosmic paradigm – the accepted explanation of how nature works and mankind's relationship to nature. In recent years this relationship has become increasingly critical and problematic. Social concern has been expressed through the environmental movement, in which science and government have been brought together to address questions of policy regarding mankind's environmental future.

The development of environmental policy has been ad hoc and opportunistic. It has been responsive to perceived crises, influenced by events and personalities, unguided at its outset by a coherent philosophy. Yet beneath its seemingly chaotic disjunctive progress there may be fundamental and even determining forces at work. Human society may be moving to a stage at which basic changes in the situation of man on earth necessitate changes in attitudes. Science opens new opportunities, but human preemption of the earth through population and technology has removed forever many options. There are no new lands to exploit, and natural abundance is no longer generally free for the taking.

The environmental movement may thus be understood as a response to a growing realization that relationships of man to earth need to move from the immature, rapacious, exuberance of earlier times to a more comprehending, sober, and conserving view of the future. Mankind may be beginning to 'come of age'. We have no guarantee, however, that humanity will reach maturity. Yet the human mind has shown its ability to respond to environmental necessities. If, as I believe, the environmental movement proceeds as if it were an evolutionary force moving the human species into a mature and sustainable relationship with nature, it may decisively shape the future, even though not all its efforts may be achieved (Boulding, 1981). But before we move to our principal theme, the process through which we will approach it requires attention.

CONCEPTUAL FOUNDATION

It is a paradox of science that scientific method alone is insufficient to interpret science. Science is a human invention and a cultural artifact. Books about science (such as this one) are not intended to be regarded as scientific, even though their arguments may be firmly based on scientific evidence. These books draw upon history and philosophy and may have (as this book has) a prophetic quality. Science, as an evolving enterprise, has no way to determine its place in human experience. To place science in context, one must look beyond science to somehow envision a course or trajectory of history along which humanity moves from past to future. This objective may be unattainable, yet something about the human mind causes humans to pursue it.

Much of the writing about science and environment is handicapped by ambiguity; words have different meanings for different readers. 'Science' is often used in an abstract sense, inclusive of several different meanings. Scientists often give 'science' their own special meaning, which is narrower than general usage. 'Environment' is even more difficult to define with precision; scientific and popular meanings may differ significantly. There is a general tendency to identify *environment* with *things* – including forces – whereas the term actually signifies *relationships*.

It is clear that science, in the sense of enlarged and tested knowledge, is changing the perception of human relationships to the earth. This change is progressing unevenly within societies and throughout the world; thus perceptual differences account for much of the controversy over environmental policy. The findings of science joined to direct experience have led to popular concern for environmental conditions and relationships reaching the proportions of a socio-ethical movement. But the movement is more disparate than coherent – a characteristic to be expected in times of conceptual change. Probabilistic pronouncements of scientists regarding environmental trends are frequently given popular interpretations which scientists regard as erroneous, causing some scientists to view the popular environmental movement with ambivalence.

Even so, public concern for environmental conditions, expressed through organization, legislation, and funding for research, has had a significant impact upon science as an enterprise. The environmental focus for scientific inquiry demonstrates the ultimate unity of the subject matter of science. No other area of human concern has drawn a greater diversity of scientific disciplines into the service of a developing field of policy nor offered greater occasion for development of inter-disciplinary collaboration. The reciprocal influences of science and the environmental movement are affecting the course of history, unobtrusively but nonetheless fundamentally.

Writings on policy for environmental science and technology are too often deficient in conceptual clarity because the writers have neglected to specify their terms of reference. Definitions may be tedious, but are necessary where failure to define may result in fundamental misunderstandings. The term 'environmental science' now in common usage, is not self-defining. Neither the words 'environmental' nor 'science' have single unequivocal meanings. 'Science' may mean knowledge or it may mean method; one reads, for example, about the findings of science and also about the scientific method. 'Science' is used to designate a profession or the professional activities of persons called 'scientists.' The word 'science' is too large and complex a concept to be defined concisely (George, 1970). Conventional definitions of science, as John Ziman (1984) observes, 'tend to emphasize quite different features, depending upon the point of view.' Summing up his introduction to the social study of science he writes:

It is indeed the product of research; it does employ characteristic methods; it is a body of organized knowledge; it is a means of solving problems. It is also a social institution; it needs material facilities; it is an education theme; it is a cultural resource; it requires to be managed; it is a major factor in human affairs. Our 'model' of science must relate and reconcile these diverse and sometimes contradictory aspects.[1]

The concept 'environment' is hardly less complex. The fundamental meaning of environment is relativistic; it denotes a relationship between a particular object and all that surrounds and directly or indirectly affects it. In common usage, however, objects environed are often unspecified or assumed to be of common knowledge. For example, in many books and articles about the earth's atmospheric or oceanic environments it seems implicit that mankind is the object environed. But in some science perspectives, objects other than humans are the focus of environmental concern. The atmosphere, for example, may be regarded as a major part of the environment of the oceans. A large part of the literature of ecology does not concern human-environmental relationships. In scientific, as well as ordinary usage, 'environment' is often applied directly to the properties, characteristics, or activities of specific entities or phenomena, with hardly more than tacit recognition of the interactive relationships which give them environmental significance. 'Milieu' is the term more appropriate to designate these entities. As physiologist Claude Bernard (1865) made clear, the human environment is both within and without the human body. The metabolic processes of life involve constant interrelating and interchange with the exterior environment. If people considered this circumstance seriously environmentalism might be the attitudinal norm.

The environmental relationship is thus often neglected in concentration on the environing objects. This selective focus may sometimes be consistent with, and even necessary for, scientific investigation. But where human behaviors, attitudes, values, and institutions are factors, the scope of inquiry must be broadened to take full account of their environmental connections. Thus environmental science tends to be multidisciplinary in character and a collaborative rather than a singular enterprise.

Environmental relationships may, of course, be investigated over a wide range of levels, from the sub-atomic to the cosmic. But the principal focus of 'environmental science' in this book is on relationships between humans (notably their organizations), and other living species and the biogeological systems within which they live. The life-supporting systems of the biosphere constitute the larger subject component of environmental science. But its concern extends to the cosmic environment from which the earth receives those energizing forces which make life on earth possible. The anthropogenic forces intermediating human-planetary relationships have already been referred to as 'cultural.' Conventional uses of the terms 'culture' and 'environment' often fail to acknowledge that all culture exists within and in relationship to a natural environment. Thus man exists within a seamless web of life within which all relationships are in some ways environmental (Storer, 1954).

ENVIRONMENTAL SCIENCE

The foregoing discussion of 'meanings' is no more than a caution against unexamined assumptions in dealing with the uses of science in environmental affairs. As with an acronym, 'environmental science' is a convenient substitute for a comprehensive but cumbersome definition. It should not be taken as a precise term, and its introduction in the 1960s was not welcomed by all scientists (Klopsteg, 1966; Etzioni, 1970; Schindler, 1976).

Would clarity and precision be gained were we to speak of 'sciences of the environment'? This seems unlikely. What sciences would be excluded? Not all science or scientific knowledge pertains directly to environmental relationships, yet there are environmental implications in all major sciences. It is those aspects of scientific knowledge and method applied to understanding relationships between a thing environed and whatever environs it that may properly be called environmental science or the sciences of the environment. Much, but not all, of the substance of the sciences is involved (National Science Board, 1971; NASA, 1988).

Environmental science provides a way to learn about these relationships, but it is not a discrete discipline such as geology, chemistry, physics, or biology which have themselves become increasingly diversified. Understanding environmental relationships requires a synthesis of many aspects of knowledge. For example, biogeochemical cycles are fundamental in a great variety of environmental relationships. How to prevent their disruption by humans involves, in addition to the 'natural' sciences and engineering, inputs from the social and behavioral sciences, economics, law, and ethics.

The sciences that advance understanding of biogeochemical relationships are essential to understanding the various environmental aspects of agriculture, forestry, nutrition, health, and ecosystem protection, and to the resolution of such problems as acidic deposition and CO_2 build-up in the atmosphere. Much of the data and understandings that result from multidisciplinary scientific research are ultimately synthesized into interdisciplinary concepts that may be regarded as the distinctive substance of environmental science and technology. The environmental content of some sciences is so considerable and their dependence upon inputs from other sciences so extensive that they may be regarded for some purposes as 'environmental sciences,' although not all of the research undertaken in their disciplines is directly environmental. Such sciences would include agronomy, anthropology, botany, ecology, geography, microbiology, paleontology, meteorology, and zoology, among others. To the extent that a body of knowledge and method can be identified as syncretic environmental science, it might more accurately be regarded as a metadiscipline, a level of research and teaching that incorporates elements from other disciplines yet is more than the sum of its parts (Caldwell, 1983).

Findings of scientific research may be environment-related and yet not in themselves be properly identifiable as environmental science. For example, the thermodynamics of the atmosphere may prove highly relevant to weather patterns and also to avionics. Yet the researchers in this field of physical science might not think of themselves as environmental scientists; nor might geologists investigating the properties of rock formation, although their findings might be environmentally significant. For example, knowledge of the properties of certain rock and its behavior under shock could have an important bearing upon urban planning decisions. Certain areas of the city of Anchorage in Alaska were totally demolished in the great earthquake of 1964 as a consequence of a predictable collapse of underlying rock formations.

Studies in sociology and psychology frequently have environmental aspects that extend beyond the immediate context of those studies and point toward more general conclusions regarding human-environmental relationships. Relevant behavioral studies may not always deal with human subjects. For example, the research of Dr John B. Calhoun (1963) on the sociology and ecology of the Norway rat produced findings regarding the effects of social and physical environmental circumstances upon this species that was suggestive of lines of inquiry that ought to be made respecting humans and other forms of animal life. Indeed, enough work has now been done to permit a few guarded generalizations on relationships between the behavior of animals and the structure of their environments. Kurt Lewin and his followers (Barker, 1968), developed a school of environmental or ecological psychology that has not only helped us to understand the ways in which people perceive their environments, but also to explain what difference those perceptions make in their attitudes and behaviors (Lynch, 1960). Ethologists have made comparable studies regarding other animal species (Klopfer & Hailman, 1967; Johnston & Pietrewiez, 1985).

Environmental science and technology provide materials and methods for constructing a bridge between the basic sciences and public policy. Among its functions, environmental science assembles and processes data from a broad range of basic sciences for application to a variety of environmental problems. In this process, gaps and inconsistencies in scientific information may be discovered. These discoveries may contribute to advancements in several basic sciences by revealing hitherto unrecognized problems or by suggesting new relationships among existing fields of knowledge. In response to the argument that science specialists know their own fields better than anyone else and do not need the help of outsiders, it may be conceded that concentration on a narrow field of investigation to the exclusion of its broader context may often be necessary for the advancement of science and yet it should also be recognized that to ignore the broader context of investigation may risk missing data essential to the narrower inquiry. Specialists are not always aware of the implications of their own work, and may fail to take cognizance of some part of their subject which they otherwise know very well (Radnitzky, 1987).

ECOLOGY AND ENVIRONMENT

There is a science, however, that in substance is distinctively and thoroughly environmental. It is the science of ecology, which has been defined as the study of organisms in relation to one another and to their surroundings. A relatively recent science, its complex and dynamic character, and its frequent dependence upon investigations in other sciences have slowed its advance. To understand many ecological processes and relationships, observation over extended periods of time has proved necessary. Funding and personal commitment for ecological studies over the time required has not always been easily obtained.

Acceptance of ecology as a valid and reliable scientific discipline was long resisted by some of the more conservative scientists. A distinguished microbiologist, Dr René Dubos, whose writings did much to win acceptance of ecology as a valid scientific discipline found, when he began to direct attention to this branch of science, that among many of his colleagues it was preferable to speak of environmental biology and to avoid reference to what was regarded as a dubious pseudoscience. Some science conservatives regarded ecology as little more than an effort to put a scientific gloss on 'nature study.' Students of ecology undertook to make their nascent discipline more scientific by subdividing it into special areas of investigation. The greater part of earlier ecological studies concerned non-human living systems. This emphasis was offset by some biologists and social scientists through efforts to develop a field of 'human ecology', and an international society was formed to advance work in this sub-field.

The term 'ecology' has acquired a wide range of meanings, not all of which pertain to science. There are differences among scientists, as well as among members of the public, regarding whether ecology should be prescriptive as well as descriptive. The findings of ecology frequently have implications for human behavior, and opinions differ over the extent to which ecologists should become advocates for the policies which their findings may suggest.

For example, scientific opinion has divided on the appropriate way to approach the problem of endangered species. One group has advocated artificial breeding under protected conditions to insure survival of a diminished stock; another believes that the fate of species, in so far as is possible, should be left to natural processes with no human interference. The latter group argues that if a species is unable to survive in the competition of the natural world its extinction, although regrettable, ought not to be prevented by human intervention. But of course it was often human behavior rather than 'nature' that has threatened extinction, and this behavior may be changed by human protective intervention. The 'let nature take its course' argument is seldom extended to members of the human species and almost never extended without substantial reservations. In 'advanced' modern societies protection is provided, often at considerable costs, for persons who would otherwise fail to survive. Yet little real protection has been provided for 'primitive' people, their culture, or their environments, endangered by encroachments from modern society. Studies in human ecology appear to have had very little influence upon public policy.

As previously noted, ecology as a term and concept has been adopted by the behavioral and (to a lesser extent) by the social sciences; ecological anthropology and ecological psychology are recognized fields of scientific inquiry. The role of ecology in science has been further complicated by extension of the word 'ecology' to a philosophy of nature and to a form of rationality (Bartlett, 1986; Dryzek, 1987). Ecological thinking and behaving are not 'scientific' although influenced by scientific ecology. Deep ecology postulated that the environment will not be protected without fundamental changes in social values and economic institutions. It is a socio-ethical perspective with distinctive political implications (Naess, 1973; Devall & Sessions, 1985; Sessions 1981).

The extension and transformation of ecological concepts is one of our more clearly defined instances of the popular spill-over effects of science. Unlike the essentially reductionist disciplines, the integrative and synthesizing characteristics of ecology preclude its confinement within conventional science. Having escaped the confines of life-science methodology, ecology as a way of seeing and understanding the world has moved through the social sciences and humanities to philosophy, to religion, and to politics.

The natural scientists have lost control of the term 'ecology', but that 'loss' is not a real loss to science, and provides a popular receptivity to the findings of scientific ecology that might not otherwise exist. The genie of ecology could not be contained in the bottle of science. Its escape into the public domain has had disturbing effects upon many attitudes and interests. With good reason it has been called 'the subversive science' (Shepard & McKinley, 1969; Hardin, 1969). More than any other field of knowledge ecological science drives the environmental movement regardless of the wishes or intentions of ecologists. Philosophical ecology has taken on a life of its own, and its values and goals may not necessarily be those with which all scientists would agree.

THE ROLE OF SCIENTISTS

Science as knowledge and method should be distinguished from the role of individual scientists in environmental policy. We will return presently to the influence of science; the case of ecology shows that it may be more than 'scientific'. Here, the role of scientists requires comment. Contention among scientists over the validity and reliability of environmental science or ecology is to some extent another version of the old controversy over the respective merits of 'pure' or 'basic' as contrasted with so-called 'applied' science. A reaction against the growth of environmental science seems to have been signaled in the United States in the National Academy of Sciences in 1980 when the recommendations of a committee appointed to forecast directions for the Academy during the ensuing decade were rejected by its membership in favor of a return to a more conservative view of 'legitimate' science.

It is not difficult to see how the system of recognition and rewards in the sciences favors achievement in basic sciences and in specialization. Nobel prizes are customarily awarded for discovery, for additions to the fund of scientific knowledge of specifics not hitherto known or understood. Contributions to the advancement of science that largely involve the restructuring of existing knowledge and the identification of hitherto unperceived relationships may also be rewarded, but achievements of this kind are more difficult to evaluate and are less often attributable to a particular individual or even to a single identifiable group. The moral for ambitious scientists who aspire to prizes and recognition is: stick to reductionist basics and avoid temptations to advance scientific knowledge through interdisciplinary syntheses.

There is an important distinction to be recognized between the role of science in the environmental movement and the roles of scientists in environmental politics. Science, understood as fact or theory, has an influence independent of the personalities or opinions of particular scientists. There are, of course, exceptions exemplified by Newton, Darwin, or Einstein, when the scientist and his work appear inseparable. Where a general science consensus exists regarding the nature and evolution of the planet, its systems of living species, and conditions affecting their survival, public opinion tends to accept generalizations and largely disregards differences among scientists over details. From cumulating findings of science emerges a popular perception of the earth and its rhythms that becomes the prevailing picture of terrestrial reality.

Science, as popularly understood, has proved to be an involuntary driving force behind the environmental movement. This is partly because, through science, cause-effect relationships are revealed and the consequences of present trends projected. But popular understanding often overlooks the reservations and qualifications upon which many scientists insist. It is probable that there are few general propositions in science upon which all scientists, without qualification, agree. And scientists, hardly less than other people, may merge their biases or preferences with idiosyncratic views of reality and truth (Goleman, 1987). So, for almost every environmental policy, statute, or regulation, there will be scientists who approve, and others who disapprove. Unlike scientists, public policymakers must ultimately arrive at some generally acceptable decision on environmental questions.

Some scientists object, in principle, to the general public and its political representatives arriving at conclusions or advocating opinions which, in their view, would be much better left to scientists. Their assumption appears to be that when sufficient evidence is available (often a point of doubt) scientists will inform the public. Yet in science all propositions are subject to challenge and revision; all evidence may never be available and new evidence may change prior assumptions. Legislative and judicial authorities, however, have less tolerance for tentativeness, and public policies require a greater degree of stability and assumed veracity than a scientific audience would find reasonable for a scientific conclusion. And so although the public looks to science and to scientists for guidance in shaping environmental policies, political choice among scientific propositions is more often sociological than scientific. Although science may provide a major input into environmental decisionmaking, it does not itself determine the decision.

Nevertheless, environmental policy decisions often depend heavily upon demonstrable scientific evidence; and so research is a necessary component of environmental policy. Resources for research, however generous, are limited. Hence public anxiety over particular issues requiring scientific investigation may have a preemptive effect upon research priorities. This has been notoriously true in medicine and hardly less for the environment. Although scientists often say that 'good' science cannot be obtained by 'telling scientists what to study,' there is ample evidence that money and facilities for research attract science talent and that where research support is absent, little research is done. Funds for scientific research have increased greatly in recent decades, but the costs of research in certain fields have grown disproportionately, for example in the construction and operation of atomic accelerators and super-colliders to study the basic structure of matter, or in the technology of orbiting laboratories for geophysical and astronomical research, or for the mapping of human genes.

Scientists must compete for research support not only within the funds allocated to science generally, but on behalf of science as against other and growing demands in society for social, medical, developmental, and military expenditures. For many scientists, the arrival of an environmental agenda for research was not welcome. For some there was a perceived threat of additional competition for limited resources; others denigrated research on environmental problems as 'applied' rather than basic science. The interdisciplinary approach required for attack upon many environmental problems has been viewed with skepticism by many science specialists. Research needed to develop a safe and sustainable energy regime has been frustrated in part by reticence of scientists to commit to a field of inquiry in which the social science disciplines and law would necessarily be involved.

The methodologies dominant in modern science have been reductionist, calling for specializations in depth. In contrast, environmental research, although possibly reductionist in incremental detail, has also sought integration in breadth, as in ecosystems research. Environmental problem-solving characteristically requires a synthesis of diverse sciences in which the experts themselves may not always be in agreement. Analysis of the environmental impacts of public policy proposals has been dismissed by some critics as making for 'bad science' – political considerations intruding (Schindler, 1976). Yet comprehensive and unprejudiced studies of environmental impact assessment do not support allegations of 'bad science,' although the state of knowledge has not always been adequate to the task (Caldwell, 1982; Carpenter, 1976, 1983).

In addition to methodological and theoretical objections to certain aspects of environmental research, hostility to the environmental movement has derived from self-serving interests of some industrial and development-mission government scientists. The professional and economic interests of scientists and engineers employed in industrial or agricultural production may be threatened by the standards and restrictions sought by environmentalists and consumer-advocates. Loyalty to employers and belief in the significance of their missions and technologies has led some scientists to become outspoken opponents of the environmental movement. Their views are shared by some university scientists who see in the growth of environmental investigation declining support for their own interests and the drawing of talent away from basic research.

These considerations suggest why the role of scientists in the environmental movement may be regarded as ambivalent. Scientists, individually and in groups, have taken major leadership roles in the environmental movement and many of them may be readily identified in the environmental literature. Their personal roles of leadership and reinforcement have been indispensable to the direction and credibility of the environmental movement. More fundamental to the movement, however, has been the influence of scientific knowledge on popular assumptions and perceptions. Even the findings of scientists who have been doubtful regarding the rationality of 'environmentalism' may add to the sum of knowledge underlying environmental concern.

INSTITUTIONALIZING ENVIRONMENTAL SCIENCE

The foregoing observations explain some of the difficulties encountered in the application of scientific knowledge to environmental aspects of human society. In principle, there is wide acceptance among the public as well as the community of scientists that it would be desirable for scientific knowledge to advance understanding of mankind's environmental relationships. There would be advantages to human health, welfare, economic wellbeing, and aesthetic satisfactions from the growth of such knowledge. But agreement is less general on how this desirable objective might be accomplished or what policy commitments, institutional arrangements, and financial allocations would be required to obtain it.

Institutional arrangements for the development and application of environmental science vary greatly. A comprehensive survey of what environment-related research is done and by whom could fill a large book. Strategies for the application of knowledge to environmental problem-solving have been described in case studies prepared for the United States National Research Council Committee on the Applications of Ecological Theory to Environmental Problems (1986). Scientific institutions for environmental research have been established by the governments of leading industrial societies, in universities, and in independent and industrial research laboratories. Because of legal requirements and popular expectations, industrial research and development has increasingly been forced to test new products and techniques before their release into the public domain. This trend has enlarged opportunities for environment-related scientific research, but voluntary research efforts (not associated with particular political or economic interests) have found funding difficult to obtain.

In the United States during the upsurge of environmental consciousness in the late 1960s and early 1970s a number of proposals were made to establish politically independent institutes or research centers for the advancement of ecological science and environmental studies. An

environmental research institute was even proposed for the government of
the United States and endorsed by President Richard Nixon in his message
on the environment, February 8, 1971. There were proposals to turn the
US National Laboratories, initially concerned largely with problems of
energy, into environmental laboratories. In 1971 a group of scientists
associated with the Ecological Society of America undertook to establish a
nongovernmental Institute of Ecology. It survived through various
vicissitudes for more than a decade until 1984 when it was at last
disbanded. Other national proposals never reached the point of implementation. Meanwhile mission-related environmental research has
been carried on by various federal units, notably by the Environmental
Protection Agency.

Application of science to environmental problems is provided in some
measure in nearly all modern countries, usually through governmental
sponsorship and frequently related to public health or physical planning.
The arrangements, however, are too diverse for useful classification.
Among countries comparability is the exception, diversity the norm. For
example, in Great Britain, the Nature Conservancy Council, established in
1949 by royal charter, has provided advice on the protection of natural
reserves and has sponsored related scientific research and services; a wider
range of scientific research is sponsored or undertaken through the
Department of the Environment, and the Department of Education and
Science, among other ministries and commissions. Summary descriptions
of the environmental programs and organizations at the governmental
level in member states of the European Community is provided by the
European Environmental Yearbook. Milan: DocTer Institute for Environmental Studies (Cutrera, 1987).

An obvious reason for organizational diversity is the diversified character
of national environments, socio-political as well as national. The variety of
institutional arrangements for environmental science reinforces the
assertion that 'environment' is not just another sector of public policy
comparable to justice, education, health or urbanization, but is contextual
to all sectors, each of which presents special sets of environmental
relationships.

International arrangements for environmental research are also
characterized by diversity. During the months preparatory to the United
Nations Conference on the Human Environment in 1972, some scientists
associated with the International Council of Scientific Unions (Scientific
Committee on Problems of the Environment [SCOPE]), proposed the
establishment of an international environmental research center. This idea
was not supported by scientists with conservative views of science in the
Council nor was it accepted by governments. The preferred vehicle for
ICSU-sponsored research continues to be multidisciplinary committees for

particular investigations, most recently the International Geosphere-Biosphere Programme (IGBP).

A successful effort on an international basis for institutionalizing environmental science has been the UNESCO-sponsored Man and the Biosphere (MAB) program (Batisse, 1980, 1982). This effort grew out of the Biosphere Conference, held in Paris in 1968, and which has generated international collaborative research and environmental protection in more than a hundred countries. MAB has sponsored an international network of protected natural areas or biosphere reserves, numbering 266 in 70 countries as of 1987. These reserves represent various types of ecosystems and serve as control points in the monitoring and measurement of ecological change. They provide a valuable resource for research in the International Geosphere-Biosphere Programme, and for public understanding and appreciation (Kellert, 1986).

The United Nations Environment Programme sponsors collaborative research-related activities that supplement the very limited UNEP funds with those of other international organizations and participating countries. There are numerous environment-related information research programs that are regional in scope, especially for tropical ecology. For example, the Latin American cooperative network Intersciencia, the Tropical Science Center in Costa Rica, the International Centre for Tropical Ecology in Venezuela or the Netherlands based Tropenobos Programme relating to tropical forests, the International Council for Research in Agroforestry in Kenya, and the Centre for Scientific Information and Documentation in Tropical Ecology in Cameroon.

As previously noted, in most modern governments environmental research units have been established in departments and ministries with natural resource development, agricultural, health, and environmental protection missions. Administrators and scientists in these units have usually objected to any central or coordinative environmental research agency that might diminish their domains or autonomy. Moreover, mission-oriented research is characteristically structured to support limited agency goals and programs, and thus risks addressing only part instead of the whole of an environmental problem. A need to match the scope of environmental research to the dimensions of the problem continues to be emphasized by some scientists, and by students of environmental policy, but resistance to this concept continues although diminishing in the face of growing threats to the global environment, e.g. climatic change.

The potential influence of government and public policy on scientific research relating to the environment may be illustrated by the experience of the United States. During the initial phase of governmental response to the environmental movement in the United States, the Congress adopted the National Environmental Policy Act of 1969 (NEPA) in which Section

102 (2) of Title I of the Act imposed obligations upon the federal executive and independent administrative agencies that could only be fulfilled by recourse to scientific information and research (Caldwell, 1982). Section 102 of NEPA 'authorizes and directs that, to the fullest extent possible: (1) the policies, regulations and public laws of the United States shall be interpreted and administered in accordance with the policies set forth in the Act, and (2) all agencies of the Federal Government shall:

(A) utilize a systematic, interdisciplinary approach which will insure the integrated use of the natural and social sciences and the environmental design arts in planning and in decisionmaking which may have an impact on man's environment;

(B) identify and develop methods and procedures, in consultation with the Council on Environmental Quality established by Title II of this Act, which will insure that presently unquantified environmental amenities and values may be given appropriate consideration in decisionmaking along with economic and technical considerations;

(C) include in every recommendation or report on proposals for legislation and other major Federal actions significantly affecting the quality of the human environment, a detailed statement by the responsible official on;

(i)   the environmental impact of the proposed action,

(ii)   any adverse environmental effects which cannot be avoided should the proposal be implemented,

(iii)   alternatives to the proposed action,

(iv)   the relationship between local short-term uses of man's environment and the maintenance and enhancement of long-term productivity, and

(v)   any irreversible and irretrievable commitments of resources which would be involved in the proposed action should it be implemented.'

In addition, paragraph (H) of Section 102 required the agencies to 'initiate and utilize ecological information in the planning and development of resource-oriented projects.'

These provisions establish the statutory basis for the environmental impact statement, an action-forcing and disclosure device which under the legal system of the United States is reviewable and enforceable by the judicial courts independent of executive policy or preference. In principle, the environmental impact statement, based on the utilization of all relevant sciences, has been adopted by as many as thirty national governments and by the Commission of the European Community (Kennedy, 1988). Environmental impact assessment has now become a professionalized aspect of applied science. It has become a focus of international training programs and seminars, for example those conducted by the Centre for Environmental Management and Planning at the University of Aberdeen. And since 1981 an International Association for Impact Assessment has provided a network for professional communication around the world.

PROSPECT

Barring destruction of its infrastructure of personnel, instruments, and institutions by war, plague, or political rejection, the momentum of environmental science is not likely to be slowed or reversed. It seems probable that, regardless of economic, ideological or behavioral preferences, growth of understanding of environmental cause-effect relationships will continue to alter prevailing assumptions regarding the way the world works. Ecology has been described as a 'subversive science,' and in view of its popular acceptance it should not be surprising if unexpected changes in what people regard as reasonable or tolerable occur in the years ahead. Major changes in perceptions and values have characterized critical periods of human history, and the circumstances of the late twentieth century support a strong inference that these times are critical.

The advancement of science has been roughly coincident with the advancement of public policies in those areas wherein growing knowledge stimulates growing social concerns. In the area of environmental policy the influence of science has been evident at all political levels from local to international. But advances in science and policy have not yet matched the progressive attrition and degradation of the environment occurring almost everywhere under the growing pressure of human numbers, economic demands, and technological implementation (cf. Pirages, 1989). The techno-economistic culture of modern society subordinates the implications of scientific findings and ecological rationality to the tenacious pursuit of poorly-defined and inadequately-considered goals of growth, development, and military security.

We appear to be in a race between the overpopulating and degrading of the biosphere and the emergence of a new and sustainable set of science-validated policies for human-environmental relationships. If humans have had intelligence and intent sufficient to reach this point in the evolution of society, one might assume that the species has the capability to overcome its self-made problems and to achieve a sustainable future of high environmental quality. The precedents and prerequisites for such an achievement are present, but so are powerful counteractive forces.

Science alone cannot save the environment. Political choice is required to translate the findings of the environmental sciences into viable policies. Scientific information, even in its limited present state, is far from being fully utilized in contemporary society. Unless political will and ecological rationality can bring about the transformations necessary to achieve a sustainable future of high environmental quality, science can do little more than to slow the pace of environmental decline and to project the consequences for a world in which not all things are possible.

1 Ziman, J. (1984). *An introduction to Science Studies: The Philosophical and Social Aspects of Science and Technology*. Cambridge: Cambridge University Press, pp. 1,2.

2
Science and governance

Although science and government represent different aspects of life and society they interrelate in ways that are complex and may be obscure. Today, more than ever, governments are influenced, often indirectly and not always rationally, by scientific findings, theories, and methods. In the drafting of laws and in the shaping and administration of public policies it is not always easy to see where the substance of science ends and the influence of other than scientific considerations begins. Lawmakers and administrators have often solicited the opinions of prominent scientists selectively in support of particular policies, although in large and complex issues the testimony of specialists alone may be inadequate or misleading. The scope of scientific input to policy ought to be no less than its relevance to the dimensions and complexity of the problem addressed. But the strength of our science has been greatest in its specialized and reductionist focus, whereas adequate answers to problems requiring scientific information characteristically involve a synthesis of all relevant knowledge to which science is seldom more than a partial contributor.

CONVENTIONAL RELATIONSHIPS

Relationships between information and policy are of course as old as the human hope to reduce uncertainty and to predict accurately. Methods and procedures that could be called science-like, if not strictly scientific, have been attributed to priestly forecasting in antiquity. Heads of state, religious authorities, and commanders of armies have ever been interested in forecasts of probabilities. When, at the beginning of modern times, methods of inquiry began to acquire the reliability that is recognized as a

characteristic of science, governments were not slow to see the advantage
in bringing these sources of information into their service.

This involvement of science in public affairs has contributed to what
might be called 'the politization of science'. Among several images, the
government scientist has been seen as an innovative public servant and an
efficient technician. Scientists have been recruited to forecast social trends
and to discover new ways of achieving economic and military purposes.
Science has been much less often seen as a means for testing the
assumptions underlying social policies. It has been commonly assumed
that science can tell people *how* to do what they have decided to do
(without benefit of scientific information) but that science could not tell
people *what*, in their own interest, they ought to do or to avoid. The
conventional relationship of science to policy was thus the application of
scientific means to scientifically uninformed ends. Since the mid-twentieth
century, however, this relationship has become increasingly under
challenge.

Uncertainty over conventional science-policy relationships grew dramatically with the advent of the atomic bomb. Other science-based
innovations followed, often with unforeseen consequences, persuading
thoughtful people, both scientists and nonscientists alike, that the
relationships between science and policy required reexamination. Dramatic innovations in biomedical technology, in plastics and pesticides, in
information systems and computers, and in space exploration, among
others, brought developments that had not been predicted, assessed, or
evaluated. Technological applications of scientific discovery were widely
hailed as progress, but many new products and processes were found to
have secondary and tertiary consequences that were unforeseen and
unwanted. These effects, described as the 'dark side of technology',
aroused the concern of informed people and contributed significantly to
the emergence of what has been called 'the environmental revolution'
(Nicholson, 1970, 1987).

Efforts to inform the public and influence government with respect to the
rising level of environmental and physiological risks were often spear-
headed by scientists, as in the formation of the Federation of Atomic
Scientists in 1945 and the Scientists' Institute for Public Information in
1963. In Great Britain, in 1972, a group of British scientists associated
with the journal *The Ecologist* published a document entitled *Blueprint for
Survival* which called for radical changes in the policies of government and
in the environmental lifestyles of people. Although widely criticized,
Blueprint showed that among scientists, as well as increasingly among
members of the public at large, there was a demand for clarification of the
relationships between science, technology, the environment, and public
policy. *Blueprint* was one of many calls for the reconsideration of public

goals and priorities in the light of scientific knowledge and the ability of science to estimate the consequences of public policies and proposals.

In retrospect, these and many other efforts to reform relationships between science and governance have fallen short of their objectives. Nevertheless, some positive results have followed. Incremental changes have occurred in attitudes and priorities within the conventional science establishment, but not without resistance. A major accomplishment of the concerned scientists was their role in calling public attention to threatening changes in the environment. This consciousness-raising had some effect. In many countries questions regarding the uses of science by government and industry began to come from voices to which elective office holders and appointed officials listen – voices of the voting public. Resultant changes in law and policy that have affected the uses of science and technology have resulted in large measure from organized public pressure influenced, often indirectly, by science.

INFUSIONARY PROCESSES

Even the socially relevant findings of science do not automatically appear on agendas for public consideration. Some scientists believe that they have fulfilled their social responsibilities as scientists when, so as to speak, they lay their findings before the public and its policymaking representatives. But unless these findings relate to some issue about which the public or its representatives are already aroused, policy implications may lie dormant. Experience has shown that injecting science content into governance through legislation, planning, and administration is itself an act of policy and requires a strategy for information transfer. The mere input of scientific information into the political process and the mechanics of policymaking does not necessarily result in the actual infusion of science into policy. In brief, information input is not always followed by policy output – a point illustrated by experience with environmental impact analysis.

Public policymaking as governance is characteristically divided among the legislative institutions of parliaments and congresses, the executive offices of presidents and ministers, their subordinate agencies, the various courts in which laws are interpreted and adjudicated and the central party committees of Soviet-style governments. These are primary institutions for governance in major modern states. Intermediary between the public at large and its government are those citizens who constitute the electorate, especially those organized on behalf of various interests. In Soviet-style socialist countries, party committees at various levels play the more important representational roles. In Western countries generally, governing institutions may receive policy-relevant scientific advice directly from various sources of which at least six have an official character.

First among these are the scientists in government. Science professionals, employed directly in governmental agencies, are engaged in fact-finding and formulation of recommendations to be considered by the political authorities. Persons trained as scientists may become project managers or administrators. When involved in the drafting of bills and governmental orders, and in the allocation of financial resources, or when called upon to advise elected officials, these scientists are advantageously situated to influence public policy. Their effectiveness however, depends upon whether the politicians and top bureaucrats who head the government understand or are in sympathy with their recommendations. It depends also upon the political insight and persuasiveness of the scientists, and perceived seriousness of the issue.

A second source of science influence within official governments are those experts or consultants who have either been appointed to councils or committees specifically advisory to governments, or who are called in to assist the political authorities of the day. Sometimes individual science advisors establish relationships with top party leaders and bureaucrats which enable them to play major roles in the shaping of public policy decision. To systematize this advisory function many governments and their agencies have established special offices. For example, in the United States the Office of Science and Technology Policy in the Executive Office of the President, and the Office of Technology Assessment reporting to the Congress, are intermediary between scientists and policymakers. Similar functions are in part provided in the United Kingdom by the Research Councils established in the Department of Education and Science.

A third source, of less direct input into science policy, are the national academies established for the explicit purpose of advising government on scientific matters. Establishment of the national academies were mileposts on the infusion of science into modern government beginning with the French Académie des Sciences in 1666, the British Royal Society (incorporated in 1661) and the Russian Academy of Science in 1724. In the United States the National Academy of Science (1865) is involved in policy chiefly through its agent, the National Research Council which draws widely upon the entire scientific community outside the Academy for research under contract to agencies of the government. The National Institute of Medicine and the National Academy of Engineering perform a similar function. In the United Kingdom, a quasi-official structure is less formal, a preeminent source of scientific information being the Royal Society which by law and custom has a somewhat less 'official' status than those academies created explicitly for national purposes. National academies of science are now constituent members of the International Council of Scientific Unions and they participate in giving information and advice to the world of nations.

A fourth source, covering far more than science-related issues, would be those national commissions appointed to investigate and report on particular questions of public policy involving science. Scientists, however, do not necessarily constitute a majority on such bodies. The royal commissions of the United Kingdom would seem to be prototypes for this source of input into public policy, and national and presidential commissions serve similar purposes in the United States.

A fifth official source of science input to policy is through legislative inquiry and investigation. For example, in the United States it is not uncommon for committees of the Congress to hold public hearings on science-related environmental issues not only in the city of Washington but, where the concern is national, throughout the country, to obtain a wide range of input from the public. Public hearings are required by many statutes not only at the federal level of government but at state and local levels as well. Issues and proposals concerning problems relating to the environment are among the more common occasions for hearings which elicit opinion from the general public and, where appropriate, receive testimony from prominent scientists whose expert opinion may be solicited. International commissions have also used public hearings to gather information, publicize their recommendations, and build public support. The International Joint Commission of Canada and the United States has held hearings pursuant to the investigations; the United Nations Commission on Environment and Development (Bruntland Commission) scheduled a series of meetings in various national capitals for the preparation and review of its report.

For the United States in particular, a sixth official source might be added – namely White House Conferences. These assemblages have been convened from time to time by presidents to address questions of major policy significance and some, such as the White House Conference on Natural Beauty convened in 1965 by President Lyndon B. Johnson, have had environmental significance. The usefulness of these conferences for the infusion of scientific ideas into public policy is at best ambiguous. They are policy-relevant in that they address public issues, and they sometimes take place with considerable publicity, enthusiasm, and fanfare; but their actual effect upon public policies does not appear to have been impressive. They may give an appearance of action and concern by government with very little tangible actually resulting.

Of course, this generalization does not hold for the work of all conferences and commissions. To the extent that the government of the day is sincerely concerned with a policy problem or in seeking a solution to it, the advice of such bodies may receive high level attention and action. The point to be made here is that scientific findings *per se*, not integrated into action recommendations in forms usable by the political authorities, are not likely to be adopted in the policy process. To the extent that scientific findings are infused into decisionable policy recommendations, the transfer may take place. The infusionary process may require an extended period of time, but meanwhile the policy implications of these reports may have a subliminal effect upon attitudes and beliefs.

Less programatic and often more generalized unofficial sources of scientific information may also influence political decisionmakers. In open societies, scientists, individually or as organized *ad hoc* groups, often try to influence governments on science-related issues. Institutions of higher education and the news media are sources for many kinds of information and opinion on scientific and environmental issues. Insofar as they are seen to influence public opinion and popular expectations they may command the attention of the public policymakers. The communications media have played a major role in bringing natural and environmental science to the general public. Nature and science have been popular topics on both public and privately-sponsored television. Even so, general public understanding of science is seldom sufficient to permit a broad public consensus on science policy. Government investment in science, almost everywhere, is influenced heavily by particular interests and with little effort to assess relative benefits to society.

More directly focused on influencing policy are the activities of volunteer nongovernmental organizations (NGOs). They seek to persuade the public and its political representatives through publications, conferences, and testimony at public hearings. The environmental movement has been strongly influenced by the activities of these organizations on local, national, regional and international global issues. Their members often include scientists, who contribute to the selection, interpretation, and dissemination of scientific information. These organizations are the divisions and battalions of the environmental movement in Western Europe and North America, are significant sources of influence on environmental policy, and are among the more effective transmitters of information from science to policymaking. Included among the NGOs, but of special character, are the professional associations of scientists, engineers, natural resources managers, and public health and medical practitioners. International federations of scientific and quasi-scientific organizations also play a major role in publicizing environmental issues and in recommending policies to national and international authorities. Prominent among those with a planetary scope are the International Council of Scientific Unions (ICSU), the World Wildlife Fund for Nature (WWF), the International Union for Conservation of Nature and Natural

Resources (IUCN), and the International Environmental Education Association (IEEA).

Science-related policy, especially in developing countries, has been increasingly influenced by the work of inter-governmental international organizations, many of which are affiliated with the United Nations. Among the UN Specialized Agencies, the World Meteorological Organization (WMO), the World Health Organization (WHO), the Food and Agriculture Organization (FAO), the United Nations Industrial Development Organization (UNIDO), and certain divisions of the United Nations Educational, Scientific, and Cultural Organization (UNESCO) carry out major environment-related scientific programs. The International Atomic Energy Agency (IAEA), and the International Maritime Organization (IMO) have science-related environmental functions. Within the UN itself the United Nations Environment Programme (UNEP) provides visibility and stimulus to research and action in environmental issues, but does not undertake scientific investigations directly.

Public expectation is, of course, a factor affecting the decisions of governing authorities on public issues. But, to a greater extent than in many other areas of policy, the relationship between public opinion and political action on environmental issues is often anomalous. Where economic and political interests become complexly involved in environmental issues, generalization about the influence of science in governance requires caution and qualification. Widespread general public concern over environmental trends revealed through science may have less effect upon governmental decisionmakers than does the persistently focused concern of agricultural, resource development, manufacturing, and financial interests.

People need not understand science to be persuaded that scientific evidence indicates that certain probabilities may follow from certain courses of action – for example, that the discharge of substantial volumes of biological or inorganic wastes into lakes and streams may ruin the quality of their waters. People may misinterpret scientific information and entertain misplaced fears (as in indiscriminate opposition to genetic engineering or to nuclear reactors in contrast to coal-fired furnaces), and there is abundant evidence of need for enlarging the public understanding of science. This need becomes evident when one considers the role of government administrators and, in some countries, of judicial courts in controversies affecting the role of science in public policies.

The content and logic of public law is not always consistent with the substance and principles of science, and frequently is slow to accommodate changing scientific findings. In controversies affecting the use of scientific methods and information, governments frequently act as 'gatekeepers', deciding what aspects of science are admissible in public affairs and what aspects should be controlled or prohibited. The position taken by the courts in the interpretation of environmental legislation has proved to be critical in the United States, where judicial review of statutory legislation and administrative rule-making has been carried to great length. On public issues wherein scientists disagree and the public is confused and divided, governments are likely to hold policy decision in abeyance.

For example, in the United States there has been widespread agreement that the complicated provisions of the Federal Clean Air Act are in need of improvement. Simplification and greater administrative flexibility could advance the policy objectives toward which legislation has been directed. Repeated public opinion surveys show strong popular support for the Clean Air Act and its objectives, but informed opinion is divided regarding changes that might improve its effectiveness. Scientists and engineers are not wholly in agreement regarding what should be done, and the testimony of economists and public health authorities is not wholly consistent. The effectiveness of legal regulations as contrasted to economic incentives for pollution control is also debatable. Under these circumstances, the Congress of the United States preferred to postpone action. The findings of science alone are insufficient to resolve all questions that include such considerations as the effect of clean air controls on jobs, taxes, and investments, for which scientific evidence is widely regarded as inadequate, and numerous legal rights and obligations which no science addresses.

Similarly, scientific uncertainties and disagreements over the causes and effects of acidic deposition have complicated and have retarded remedial action by governments in Europe and North America. In the world today a much higher standard of predictability is required of environmental science than is expected, for example, from economics. The infusion of science into public policy is characterized by reservations and contingencies, frequently having economic implications.

PHILOSOPHICAL FACTORS

The foregoing discussion may have oversimplified relationships by ignoring the effects of personal knowledge and belief on the part of scientists, politicians, and administrators. As with the public generally, public officials differ greatly in their knowledge of science and their receptivity to scientific concepts and information. In nearly all modern states a high proportion of the incumbents of legislative, judicial, and top executive offices are held by persons trained in the law and whose formal education has little if any science content. Economists are especially influential in the bureaucracies and their science background tends to be very limited. Yet the weight that an important public decisionmaker gives or does not give science in the scale of his beliefs and values can sometimes make a difference in the formulation and execution of public policies, notably with respect to those environmental issues where scientific evidence appears to be inconclusive. Political and economic ideology can be formidable thought conditioners. Two biasing mind-sets in the consideration of science policy questions have been respectively identified as 'economism' and 'scientism'.

Economism is the placing of an exceptional and inordinate emphasis upon economic values in contradistinction to all others – a priority implicit in the more doctrinaire interpretations of both capitalist and socialist ideology. This anthropocentric ideology places little or no value upon nature apart from its immediate utility for economic purposes. There are no 'rights' in the natural world that humans have a moral obligation to respect; nature has no value other than that which can be turned to human purposes, essentially materialistic purposes. The labor theory of value is one of the more explicit expressions of economism.

Those technocrats, bureaucrats, and economic developers who are indifferent to environmental values, and believe that they act in the service of economic welfare do not appear to regard themselves as despoilers of the environment, but rather as expediters of human efforts to realize mankind's destiny on earth. To the extent that scientific knowledge and technique advance the goal of bringing all earthly creation under purposeful human control, science will receive a hearing. Thus the proper role of science is to assist in the advancement of these materialistic values – not to examine their wisdom (Federov, 1963).

The second ideological barrier to the appropriate use of science in environmental policy is, paradoxically, 'scientism'. This belief, that science, in its several meanings, is inherently capable of solving almost all human problems, ought to be regarded as a science heresy. It is an unwarranted extrapolation from the unquestioned achievements of science, and reflects an over-simplification of the ways in which science relates to the social and political issues of human society. Scientistic assumptions are harmful to environmental policy when protection of species or ecosystems is disparaged on the assumption that whatever nature has done, science can do as well or better. That science can sometimes improve on nature does not justify extending this potential to a general principle.

So closely related to scientism as to be regarded as an extension of its assumptions is an exaggerated reliance on technology to solve mankind's environmental problems. 'Technocracy', as it is sometimes called, represents an effort to achieve policy solutions by recourse to technological innovation or through what is sometimes called a 'technological fix'.

Technology may indeed play an important, even indispensable, role in coping with many environmental problems, man-made or natural, but difficulties arise when technological solutions are not adequately informed by science and by a broader range of humane values.

Single-purpose technological applications, in particular, carry substantial risk where complex ecological interrelationships are encountered. As with economism and scientism, technologism results from linear-track thinking that pushes legitimate and important considerations too far, to the exclusion of other equally significant factors. Large scale agricultural and water power developments intended to promote economic growth have often been advanced with insufficient critical examination of the alleged benefits of their ostensible multipurposes, possible incidental effects, and allocation of costs.

INSTITUTIONAL ARRANGEMENTS

At least three very different types of institutionalized procedures have been developed to facilitate the infusion of scientific information and method into the processes of governance. In summary, these are arrangements to: (1) mobilize concern, (2) analyze proposals, and (3) evaluate findings and hypotheses. Each of these procedures implies some formal structuring of relationships; none purport to make policy, but all are intended to inform or influence it.

To mobilize concern

We have noted that certain types of organized efforts (e.g. conferences or commissions) have been sources of scientific input into the public policy processes. Royal and presidential commissions have focused attention, raised consciousness, and formulated recommendations on a wide range of policy issues, some of them environmental. Similar institutional arrangements have been utilized for the same purposes at the international level.

International conferences or congresses are often called to mobilize concern, disseminate information, and formulate recommendations. A specialized subset of the conference device, often described as a technical meeting, has been used for the exchange of information among science experts. National and international policies may be implicit in the recommendations of international scientific congresses and symposia but, historically at least, the main purpose of these gatherings has been to assess the state of scientific knowledge and not primarily to make policy proposals. Throughout the nineteenth century numbers of these international congresses were held for a wide range of scientific purposes and were forerunners of the formation of permanent bodies such as the International Council of Scientific Unions and its constituent members (Gregory, 1938).

Although governments sometimes hosted these conferences they were almost always initiated by nongovernmental organizations of scientists. Agendas normally adhered strictly to scientific questions and political issues were usually regarded as out-of-bounds. Many scientists have regarded science as beyond the competence and concern of politics, and have viewed public science policy debates as deliberations over matter with which scientists were better able to deal. With a growing perception of environmental threats, scientists have become less diffident about entering the turbulent field of policy development, more often through non-governmental organizations concerned with science policy issues.

When the International Union for Conservation of Nature and Natural Resources (IUCN) was established in 1948, its role was seen as mobilizing concern for the growing hazards to nature. Through the Union and its members, efforts were organized to bring protection to endangered species and the IUCN organized a survival or rescue service and undertook to 'inform' governments with respect to threats to nature and natural resources in areas under their control (Boardman, 1981). Efforts to move the IUCN toward a more explicit role in policy formation were for some years resisted, the argument being that such activity would adulterate the scientific functions of the Union. In 1971, the IUCN established a Commission on Law, Policy, and Administration and subsequently was involved in the drafting of the United Nations resolution on the World Charter for Nature, and the development of the World Conservation Strategy in cooperation with the United Nations Environment Program. The IUCN had formerly been prepared through its Commission on Legislation to advise governments at their request upon desirable statutes for nature protection. Now, however, it was engaged in what might be called proselytizing in the sense of undertaking to persuade national governments to adopt national conservation strategies and to examine their environmental circumstances in light of the considerations set forth in the strategy.

To analyze proposals

Four types of science-based analyses have been developed to assist policymaking through ascertaining the environmental consequences of the implementation of particular policies or proposals. They are respectively: testing of products for health and safety, impact analysis, technology assessment, and risk analyses. In actual practice, these techniques sometimes employ similar procedures; yet each does have distinctive characteristics. Each requires the assembling of interdisciplinary teams of experts and the establishment of consistent rules of procedure and analysis. Their successful application therefore calls for some formal institutional structure.

Although not initially perceived as 'environmental', the testing of food, drugs, and industrial equipment for possible harmful effects may be regarded as a use of science in governance. From the perspective of physiology as described by Claude Bernard, all external impacts on the human body may be regarded as environmental. The campaign against cigarette smoking is clearly a case of scientific analysis having significantly altered public policies. Even when analytic methods are not wholly scientific they have become major media for infusing scientific methods and findings into political decisionmaking. It is becoming increasingly difficult for governments to ignore scientific inferences strongly supported by tested data.

During the past two decades, impact analysis has been extended in substantive scope and in jurisdictional adoption. Social and economic impacts are now widely assessed, and environmental impact analysis in some form has been adopted as of 1988 by thirty national governments (including the European Community) and by many more provincial and municipal jurisdictions. Impact analysis is one of the clearer examples of the institutionalization of scientific information and procedures for the purpose of informing the policies and practices of governance. Environmental impact assessment has been considered in Chapter 1, but this technique has been broadened to include social and economic factors which from some viewpoints might also be considered environmental. Inclusion of non-quantifiable values in analysis and the public review of impact statements indicate that much more than the application of scientific information and method may be involved. Indeed the procedure itself is not to be regarded as wholly scientific even though good science is essential to the fulfilment of its purpose. Nonetheless it represents an infusion of scientific method and finding into the governing process.

Technology assessment is another analytic procedure requiring an organizational infrastructure. Its purpose is to examine the consequences of the deployment of specific technologies into the environment. In the United States government, the term technology has been broadly interpreted in the Office of Technology Assessment which was established by the Congress in 1972. Technology assessment, in practice, has not only involved the use of multi-disciplinary staff, but has also drawn upon multi-disciplinary advisory panels for guidance during the assessment and for a review of findings. Although the scope of a technology assessment might go beyond environmental impacts as commonly understood, it is those impacts (e.g. on health and safety), that have often been the particular objects of inquiry.

Formal impact analysis and technology assessment have been initiated only within the past two decades. Each technique has led to the emergence of professional practitioners, professional organizations, and journals – national and international. They play a significant role in the process of environmental policy analysis and must be regarded as major sources for the infusion of scientific information and procedures into environmental policy and planning. These techniques for policy analyses have been built into the administrative procedures of the more advanced forms of governance.

Environmental policies and proposals are subject to other forms of analysis which make fewer demands of an institutional character, among these are risk assessment and cost-benefit analysis. These analytic procedures are less likely to require large interdisciplinary inputs or to require extensive literature searches and field investigation. Analysts using these techniques are not necessarily scientists, but to the extent that they are based upon pertinent scientific information, their findings are more credible.

In addition to scientific information, risk assessment relies heavily on statistical analysis and probability theory. It is helpful in indicating where the allocation of attention and funding for environmental protection is likely to show the greater probable benefit and the lesser probable risk. To the extent that the public understands where its greater uncertainties lie, the task of choosing policy priorities is facilitated. Cost-benefit analysis relies less on science than on economic calculations. Although widely used in the past by some governmental agencies, it does not necessarily employ or always require scientific information.

To evaluate findings and hypotheses

Studies of policymaking and administration-making reveal that the art of responsible judgment involves more than a weighing or even weighting of facts (Vickers, 1965; 1980). One can seldom know what facts relevant to a decision may be missing at the time that a judgment must be made. Moreover, facts, as such, are never self-explanatory; facts require interpretation. The more complex and ramifying an issue, the less certain it is that all of the facts necessary to make a sound decision will be available or will be considered.

A major cause of ambiguity between science and governance lies in the difference in their approaches to decisionmaking and evaluative judgment. Generalizations never apply to all instances, but in cases involving major policy decisions it is safe to conclude that the scope of relevant considerations is much greater in governance than in science. The makers of public policy need to consider many things beyond the purview of the sciences. Thus as between the bases for arriving at a scientific finding on the one hand, and at a political judgment on the other, there are significant quantitative and qualitative differences, and the reliability of relevant evidence as between the presumed 'facts' of science and politics may be expected to differ. Politically relevant evidence is often beyond the reach of science and scientifically relevant data may be unknown to or uncomprehended by political decisionmakers.

The 'facts' of science are often incomplete and subject to unforeseen change; they are nevertheless more often verifiable than is some of the ostensible 'factual' information that policymakers must take into account. On controversial issues, evaluative approaches of contesting parties may be incommensurable and so uncompromisable. Scientific findings and hypotheses may be subjected to tests of falsification that are politically inapplicable to many propositions regarded as axiomatic in public affairs. If a statutory law or a judicial opinion declares a certain proposition to be factually true, the public decisionmaker will need to take account of that political 'fact' in his or her evaluation of policy alternatives. If large numbers of people believe something to be true which science has shown to be false, their belief is nevertheless a 'fact' with which policymakers must reckon.

Environmental science has been changing popular perceptions regarding mankind's environmental relationships. Yet the depth and extent of environmental perceptions and understandings differs widely among people in a given society and among different countries and cultures. Practitioners of the same fields of science, although from different countries and cultures can, for the most part, communicate effectively with one another and work together in international conferences and multinational scientific investigations. They all understand and speak the common languages of the sciences. Within the realm of politics and diplomacy circumstances are very different. Here, national languages, traditions, cultural values, assumptions, and ways of life obstruct common understandings and often misdirect communications. In the sciences, controversies, contentions, and misunderstandings are not uncommon and are sometimes spectacular. But they are less prevalent and, in the long-run, usually less difficult to resolve than are the often emotion-laden issues which divide opinions in politics and international affairs. The sciences have methods that can be applied to resolving questions of probability of propositions that are regarded as scientific; but the truth of many social and political beliefs can sometimes only be resolved, if at all, in the ultimate court of history.

ENLARGING THE CAPABILITY OF SCIENCE TO INFORM

An obvious benefit of science is its ability to forecast future opportunities and risks and to explore ways to realize the former and avoid the latter. Yet it is also useful to understand why the important and growing role of science in governance is, nevertheless, limited. Many aspects of life are not adequately informed by science; some probably cannot be. This is notable in matters of values, ethics, and personal choice, especially to the extent that consequences or outcomes are not foreseeable. The sciences are also of limited help where their findings appear to contradict one another or reveal qualitatively equal but different alternative courses of action. Science may also be of little help where immediate social, political, or military pressures force decisions, with insufficient opportunity to consider or consult.

There is no easy or rapid way to bring science to bear more effectively on public decisions – environmental or otherwise. Yet strategies are available that if applied could help. One is to improve the quality of decision support systems. Formal methods, some of which we have described, are needed to offset human tendencies toward preconceived, inadequate, or erroneous perceptions of the problems which public policymakers proposed to address. Advances in scientific instrumentation and notably in computer technology have vastly enlarged capabilities in gathering, testing, sifting and collating information with respect to environmental status, trends, and effects. Advances in information technologies generally are almost certain to affect the accessibility of environmental information systems.

Measurements and estimates of multiple environmental interactions have become possible with the development of ever more powerful and sophisticated computers. Since the first published projections of complex interactive trends by Professor Jay Forrester of the Massachusetts Institute of Technology (World Dynamics, 1971) the art and science of computer modeling, simulation and forecasting have been developed to a point where many policymakers have begun to regard models as 'oracles' (Meadows & Robinson, 1985). If not taken as literary guides to action the models may greatly assist policymaking, but they are more reliable as indicators of general trends than of detailed probabilities (OTA, 1982).

Since the 1972 report to the Club of Rome entitled *The Limits to Growth* (Meadows, 1972), much mathematical modeling has been undertaken to simulate global environmental, demographic, and socioeconomic trends

(*Global* 2000 *Report*, Meadows, 1982; OTA, 1982; Bremer, 1987; Toth, Hizsnyik & Clark, 1989). Although differing in method and detail, the general outcomes projected by these various independent efforts tend to be, in principle, mutually consistent. All predict serious difficulties for mankind if present technoeconomic and demographic trends continue unmodified. Among scientists and even more among economists and politicians there are sharp differences of opinion regarding the reliability and even the desirability of this type of trends forecasting. It is not always clear from the comments of some critics whether it is the method or the message that most offends them.

Clearly, many are put off by the generally negative conclusions of the several models. Critics, including many scientists, discount the limits-to-growth implications of some models, alleging that they underestimate the innovative capabilities of science and technology and take no account of the 'indomitable spirit of mankind' (Simon, 1981). In the United States, the most recent *official* effort to project the future was made in the *Global* 2000 *Report* commissioned by President Carter and published in 1980, his final year in office. The cautionary and pessimistic tenor of the *Global* 2000 *Report* won hostility in the business community and among political conservatives and liberals alike. Members of the incoming Reagan administration undertook to commission an official refutation of the report. This effort miscarried but was taken up by the private Heritage Foundation which sponsored a so-called counter-report prepared and edited by Herman Kahn and Julian Simon (1984). Largely compiled from work published elsewhere by a number of reputable scientists and economists, most of the contributions were not in fact directed toward the *Global* 2000 *Report* or its forecasts. In many cases initial publication of the papers had preceded the alleged refutation and in some instances could be read as contrary to the viewpoint of the editors.

The earlier attempts at global modeling were inevitably gropings in the dark (Meadows, et al., 1982). There are almost certainly limits to the reliability of predictive models. Nevertheless the simulation model can become a powerful tool of policy if it does no more than alert the public and its policymakers to the possible outcomes of alternative courses of policy.

Some critics of trend analysis and forecasting regard such developments as unreliable, undesirable, and even dangerous. Some political conservatives and libertarians see in the development of forecasting capabilities a foundation for planned economies. Some objectors fear that such forecasts may become self-fulfilling and may deflect or diminish the creative potential which they believe to be inherent in an undirected system of free enterprise. At the conservative extreme, comprehensive long range science-based forecasting is seen as a giant step toward socialism.

Not only do some critics of forecasting declare it to be a very bad idea, but some go so far as to assert that government ought not to warn the public or otherwise inform them regarding the prospect of impending hazards. Severe storm or flood warnings are presumably excepted. The argument here, usually citing past failures to predict accurately, is that to disturb the public with rumors or allegations that may prove false is harmful to the economy, to public confidence, and to national morale. If difficulties become imminent, it will then be time to address them, but meanwhile domestic tranquility should not be disturbed by prophecies that may prove false (cf. Miller, 1963).

It is hardly coincidental that the more outspoken critics of forecasting have often been vigorous opponents of the environmental protection movement. It seems fair to conclude that their view of the proper relationship between science and governance is to confine science largely to unexceptional activities such as improving weapons systems, advancing the productivity of agriculture, enlarging medical capabilities, and generally contributing to the growth of the economy. Under this scenario science would be relegated to its traditional role as servant to human purposes. From this viewpoint it is not a legitimate function of science to undermine public confidence in the social, economic, and political systems through which science is itself supported. Socrates was condemned for such mischief.

It seems probable that the adverse trends that the critics of forecasting discount or deny will force continuing development of the science-based methods of analysis and projection which they deplore. If trends forecasting can be demonstrated to be even partially valid, if miscalculations prove significantly fewer than those resulting from traditional trial and error, the advantages of the new science-based prognosis will surely win acceptance. It is not necessary to believe that humanity will be able decisively to shape its future to believe that it may be able to utilize science to avoid some of the worst possible consequences of its own inadvertent making.

3
Geosphere and biosphere

Before the Earth today can become an object of human respect and concern it must first become an object of awareness and understanding. Today the presence of the Earth is assumed by most of mankind much as a fish in a fish-bowl accepts its environment. Planetary awareness has increased greatly since human entry into outer space; yet few people have reached the level of appreciation expressed by Adlai Stevenson, upon retirement as US Ambassador to the United Nations:

We travel together, passengers on a little space ship, dependent upon its vulnerable reserves of air and soil; all committed for our safety to its security and peace; preserved from annihilation only by the care, and the work, and I will say the love we give to our fragile craft.[1]

The view of the Earth from outer space, first revealed by the astronauts of the Apollo VIII on Christmas Eve 1968, created a powerful image that became a symbol of the environmental movement. From that time onward that image of the Earth was conceptual as well as visual. Anne Lindbergh (1969) found in this image a spiritual dimension:

We can see our parent Earth with detachment, with tenderness, with some shame and pity, but at last also with love. With adult love comes responsibility. We begin to realize how utterly we are Earth's children. We can accept our responsibility to Earth, and our heritage from it, which we must protect if we are to survive.[2]

These informed and sensitive reactions were not those of a less knowing, less caring, and less articulate public. The view from space did not exert an obvious or immediate influence on political or economic behavior. Yet a subliminal change in basic attitudes toward the Earth appears to have followed from the Apollo flights. Further probes into the solar system, and especially of the plant Mars, strengthened the impression of the very exceptional nature of Earth's biosphere.

The integrative concept of a life-sustaining planet – of the biosphere – had entered the domain of scientific discourse more than half a century before the Apollo flights or the intergovernmental Biosphere Conference which took place in Paris in September 1968. The concept, as will presently be detailed, was not new to science, but not until after mid-century did the biosphere enter the public domain of ideas. An integrative and dynamic intimation of a living planet had been growing, but was given visible expression through Apollo. Advances in geophysical and evolutionary sciences added content to the image of the blue planet, beyond the image of spaceship Earth, to Gaia, the self-organizing self-maintaining biosphere, evolving on a geosphere which provided an environment in which life could begin.

EARTH AND WORLD

Science, and the Apollo program, reinforced a distinction between the Earth of nature and the world of man. Although the distinction had been clear among many ancient peoples and primitive societies, it became blurred in modern times to near indistinction in the conduct of political and economic affairs. The difference was not lost among physical scientists whose business it was to comprehend the planet. But, with the partial exception of the theory of geopolitics, presently to be described, the planet Earth *per se* was not an object of public policy. Earth and world were, and for many people still remain, interchangeable concepts. However, by the time of the International Geophysical year of 1956–7, science was well on the way to reaffirming the distinction.

The difference is simple and should be apparent. The Earth is a creation of the cosmos and is independent of man. The world is a human artifact; it is a conceptual creation of human experience and information. Today the human world is geographically congruent with the physical Earth, its political subdivisions marked off on maps or globes. Maps of the geophysical Earth show rivers, lakes, mountains, oceans, and deserts among those geographical features that have been characterized during the course of planetary evolution. Geopolitics in its broader sense partially unites the concepts of Earth and world in analysis of the strategic importance of the location, extent, and resources of lands and seas.

Geopolitics has been described as a study of the influence of geographical features on the political evolution, opportunities, and vulnerabilities of states and nations. The term should be distinguished from political geography, as geopolitics, in a special historical context, has historically referred predominantly to control and exploitation of the natural environment in the interest of national policy. Its focus has been upon the strategic geographical positions of nations in foreign relations and military affairs. Today, however, it may gain a new meaning. The political response to changing conditions in the geosphere, especially the possible effects of a planetary warming caused by an atmospheric 'greenhouse' effect, could take the form of international politics driven by geophysical forces. Political response to climate change is a case in point.

'Geopolitics' appears to have originated with a Swedish political scientist Rudolph Kjellin, following the lead of a German geographer Friedrich Ratzel (1844–1904) who developed a theory of geography closely related to geomorphology, climate, and biological evolution. Ratzel, but more particularly some of his followers, pushed the theory of geographical determination to the edge of supportable evidence. An American geographer Ellsworth Huntington (1945) developed a hypothesis regarding the influence of climate on civilization which critics regarded as questionable. A reaction followed among geographers against what was called 'environmentalism' (Platt, 1948; Lewthwaite, 1966; James & Martin, 1972). As with many reactions, this one may have gone too far in separating influences of the geophysical environment from human culture and political development. When the popular environmental movement in the 1960s looked to science for guidance, geography as a discipline was unprepared (some individual geographers excepted) to take a role of leadership. Among the sciences this role instead was largely assumed by investigators within the science of ecology.

Ecological investigations by the 1970s had laid a broader and firmer foundation for identifying and evaluating relationships between human societies and their biophysical environments. Ecosystems theory embraced geomorphology, biogeochemical relationships, climate, and much more. The extension of ecosystems theory to the global Earth was scientifically inevitable, and man was progressively revealed to be an agent of change throughout the biosphere or ecosphere (Cole, 1958). Thus the relationship between human societies and the geosphere-biosphere of the planet Earth was approached on a basis sounder and more comprehensive than in earlier theories.

There is much yet to be learnt regarding the biogeochemical systems and cycles that form the living Earth. But enough is now known to inform the policies of governments and the behavior of humans regarding opportune and sustainable uses of the Earth. This includes knowledge of the risks, hazards and limits of exploitation of what are called 'natural resources'.

A 'resource' is of course an economic concept: a substance or a source of energy derived from the Earth and useful to humans. From an economistic point of view, the Earth is perceived as a storehouse or supermarket of raw materials (i.e. resources). Throughout modern times this materialistic and utilitarian view of the Earth has been dominant. In the religions based on the dualistic Hebraic tradition, God's Earth was created to serve man's world. Thus a religious tradition and modern materialism combined to subordinate the Earth and its natural systems to the world of man and his cultural artifacts.

Mankind's concept of the world has been one of those artifacts. Anthropologists, historians, and cartographers have described the differing perceptions of the world held by humans. The world was that part of the Earth known to particular societies. Some ancient geographers knew the Earth to extend beyond their world: terra incognita on their maps. The world was the domain of humans, and when the term was used to include the whole Earth, as in 'the world of nature' or the 'natural world', human dominion was implicit. Earth and world were nevertheless separable, and when the words were used interchangeably without regard to their difference, confusion of meaning was risked.

Identification of the Earth, as separate from man's world, but indispensable to it, has progressively emerged during modern times. Seeing the human species as a component within the living systems of the Earth marks a shift in modern perspective. It affects significantly the way that people see and evaluate their relationship to their environment. In affecting this change, symbolic imagery has been important. The psychological effect of the view of Earth from outer space may have been the most significant impact of the Apollo venture, changing man's mental image of the Earth for all future time. Human society having spread over the entire planet, Earth and world must now be considered as congruent in human plans and expectations. Men could once boast of conquering worlds and of becoming their master: no man or living species can become master of the Earth. The contest of the United States and the Soviet Union for the 'conquest of space' has had a reactive effect that was not anticipated. The hubris of space conquest has induced in thoughtful humans a humility born from an appreciation of the immense im-probability of a living Earth, and the moral imperative to take care that its life-sustaining capabilities are guarded and preserved.

PROCESSES OF DISCOVERY

The roughly five hundred years between the discovery of America by Christopher Columbus and the landing of the Apollo XI astronauts upon the moon will surely appear in retrospect as a defined and bounded era in the history of man and the Earth. In our times, this half-millennium is

called *modern* – whatever name future eras may give it. The Earth can
never again be seen as it was when the era began, nor can prospects for
the era to come be forecast by precedents that have given reliable
predictions in the past. Science and human impact on the Earth have
caused irreversible changes in the world view of growing numbers of
informed peoples.

'In the twentieth century, man, for the first time in the history of the
Earth, knew and embraced the whole biosphere, completing the geographic
map of the planet Earth, and colonized its whole surface. *Mankind became
a single totality in the life of the Earth.*'[3] Thus the Russian scientist V. I.
Vernadsky in 1938 summarized the end of a process of discovery which
began at least seven thousand years earlier when man began to record
impressions of the natural world.

At the beginning of modern times, large areas of the world had no
permanent human settlements. The major areas of human habitation
were isolated and developed distinctive cultures. Farming and herding
relied largely upon natural systems, modified only marginally by public
works for water supply, flood control and irrigation. Today large urban
concentrations are absolutely dependent for survival on the continuous
operation of artificial systems. Modern society cannot exist without a
steady flow of electricity and fuels. As population has grown, the world's
peoples have become increasingly homogenized physically and culturally.
Nearly all major premodern cultures have been extinguished or acculturated by the dominant civilization.

The modern age has been characterized by an explosive increase in
human populations, institutions, and knowledge, especially technology.
Through technology, the impact per human individual upon the biosphere
has increased exponentially, accelerating toward the end of this century.
Distinctive among the many forms of institutionalized human dominion,
the nation-state and corporate enterprize have been the characteristic
structures for extending human preemption of the Earth. They developed
in Europe and accompanied the expansion of the European peoples into the
Americas, into South Africa and Australia, and across northern Asia to the
Pacific Ocean.

The socio-biological phenomenon distinguishing this era has been the
human preemption and discovery of the biosphere. This is a simple way of
stating a logically backward paradox: the biosphere was occupied and its
exploitation well advanced before it was really 'discovered;' before its true
nature – resilient, vulnerable and finite – was understood. Before AD 1500
man's knowledge of the nature of the Earth or its relationship to the rest
of the universe was very limited, and much of what was believed was
untrue. Today, near the end of this era, humans have achieved

experiential knowledge of the Earth and its place in space, and have gathered some clues as to its evolution in time.

Popular awareness of the biosphere, which has only occurred during the latter half of the twentieth century, has come none too soon for its survival and mankind's with it. By the 1960s, it was becoming evident that the uncontrolled indiscriminate impact of human activity upon the biosphere could not long continue without endangering the basis of life itself. Yet, opinions differ about the imminence of danger and the prospects for avoiding it. To understand the changes in human beliefs and in the substance of knowledge required for comprehension of the true nature of the planet Earth, it may be useful to trace the discovery of the biosphere as an evolved living system, with tolerances and limitations that human exactions cannot exceed without risking – or in some cases causing – disaster.

LOCATING AND MEASURING THE EARTH

Discovery of the true nature of the biosphere was preceded by the discovery, description, and investigation of the inorganic Earth or geosphere. The sciences and mathematics needed to describe the physical Earth appeared earlier than did those life sciences necessary for comprehension of the biosphere. A motivation for surveying and measuring the Earth arose from the economic and political developments of early modern times, notably the rise of commerce and of national states with geopolitical ambitions. Men were obviously aware of the living world, but as a practical matter it was not understood as an interactive self-maintaining dynamic system. From a religious or philosophical perspective, living creatures constituted an extended chain of being uniting all life in a divinely-ordained plan in which man was exceptional. Practical people were primarily concerned with ascertaining the dimensions, configurations and exploitable resources of the geophysical Earth which, although linked in fact with nature, were viewed largely from a utilitarian perspective.

The first records of man's knowledge of the extent of his environment are maps. The oldest known were found on Sumerian and Babylonian clay tablets in the Tigris-Euphrates Valley. The Greeks seem to have been the earliest to try to ascertain the shape of the Earth: they first believed the Earth to be circular and, subsequently, they thought it to be an elliptical plane. Pythagoras (c. 532 BC) and Aristotle (384–322 BC) appear to have believed that the Earth was a sphere, but the first globe that we know of appears to have been made by Crates of Mallus about 145 BC. The science of geodesy may be said to have been founded by Eratosthenes of Alexandria (c. 276–194 BC), the first man known to have measured the size of the planet. Eratosthenes' calculation were not substantially improved upon until AD 1615 when the Dutch scientist Willebrord Snell measured the Earth by triangulation.

Ptolemy of Alexandria (c. AD 150), established the concepts of the world that prevailed into early modern times. Maps of the fifteenth and sixteenth centuries generally followed the Ptolemaic projections, and, in 1492 in Nuremberg, Martin Behaim constructed one of the first modern globes following the Ptolemaic concepts. During the latter years of the European Middle Ages, collections and translations were made of the astronomical and geographical works of Greek and Arab scholars.

The great European voyages of discovery beginning during the latter half of the fifteenth century stimulated the development of techniques of location and measurement. Between 1500 and 1600 the sciences of navigation and cartography developed rapidly. In 1569 the Flemish cosmographer Gerard Mercator published his famous projection, which was further refined in 1599 by the English mathematician Edward Wright for purposes of navigation. The needs of maritime commerce became so urgent that in 1713 the English government appointed a special Commission for the Discovery of Longitude at Sea and offered substantial rewards for relevant innovations. The invention of the marine chronometer by John Harrison followed in 1735. This incremental development of instrumentation was essential to discovery of the true nature of the Earth although this was not its immediate purpose.

The extended voyages of Christopher Columbus, Vasco Da Gama, and Ferdinand Magellan began a process of discovering, describing and mapping the surface of the Earth, a process which continued through space technology to the end of the twentieth century. In 1891 a Geographical Conference in Berne received a proposal to construct an accurate map of the world on a uniform scale. A committee was appointed to pursue the project, and it reported consecutively to Geographical Congresses held in London in 1895, in Berlin in 1899, and in Washington in 1904. Finally a special conference convened in London in November 1909 adopted proposed standards for the map, and rules to govern its production. In 1913, a general international conference in Paris, at which thirty-four nations were represented, accepted the project of the *Carte du Monde au Millionième* on a scale of approximately 1 inch to 15·8 miles. Today aerial photogrammetry and imaging from extraterrestrial satellites obviates most of the earlier controversies over map-making. Changes in the Earth's surface can now be monitored and cartography can assume a dynamic character.

Exploration of the sea floors required further technology and instrumentation. The scientific voyage of HMS Challenger around the world (1872–6) provided the first comprehensive survey of the physical and biological conditions of the oceans. The laying of submarine telegraph cables required accurate measurements of the ocean depths and added to knowledge of submarine conditions. Submarine technology advanced dramatically during the late twentieth century allowing not only more accurate mapping of the ocean floor, but also new and unsuspected insights into the range and diversity of life in the marine depths of the biosphere.

The discovery, description, and measurement of the surface of the Earth were matched by advances in knowledge of the relationship of the Earth to the cosmos. Modern astronomy adopted the theories of Nicolaus Copernicus (1473–1543), who held that the planets together with the Earth revolved in circular orbits around the sun. Advanced by the work of Galileo, Huygens, and Kepler among others, the dynamics of the universe were first satisfactorily formulated by Isaac Newton (1642–1727) in his *Philosophiae Naturalis Principia Mathematica* (1687). Cosmic mechanics as formulated by Newton and modified and refined by his successors remained a dominant explanation of the behavior of the universe until Albert Einstein (1879–1955) proposed his theories of relativity.

In the twentieth century, the measurement and description of the universe was extended to the galaxy which encompasses the solar system to which the Earth belongs. But the scope of twentieth century astronomy rapidly transcended the limits of our immediate galaxy to a presently incalculable, but seemingly immense, number of external galaxies or island universes extending infinitely into space. Exploration of deep space was advanced by the discovery by Karel Jansky in 1931 that radio waves, apparently from the farthest reaches of the universe, can be received and interpreted upon the Earth. Giant radio telescopes are now augmenting our knowledge of the cosmos.

Thus, by the latter third of the twentieth century, man was not only able to locate himself at whatever point he might happen to be on the surface of the Earth, but also to a degree undreamt of at the beginning of the modern era, was able to locate his planet with some accuracy in the nearer regions of a universe of incomprehensible size. This process of discovery involved the interaction of virtually all of the physical sciences, discovery in any one of which frequently advanced discovery in others.

Before the mid-twentieth century, different geodetic systems of measurement were in use in a number of different countries, but a world system of control points and coordinates has now been devised with the assistance of the International Union of Geodesy and Geophysics and the United Nations. Scientific exploration of the Earth was greatly advanced by innovations in instrumentation, such as radar, sonar, and remote sensing by satellite, and the development of new methods of photogrammetry which enormously increased the speed and accuracy of determining the configuration and topographical properties of the physical world, of its climate and oceanographic conditions, and of the extent and condition of its vegetation.

A major step toward understanding the physical Earth was the International Geophysical Year (IGY), 1957–8, sponsored by the International Council of Scientific Unions and the World Meterological Organization. One consequence of the IGY was the Antarctic Treaty of 1959 which established the Antarctic continent as the world's first international scientific reserve and set a precedent for the UN Treaty on the Peaceful Uses of Outer Space. Yet as of 1988, a proposal by the Antarctic Consultative Parties to open the continent to minerals development, and the United States Strategic Defence Initiative, indicated the fragile nature of these earlier environment-protecting agreements (Shapely, 1985; Vicuña, 1985; Child, 1985; Mitchell, 1988). But the proposed minerals convention has been blocked by refusal of Australia and France to ratify.

In recent years, technology essential to obtaining an evolving picture of the Earth in cosmic context has advanced extraordinarily. A detailed list of scientific and technical developments could fill many pages, including telescopes, (refracting, reflecting, and radio); microscopes of several varieties, (including the electron microscope); cyclotrons, accelerators, and colliders in high-energy physics; chromatographs for the analysis of chemical substances; and the instrumentation for deep sea and space exploration. The very mass of the forthcoming findings and their frequently specialized character have made coherent synthesis difficult, especially for the general public. Research technology has facilitated exploitation of Earth's resources and, in theory, has provided a foundation in knowledge that might enable man to act prudently towards Earth seen as a whole. These advances in the physical sciences initially had only marginal or indirect effects upon environmental policy, but their influence may grow in the years ahead. Problems of energy, climate change, and environmental contamination almost assure this.

INTERDEPENDENCIES OF THE LIVING WORLD

In 1807 the naturalist Alexander von Humboldt wrote, 'In the great chain of causes and effects no thing and no activity should be regarded in isolation.'[4] This interconnectedness of the living world had long been recognized intuitively but not until the twentieth century did standard terminology to designate the specific, systematic interconnections of the natural world come into general use. In 1867 Ernst Haeckel put forward the word 'ecology' to designate the study of living systems in relation to their environment, but, like 'biosphere,' it was slow to find common usage. The term 'ecosystem' did not appear before A. G. Tansley used the term in an essay published in 1935 in the journal *Ecology*. The ecosystem has also been known by other names, notably 'biogeocoenose,' especially in the Russian literature. It means a definable or bounded system of complex and dynamic biological and physical interrelationships that vary greatly in size and complexity from the minute or simple to the very large and complex. The term 'ecosphere' has been used to summarize the totality of living systems that envelop the Earth and may be regarded as synonymous with 'biosphere'. And, as noted in Chapter 1, the terms ecology and ecosystem have acquired popular and philosophical meanings beyond the more precise definitions in science.

In the course of discovering the interdependencies of the living world, the organisms of which it is comprised have been classified, located, and described, although this task is yet far from complete, especially for the tropical rain forests. Taxonomy and systematics, classification and description of species, were major concerns of biological science in the eighteenth and greater part of the nineteenth centuries, a work particularly associated with the name of the Swedish botanist, Carl von Linné (Linnaeus, 1707–78). Exploration of the continents and the seas and the collection of plant and animal specimens laid foundations for the geography and ecology of living species and for more sophisticated understandings of their habitat requirements, genetic characteristics and interspecific behavior. Today, this area of investigation has attained a new and critical importance in relation to applied molecular biology, and biotechnology.

The distribution of plants and animals was discovered to be neither random nor static. The reasons for the habitat of a particular species were often found to be complex, involving behaviors of other species. Spatial locations were found frequently to be related to biological parameters among which competition, symbiosis, and preference for food and territory were factors. At any given time the network of interdependencies in the living world was found to be in a state of approximate, although dynamic, equilibrium. This homeostatic state was subject to change through forces acting not only in the physical environment external to organisms, but through genetic changes in the organisms themselves. The consequences of this process of change were discovered to result in the evolution of the species, and theoretical mechanism of this process were described by Charles Darwin in 1859 in *On The Origin of Species by Means of Natural Selection*, by Alfred Russell Wallace in 1870 in *Contributions to a Theory of Natural Selection*, and by the sciences of paleontology and genetics after 1900.

The transplanting of species into areas in which they had not naturally occurred, if it did not fail, frequently had disruptive and calamitous results. The homogenizing and impoverishing of the ecosystems of the Earth was an easily measurable consequence of human interference with natural interrelationships. At almost no time and place in the expansion of populations, and especially of European populations in modern time, did an ecological awareness or an ecologically-oriented policy guide the behavior of the explorers and settlers. By mid-twentieth century, however, the disastrous record of untested and unguided human intervention had been well documented, and there was a growing popular awareness of the dangers of uninformed disruptions of natural systems. Nevertheless, individual and institutionalized human behavior was slow to catch up with scientific understanding.

Less readily understood than the interconnectedness of things in space was their interconnectedness in time. The theory of evolution dealt with intervals of time far greater than the experiences of any human individual and beyond the comprehension of most. Yet, in part because of the work of Albert Einstein exploring the relativity of time and space, the significance of time in human affairs was changing. Past expectations in relation to time have become less and less reliable as guides for expectation in the future. Cultural change, influenced heavily by innovation in science and technology, accelerating through the nineteenth and twentieth centuries, has contributed to the impact of human behavior upon the natural world, and has created tension and discontinuities in personal life and society. Is perceived human time accelerating?

The biological and behavioral sciences have identified chronological sequences, periodicities, and interdependencies among organisms that must be respected to avoid harmful consequences. For example, because of an almost universal failure to appreciate the significance of exponential growth, societies have failed to take timely action to prevent the catastrophic explosion of human populations. In the framing of environmental policies the necessities for foresight and lead time, the inevitability of ramifications, and the effects of time lag have become concepts essential to guiding human behavior in relation to the biosphere.

The discovery of the nature of the biosphere inevitably involved man in a process of self-discovery. As the profound and often destructive impact of human behavior upon the Earth became more apparent, the need to know more about human nature became increasingly evident. The seeming growth of aberrant behavior among individuals and societies strongly suggested that the human adjustments required by man-made changes in the modern world might be exceeding the adaptive ability of many individuals.

THE BIOSPHERE CONCEPT

In 1913, biochemist Lawrence J. Henderson published a study of the physio-chemical circumstances under which life could exist. His conclusions regarding the inorganic basis of life and the planetary conditions necessary for life to arise and continue have been modified in particulars but not in general theory. Thirty-five years later, Harold S. Blum in *Time's Arrow and Evolution* (1951) explored the relationship between the second law of thermodynamics and organic evolution, and largely reaffirmed Henderson's thesis that the evolution and present condition of life as it has developed on the Earth is an extremely improbable phenomenon, although the enormous size of the universe permits the statistical probability of other planets capable of sustaining life. Blum concluded, 'If we think, however, of the delicate balance of conditions our earth enjoys, and to what extent chance has entered repeatedly into biological evolution, it seems that the probability of evolving a series of living organisms closely resembling those we know on earth may be a relatively small number. This becomes poignantly evident when we think of all the chance events concerning the evolution of the human brain – which occurred only once on our planet.'[5] As true today as when it was written was Blum's observation:

And perhaps for this reason alone, this life-stuff is something to be cherished as our proper heritage. To be guarded from destruction by, say, the activity of man, a species of living system that has risen to power and dominance through the development of a certain special property, intelligence. Such a development – vastly exceeding that of any other species – has apparently given this particular system the ability to determine its own destiny to a certain extent. Yet at the moment there are all too many signs that man lacks the ability to exercise the control over his own activities that may be necessary for survival.[6]

Mankind's understanding of its place in nature, and an awareness of the predicament in which its efforts to reshape the Earth have placed it, have grown gradually as the concept of the biosphere itself has been built up by successive enlargements of scientific knowledge. An Austrian geologist, Edward Suess (1831–1914), has been credited with first use of the term in the concluding chapter of a small book entitled *Die Entstehung de Alpen* (1875); there he introduced the 'biosphere' in a description of the concentric layers enveloping the Earth. The development of the term in modern scientific thought is particularly associated with the work of V. I. Vernadsky (1863–1945), Russian minerologist and a forerunner in modern biogeochemistry. Although Vernadsky attributed the concept to the French scientist Lamarck (1744–1829), the term gained currency through the publication of Vernadsky's book, *Biosfera*, in Leningrad in

1926, and a French edition, *La Biosphére*, published in Paris in 1929 (Bailes, 1981; Grinevald, 1985; Serafin, 1988).

Vernadsky's ideas appear to have grown out of his study of biogeochemical phenomena, were developed during the period of World War I, and first outlined in 1922–3 in lectures at the Sorbonne in Paris. The elements of Vernadsky's concept of the biosphere have been stated in a paper published in English translation in the *American Scientist* (1945). He distinguished the biosphere as the area or domain of life, a region where the prevailing conditions are such that incoming solar radiation can produce the geochemical changes necessary for life to occur. The biosphere included the atmospheric troposphere, the hydrosphere or oceans, and the upper layers of the lithosphere – a thin layer of rock and soil extending below the surface of the Earth.

Vernadsky identified sixteen propositions distinguishing living from inert material. Among them are the following. The processes of living natural bodies are not reversible in time, and the vast majority of living organisms change their forms in the process of evolution. The processes of changing growth in living matter tend to increase the free energy of the biosphere, and the number of chemical compounds produced by living organisms probably reaches many millions, where the number of different kinds of chemical compounds in inert bodies is limited to a few thousand. New living natural bodies are born only from preexisting ones, and have a common nature in their cellular morphology, substance, and reproductive capacity. All living matter is, therefore, ultimately genetically connected throughout the course of geologic time. Living organisms arise and exist only in the biosphere, and only as discrete bodies; no entry of life into the biosphere from cosmic space has ever been observed.

These propositions were not novel, but upon them Vernadsky based a summation which had never before been so concisely and pointedly stated:

> In everyday life one used to speak of man as an individual, living and moving freely about our planet, freely building up his history. Until recently the historians and the students of the humanities, and to a certain extent even the biologists, consciously failed to reckon with the natural laws of the biosphere, the only terrestrial envelope where life can exist. Basically man cannot be separated from it; it is only now that this indissolubility begins to appear clearly and in precise terms before us. He is geologically connected with its material and energetic structure. Actually no living organism exists on earth in a state of freedom. All organisms are connected indissolubly and uninterruptedly, first of all through nutrition and respiration, with the circumambient material and energetic medium. Outside it they cannot exist in a natural condition.[7]

Apparently influenced by the French mathematician and Bergsonian philosopher Edouard LeRoy (1870–1854) and the French Jesuit, geologist, and paleontologist Pierre Teilhard de Chardin (1881–1955), Vernadsky adopted the concept of the noosphere as the state toward which the biosphere is now evolving (Serafin, 1988). The noosphere, or realm of thought, declared Vernadsky, 'is a new geological phenomenon on our planet. In it for the first time man becomes *a large-scale geologic force*. He can and must rebuild the providence of his life by his work and thought, rebuild it radically in comparison with the past.'[8]

As man propagates the noosphere, he extends and transforms the biosphere. Vernadsky observed prophetically that:

Chemically, the face of our planet, the biosphere, is being sharply changed by man, consciously, and even more so, unconsciously. The aerial envelope of the land as well as all its natural waters are changed both physically and chemically by man. In the twentieth century, as a result of the growth of human civilization, the seas and the parts of the oceans closest to shore become changed more and more markedly. Man now must take more and more measures to preserve for future generations the wealth of the seas which so far have belonged to nobody. Besides this, new species and races of animals and plants are being created by man. Fairy tale dreams appear possible in the future: man is striving to emerge beyond the boundaries of this planet into cosmic space. And he probably will do so.[9]

Vernadsky followed his colleague the geologist A. P. Pavlov (1854–1929) in saying that we had entered the *anthropogenic era of geologic time*, 'That man, under our very eyes, is becoming a mighty and ever-growing geological force'. Nevertheless, man was bound by a seemingly infinite number of ties to the biosphere and was, except as his existence was modifiable and modified by his thought and effort, subject to its physical limitations. Within the parameters of the natural world, man's mere presence, as well as his deliberate and inadvertent impact, transforms its properties and conditions. There thus arises, as Vernadsky concluded, 'the problem of the *reconstruction of the biosphere in the interest of freely thinking humanity as a single totality*'. The problem was, how to adapt the biosphere to man's needs and desires without impairing its viability. In discovering the nature of the biosphere man was creating and simultaneously discovering the noosphere, which, declared Vernadsky, is 'this new state of the biosphere, which we approach without our noticing it'.

Although Vernadsky developed the scientific concept of the biosphere, and posed the problem which makes it an object of policy, popular awareness of the biosphere was also enhanced by the writings of Pierre Teilhard de Chardin, whose principal work, *Le Phénoméne Humain* (*The Phenomenon of Man*, 1938), took a poetic and metaphysical approach to the concept of the biosphere, which is evident in the following passage describing the fundamental unity of living matter:

However tenuous it was, the first veil of organised matter spread over the earth could neither have established nor maintained itself without some network of influences and exchanges which made it a biologically *cohesive* whole. From its origin, the cellular nebula necessarily represented, despite its internal multiplicity, a sort of diffuse super-organism. Not merely a *foam of lives* but, to a certain extent, itself a *living film*. A simple reappearance, after all, in more advanced form and on a higher level of those much older conditions which we have already seen presiding over the birth and equilibrium of the first polymerised substances on the surface of the early earth. A simple prelude, too, to the much more advanced evolutionary solidarity, so marked in the higher forms of life, whose existence obliges us increasingly to admit the strictly organic nature of the links which unite them in a single whole at the heart of the biosphere.[10]

To resolve the problem that Vernadsky posed regarding man's transformation of the Earth, the biosphere must first become a subject of social concern and then an object of public policy. Recognition of the biosphere as an object of international policy began with a resolution adopted in November 1966 by the General Conference of UNESCO at its fourteenth session. Pursuant to this resolution, an Inter-governmental Conference of Experts on the Scientific Basis for Rational Use and Conservation of the Resources of the Biosphere was convened in Paris, September 4–13, 1968. This gathering, known for convenience as the Biosphere Conference, was organized by UNESCO with assistance from the United Nations secretariat, the Food and Agriculture Organization, the World Health Organization, the International Union for Conservation of Nature and Natural Resources, and the International Biological Pro-gramme. The significance of this conference and its recommendations for institutional development will be considered in subsequent chapters of this volume. Here the conference is mentioned as evidence of a transnational awareness of the loss of environmental quality and integrity that had been occurring throughout the biosphere.

In summarizing recurring themes which had emerged during the conference, the final report declared that although some of the changes in the environment have been taking place for decades or longer, they seem to have reached a critical threshold, and are now producing concern and a popular demand for correction (UNESCO, 1969). 'Parallel with this concern', the report continued, 'is the realization that ways of developing and using natural resources must be changed from single purpose efforts, both public and private, with little regard for attendant consequences, to other uses of resources and wider social goals'. The report emphasized that human exploitation of the Earth 'must give way to recognition that the biosphere is a system all of which may be affected by action on any part of it', an observation made by von Humboldt 150 years earlier. The problem was not one for science alone. A further consequence of a new awareness that man is a key factor in the biosphere was 'That natural science and technology alone are inadequate for modern solutions to resource management problems; one must also consider social sciences in particular, politics and public administration, economics, law, sociology and psychology, for, after all, it is resources as considered by man with which we are concerned'.

From 1968 onward, the concept of the biophysical changes necessary for life to develop as an evolving, self-renewing planetary system was implicit even when not explicitly stated in declarations of international environmental policy, such as that issued by the United Nations Associations of the Scandinavian countries and the 'Declaration on the Management of the Natural Environment of Europe' by the European Conservation Conference in 1970. On January 1, 1970, the term 'biosphere' was incorporated into the public law of the United States in the Preamble of the National Environmental Policy Act of 1969 (PL 91–190), which declared that it is a part of national policy to 'promote efforts which will prevent or eliminate damage to the environment and the biosphere...'

THE GAIA HYPOTHESIS

In 1979, publication of a book by a British scientist, J. E. Lovelock, carried the biosphere concept one step further toward a unifying and dynamic synthesis. In *Gaia: A New Look at Life on Earth*, Lovelock (1979), developed the proposition 'that the biosphere is a self-regulating entity with the capacity to keep our planet healthy by controlling the chemical and physical environment'. Gaia, Grecian goddess of the Earth, was chosen as a convenient shorthand symbol for the hypothesis.

The Gaia hypothesis is a logical progression from the Vernadsky biosphere-noosphere synthesis, and provides a unifying interpretation of relationships between the inanimate and animate aspects of the Earth. Lawrence Henderson theorized that the evolution of the geosphere proceeded to a stage at which life on Earth became possible, and thereafter life emerged and, according to Lovelock's hypothesis, began to transform the geosphere, making it more hospitable to life. The biosphere thus took form as a self-organizing, self-renewing systemic process with homeostatic capacities for buffering or deflecting attacks upon its integrity.

The Gaia hypothesis has led to two consequences which, although dissimilar, reinforce a biospheric paradigm of man's relationship to Earth. The first has been a stimulus to work already ongoing in the sciences; the second has been involuntary support from science for the growing ethos of popular ecology (Serafin, 1988).

The first general response to Gaia from the scientific community was skepticism accompanied by a stimulus to further inquiry (Kerr, 1988). Investigation of the Gaia hypothesis or of the interactions that it posited, necessitated an interscience interdisciplinary effort. Impetus toward a major coordinated effort had been building, notably since the International Geophysical year (July 1957–December 1958) reinforced by collaborative programs that followed (e.g. International Year of the Quiet Sun (IQSY), the Upper Mantle Program (UMP), the International Magnetosphere Study (IMS), the Global Atmospheric Research Programme (GARP), the International Biological Programme (IBP), the Man and the Biosphere Programme (MAB), the International Hydrological Decade (IHO), and the International Decade of Ocean Exploration (IDOE). As previously noted, the International Council of Scientific Unions (ICSU) in 1969 established the Scientific Committee on Problems of the Environment (SCOPE) which has since carried on interdisciplinary attitudes that led logically to initiation by ICSU in 1983 of the International Geosphere-Biosphere Programme (IGBP), (Malone & Roederer, 1985).

IGBP sets a very broad and long term agenda of global dimensions for the sciences. To the onlooker outside the community of science it appears as if scientists in large numbers have overcome an earlier skepticism of the environmental movement, and are now prepared to participate in collaborative interdisciplinary research. Summarizing the proceedings of a symposium on global change and the International Geosphere-Biosphere Programme, Canadian geologist W. S. Fyfe (1984) concluded:

Eventually, IBGP must be done. Many of the problems with which it is concerned are too complex to be solved by the traditional disciplines. Members of our very traditional universities always have a little fear of moving out from the secure havens of specialisation but, when the best minds are involved, I think the rewards which follow from such motion are great. We are involved with new science.

The societal effect of Gaia was to provide an image or symbol for the more philosophic concerns of the environmental movement. From the viewpoint of 'deep ecology' Gaia incapsulates or integrates the complex dynamic geo-ecological processes that ought to be the subject of human regard and respect. J. E. Lovelock warned that Gaia should not be taken as a sentient being, but neither, in some of the more sophisticated theologies, is God so regarded. If Gaia is a symbolic expression of the life-force manifest in creation, it fulfills a role attributed to traditional gods. It adds empirical substance to the evolutionary theology of Teihard de Chardin. Out of understanding and respect for Gaia, humanity may evolve toward a spirituality of natural religion that is consistent with the reality of the cosmos as discovered through science (Brown, 1984; Toulmin, 1982).

PLANETARY POLITY

It follows from the growing understanding of the geosphere-biosphere that the politics of nations and increasingly of non-governmental organizations will find the planetary globe to be their ultimate sphere of action. Earth and world have now become physically congruent, but not yet universally conceptually identical. The United Nations Commission on Environment and Development opened its report on *Our Common Future* (1987) with the phrase: 'The Earth is one but the world is not'. Although the world of man now covers the entire surface of the planet, relatively few people yet see the Earth as an object of concern, respect, and responsibility. In the minds of too many people a line is still drawn between their lives and the rest of the Earth. To safeguard the future of man and biosphere, the Commission urged the need to bring the disparate policies of nations into conformity with the imperatives of the planetary systems upon which life depends. This task, however, entailed the art of politics, a subject beyond the agenda of the Commission.

Meanwhile, geopolicy, even when tacit rather than explicit, has characterized the strategy of both greater and lesser states. Biopolicy, which has hitherto been a relatively minor aspect of statecraft, has been growing in significance since the international conference on the Biosphere (Paris, 1968) and United Nations Conference on The Human Environment (Stockholm, 1972). Heretofore, the roles of science in relation to the politics of geosphere and biosphere have differed. Geopolicy, distinguished from, but including, geopolitics, has employed science as a servant of economic and military strategy. Biology has served the concerns of agriculture and public health, and biopolicy was implicit in the population theories of Robert Malthus. The voyage of Charles Darwin on the Beagle (1831–6) joined geosphere and biosphere in a common investigation. The voyage was intended primarily for geodetic surveys useful to the British Royal Navy and commercial navigation. Yet Darwin's observations, as the expedition naturalist, marked a major advance in the concept of the living world and the evolution of species.

Geopolicy dominated the strategies of the great world powers of the nineteenth and twentieth centuries (Parker, 1985). The British achieved political dominion circumscribing the geosphere: the sun never set upon the British Empire. Other regimes as well – Russia, Germany, France, the United States and Japan – were competitors for the control of strategic navigation routes, straits, isthmuses, harbors, and ice-free ports. Access to raw materials was another goal of geopolicy to which science in agriculture and geology contributed. The science of meteorology was state-sponsored for its obvious bearing upon agriculture, commerce at sea, and military maneuvers. Astronomy and geodesy contributed to the practical art of navigation. Thus the discovery and comprehension of the geosphere in its various aspects served the mercantilist, industrialist, and strategic interests of political states. Political strategy for dominion in the geosphere was competitive and antagonistic. Global awareness in the context of the old geopolitics induced conflict rather than cooperation and was a factor in the two World Wars and many lesser conflicts (O'Sullivan, 1986).

Biopolicy, conversely, required cooperation even though that relationship was as often antagonistic as amicable. Initial steps toward biopolicy were directed toward preventing the spread of disease, first in humans and later in domestic animals and in plants. Epidemiology was science in the service of national interest and its initial tool was quarantine. A global view of transmissable disease was not necessary until national authorities began to realize that the surest protection against epidemic disease was to prevent or contain it at its source. Ironically, a century passed before this obvious lesson was applied to the prevention of environmental pollution. The international sanitary conventions from 1892 onwards developed a worldwide system of protection against contagion. A conference in Paris in 1903 led to the establishment of the International Office of Public Health four years later, and in 1923 the Health Section of the League of Nations was established not only to prevent epidemics but to investigate the etiology of disease and assist the organization of national departments of health. These offices and the Pan American Sanitary Bureau were incorporated in the World Health Organization (WHO) following its establishment in 1946. Human health-related environmental conditions are now surveyed and reported in UNEP's Global Environmental Monitoring System (e.g. *Global Pollution and Health*, WHO & UNEP, 1987).

The cooperative measures did not grow from or require an explicit biospheric comprehension of the world. They did, however, initiate a process of international cooperation that not only provided experience in collaborative efforts, but provided precedents upon which further initiatives could build. An important role of science throughout the twentieth century was to enlarge progressively the areas and subjects in which national interests required international cooperation. As knowledge of the living world increased, a realization has grown that whereas the geosphere was at base indestructible by man and, relative to human time, eternal, the biosphere was vulnerable to improvident exploitation and to man-induced changes in the geosphere.

Withal, the forces, cycles, and sequences of the geosphere require greatly enlarged understanding. Science must be advanced on all fronts and to this end international collaboration is essential. Nowhere have the implications of geo-science for a planetary policy been better expressed than in the recommendations of the Advisory Committee on Earth System Science of the United States National Aeronautics and Space Administration (NASA, 1986). The concluding and international portion of its recommended program deserves replication in full:

INTERNATIONAL COOPERATION

International Cooperation is essential to the global study of the Earth and to the success of the Earth System Science initiative proposed here, for two reasons. First, detailed global observations from space and from a variety of locations on the Earth's surface are required; the nations concerned must be included in the planning and execution of observational programs that affect them. In addition, other nations are planning major space systems for remote sensing of the Earth, which will provide significant data relevant to Earth System research.

International collaboration proceeds at three levels, all of which must be carefully coordinated. First, there is the traditional communication of scientists among themselves concerning scientific problems and the strategies for addressing them. This process is promoted at the international level (e.g. the International Lithosphere Program) primarily by the International Council of Scientific Unions (ICSU), as well as by a number of other organizations. Secondly, for any activity requiring systematic exchange of data or for access to the territory, airspace, or economic zones of other nations of Earth-science observations, there must be specific international arrangements. These are facilitated by an endorsement of such scientific activities by an established international agency or other appropriate body. International action to address the issues of physical climate change has already begun, but arrangements for study of the biogeochemical cycles have not yet been initiated.

Finally, the program will benefit from the increasingly explicit collaboration between governments in the instrumentation and operation of spacecraft. Bilateral agreements between space agencies are a proven mechanism for such collaboration. The European Space Agency (ESA) and NASA cooperated on early Space Shuttle scientific missions, and the number of collaborating nations is now increasing....

Coordination among US and foreign agencies planning remote-sensing satellites for the near term is already well developed, implemented through such groups as the Committee on Earth Observations Satellites (CEO).This coordination seeks to assure compatibility and international availability of data sets from the various systems. For the longer term, discussions among Canadian, European, Japanese and US government remote-sensing specialists have revealed substantial commonality of measurements objectives for Earth observation from polar platforms of the Space Station. These discussions are expected to result in significant collaboration both in instrument development and in exchange and analyses of data.

A number of major international research programs relevant to Earth System Science, which involve (or should involve) US participation, are now in place. The World Climate Research Program sponsored by ICSU and the World Meterological Organization includes the following programs fundamental to ESSC [US Earth System Sciences Committee] goals:

- The Tropical Ocean Global Atmosphere (TOGA) program, recently instituted to determine the causes and establish the predictability of El Niño and Southern Oscillation events.
- The International Satellite Cloud Climatology Project (ISCCP), recently established to provide a global data set on the interactions of clouds and radiation, with applications to climate models.
- The International Satellite Land Surface Climatology Project (ISLSCP), recently begun to measure the interactions of land-surface processes with climate in specific biomes.
- The World Ocean Circulation Experiment (WOCE), now being organized within the World Climate Research Program to permit development of improved models of global ocean circulation on timescales of decades and longer.

Other programs important to ESSC goals include the following:

- The International Geosphere-Biosphere (or Global Change) Program (IGBP), now being formulated within ICSU to lead a worldwide study of global change.
- The Crustal Dynamics Project, begun in 1979 and involving NASA and bilateral agreements with 23 countries, designed to measure global plate tectonic movements.
- The International Working Group on Magnetic Field Satellites, recently formed to define and integrate measurements of the secular variation of the Earth's magnetic field.
- The Global Ocean Flux Study (GOFS), proposed to extend our understanding of processes responsible for production and fate of biogenic materials in the sea from regional to ocean-basin and global scales.

Evidence from the sciences now permits the conclusion that if the basic physico-chemical properties of the geosphere are beyond the power of humans to destroy, human activities can alter the balance of those properties in atmosphere, water, and soil so as to impair their life-support capabilities. Living species and systems are more directly vulnerable. They may be diminished or destroyed in any of several ways: through ignorance and inadvertence or through perverse or reckless behavior. International efforts to stop the attrition of the ozone layer caused by release of trace gases illustrates the emergence of a new political awareness of bio-geochemical realities (Dorfman, 1987). This may be described as a new form of geopolitics – political response to the threat of geophysical cataclysm.

Meanwhile a wide discrepancy between ecological literacy and technological capabilities presents serious danger when associated with political or ideological fanaticism. Mass insanity has gained dominance in certain political states which could deploy weapons that could destroy the greater part of mankind and the more sensitive systems of life on earth. Crazy states have now become a menace to the entire world and to the biosphere (Dror, 1971), but mankind has not yet learnt how to deal with them – how to protect the many from terrorism by a few. Yet if this only were achieved, it would not be enough to protect against perversity.

There is another more subtle and pervasive threat to the biosphere and to ecological stability. It is the outward pressure of people from those regions of the Earth devastated by the convergent forces of ignorance, poverty, overpopulation, and impelled by an innate urge to survive. Over large areas of the Earth, human populations have (metaphorically) scraped the Earth to its bare bone or rock. Life-sustaining capabilities have been deeply impaired or lost in many countries while their human populations continue to grow. Ill-conceived colonization schemes have spread the process of environmental degradation. Famine relief from nations with food surpluses temporarily alleviates the situation, but in the absence of other measures does not cure its causes, nor prevent its recurrence. The outmigration of destitute millions into unspoiled lands and into the developed world is a phenomenon with which democratic governments seem unable to cope. Jean Raspail in *The Camp of the Saints* (1975) provides a terrifying fictional scenario of a 'peaceful' invasion which the moral and political ideologies of modern liberal states deprive them of power to resist.

The implication of present trends for the future of humans in the biosphere are hardly beyond question: only if people through governance cooperate in informed, collective, firm self-discipline can they overcome threats to the integrity of the biosphere. In the present state of the world this implies antagonistic cooperation. If the biosphere is not to suffer progressive degradation, politically unfriendly regimes will have to put aside their differences to the extent necessary to overcome a common danger, as eighteen states now are attempting to do for the Mediterranean Sea.

We have no assurance that humans will succeed. The rhetoric of the United Nations' World Charter for Nature would seem to commit the majority of nations to policies of international environmental responsibility. Even the sole dissenter to the Charter, the United States of America, in its preamble to the National Environmental Policy Act of 1969 declares a national purpose 'to promote efforts which will prevent or eliminate damage to the environment and biosphere...' But unenforceable statements of good intent are not binding upon the makers of policy. Sectoral and nationalistic interests remain strongly focused on the pressure points of political power – military, demographic, and economic. Economism is still the dominant basic ideology underlying capitalism and socialism alike. As the world appears today it is possible but unlikely that the biosphere can be preserved in its present state of richness and variety.

Belief in the possibility of protecting some significant part of the biosphere rests on the often observed counter-intuitive behavior of human societies. People do learn and attitudes do change. Science alone may be insufficient to displace the counting-house psychology that has dominated modern society. An emotional acknowledgement that man is of the Earth, in the full meaning of this axiom, could be a potent force toward planetary policy. What may be needed is an intangible quality of perception – spiritual, aesthetic, even awesome and expressed in these lines by Walt Whitman, from *Leaves of Grass*:

> Earth! my likeness!
> Though you look impressive
> ample and spheric there
> I now suspect that is not all.

NOTES

1. A. Stevenson (1965). *Official Record of the 39th Session, (30 June–31 July 1965) 137th Meeting of the United Nations Economic and Social Council held in Geneva*, 9 July 1965. New York: United Nations, 90 para. 42.
2. A. Lindbergh (1969). The Heron and the Astronaut. *Life* 66 (28 February 1969): 26
3. V. I. Vernadsky. The Biosphere and Noosphere. *American Scientist* 33 (January 1945): 8.
4. A. von Humboldt und A. Bonpland (1807). *Ideen zu einer Geographie der Pflanzen nebst einem Naturgemälde der Tropenländer*. Tübingen: Berj F. C. Cotta, 1807. Humboldt's observation actually read: 'In der grossen Verkettung von Ursachen und Wirkungen darf kein Stoff, keine Thätigkeit isolirt betrachtet werden,' p. 39. Reprinted in 1963 by Wissenshaftliche Buchgesellshaft, Darmstadt.
5. H. S. Blum (1962). *Time's Arrow and Evolution*. New York: Harper Torchbook 212: A.
6. Ibid.
7. V. I. Vernadsky. Op. cit., 4.
8. V. I. Vernadsky. This and the following quotations from Vernadsky are from Ibid., pp. 9–10.
9. V. I. Vernadsky.

10. P. Teilhard de Chardin (1961). *The Phenomenon of Man*. Trans. from the French by B. Wall. New York: Harper & Row, pp. 94–95.
11. W. F. Fyfe (1985). In Malone & Roederer (eds.) *Global Change*. Cambridge: Cambridge University Press, p. 507.

PART II

Developing a planetary paradigm

Belief and behavior are not always consistent, and yet belief conditions behavior in many ways. Beliefs and assumptions regarding the Earth and the ways that nature and the perceived worlds of man work are fundamental to all human cultures. Perceptions of reality are built into the language that expresses them. Words and phrases tend to perpetuate the image of belief long after those beliefs have changed. We still speak of the rising sun and of the approaching night even though we know that it is the rotation of the Earth causing these events.

Century-old metaphors may be more expressive of how we understand relationships than are new terms, adopted to give identity to scientific discoveries and social innovations. 'Paradigm' is, for example, an uncommon term used to identify an aspect of human culture which no other expression fits exactly. It saves words, and focuses meaning when applied to patterns of belief about the nature of the Earth and the worlds of man upon it. In the twentieth century the rapid advance of science has not been matched by changes in popular language and understanding. Language biases our thoughts; we cannot deal with concepts for which we have no words. The words we use are tools of perception and analysis which may shape our assumptions and limit or distort our assessments of trends and possibilities. Educated incapacity is a danger to all literate cultures facing challenges of transition.

Thus roots of the problem of consensus on man-environment relationships extend into the terrain of cognitive psychology and linguistics. There appears to be a reciprocal relationship between cultural norms and the way in which ordinary environmental relationships are interpreted. From the prevailing viewpoint, man is seen apart from nature and largely an exception to 'nature's rules.' The interpenetration of the human interior and exterior environments may be a commonplace of physiology, yet it is not an assumption guiding the daily behavior of most people. If it were, the concept of man-in-biosphere would be axiomatic and people might see their relationship to the earth differently. As with parallax, a small change of individual viewpoints can extend to large changes in public policies.

If, indeed, the future of man and biosphere are threatened by the failure of modern society to have achieved a sustainable relationship to the Earth, the development of an appropriate societal paradigm regarding that relationship becomes an imperative for survival. Modern civilization has radically changed the relationship of man to Earth. The prevailing paradigms of society have yet to catch up with this reality. Nevertheless, a science-related alternative interpretation of man-Earth relationships has been developing and is already influencing public discourse on mankind's environmental future.

4
Perspectives and priorities

Insofar as we can read the record of human experience it seems that what almost everyone believes is not necessarily true. Yet those beliefs, right or wrong, are themselves 'truths' which leaders and governors of people must consider. Whatever the ultimate truths may be, until some critical number of people accept them they are politically irrelevant, although perhaps important in other ways. That critical number is dependent upon character of a culture, and especially its structure and allocation of social power. In the large and complexly changing societies of the modern world it is difficult to foresee which, if any, of the competing values and attitudes is becoming dominant. Forces of circumstance in the natural world could be the decisive factors in changing people's expectations and behaviors. Predictions of changing paradigms are risky, however, because humans, being susceptible to error, have often misinterpreted the course of events. It is a truism of politics that to be right prematurely is to be wrong. But it is also true that to persist too long in an erroneous assessment of events may be fatal not only for political leaders, but for the whole society.

STRUCTURE OF PRIORITIES

Because the state of the environment has seldom been a major political concern in the past, its emergence in the present implies and necessitates two kinds of social change. First, there must be a change in societal perspectives – in the way people see the environment in relation to their interests and values. Second, there must be a change in institutional priorities – in the relative importance attributed to the issues with which people are concerned. The role of science in society is more clearly marked in the first aspect of change than in the second. Bringing about change in social attitudes is not easy, but it is almost always less difficult than redirecting and reprogramming governmental institutions. Institutional change seldom precedes social reorientation, and then usually as an incident of war or top-down revolutions in which new perspectives are imposed upon society by a dominant, militant elite (e.g. the Russian revolution of 1918).

The ultimate direction of the environmental movement is toward a restructuring of social priorities. This objective has analogies in proselytizing religions and political ideologies. Such analogies are generalizations and accordingly imply exceptions. For example, not all environmentalists, as with adherents to other systems of belief, think alike. Persons having a commitment in common to particular policy goals may differ in doctrine and strategy and yet may share assumptions about the way the world works and what is important in human life. Today it seems valid to generalize that in all major modern religious and ideological movements, the intended direction is transnational – the destination ultimately universal.

For the environmental movement, at present, an *international* perspective is a practical expediency. Governance in the world is divided among nations. There are presently no institutionalized political means for direct action in dealing with transnational environmental issues other than national governments or their intergovernmental agents. Embryonic transnational arrangements may, however, be developing. Nation-based non-governmental international organizations are now beginning to offer the possibility of alternatives to international intergovernmental initiatives. This possibility is becoming more significant because international non-governmental organizations (NGOs) have increasingly influenced the rhetoric and even the actions of national governments and intergovernmental organizations, notably those within, or in various ways associated with, the United Nations system. Some are even beginning to share functions with governments.

Non-governmental organizations have increasingly sought ways to influence the policies and actions of intergovernmental agencies. It is now to be expected that each major intergovernmental conference on environment-related affairs will be paralleled by one or more unofficial non-governmental forums meeting at the same time in the same city. Parallel meetings were conspicuously evident on the occasion of the United Nations Conference on the Human Environment in 1972 at Stockholm. Similar dualities of official–unofficial representation have characterized United Nations conferences on population, food, energy, and science and technology. Why this dualism in representation?

Explanation may be found in popular beliefs regarding the perspectives and priorities that may be expected to dominate intergovernmental conferences. The non-governmental groups which gathered at Stockholm were there primarily because they did not trust the official representatives of governments, in the absence of external pressure and exposure, to achieve more than non-committal declarations and equivocating comprises. The differences between the two types of representation were reflected in their choice of priorities. The non-governmental groups viewed the issues before the UN conference largely from a one-world, transnational perspective. Governmental delegations were confined to official positions and generally reflected the assumptions and values politically dominant in the governments of their countries. Science advisers to the official delegations were reported to argue for policy positions reflecting scientific understanding of the impacts of humans on the biosphere. But for every scientist urging positive action there were foreign office and military advisers urging caution. There were fundamental differences in perspectives on man-environment relationships and what the present state of the world required of people and governments.

To understand the problems of choice that the environmental movement presents to society and government it is necessary to distinguish the basic from the incidental in the structuring of priorities and values. One need not discount important differences among modern societies to recognize that they may be similar in certain fundamental ways. In the modern world science, and science-based technology, have materially changed the ways in which many people live, but have had much less effect upon their social attitudes and institutions.

It is a paradox of modern times that unprecedented advances in science and in comprehension of the nature of the world and man have proceeded in association with political assumptions that the logic of science would seem to refute. Science is least developed and least reliable in the very area in which it might best inform humans regarding their options and limitations in social choices and governance – at the interface of the natural and social sciences. As a consequence, science and technology have been put to the service of purposes and policies for which science provides no adequate criteria for evaluation. Economics and military security are primary concerns of modern governments and it seems safe to predict that neither of these concerns nor their associated problems will find satisfactory solutions until the underlying causes of concern are realistically addressed. This seems unlikely to happen in the absence of a broad, interdisciplinary examination of risks and opportunities within the context of real-world perspective.

It is curious, in a world in which scientific analysis and rationality are ostensibly valued, that dominant beliefs regarding political economy are arbitrarily and selectively constrained by narrow interpretations of rational behavior. At present, the polarized positions regarding the political economy of modern societies are those in which market forces are viewed as the primary agents of societal development, and those in which the unfolding of immutable laws of history, assisted by centralized planning, determine mankind's future. The former, variously modified, characterizes the liberal democracies of the industrial world; the latter is basic to radical Marxist ideology and its expression is idealist as contrasted to practical socialism (e.g. of Mikhail Gorbachev) which more readily comprises with existential realities.

From the perspective of an international environmental movement, a similarity basic to the capitalist free market and to Marxist socialist planned economies is as significant as is their differences. A denominator basic to both societies is the dominant role of technology. Each economy, in its own way, suggests Jacques Ellul's (1964) description of a technological society. Technique became a dominating social value during the development of industrialism. Mechanization was only one of a growing number of techniques that were developed to meet the needs of a mass society shaped by processes of production and consumption. The partial displacement of mechanized industrial order by the electronic post-industrial era has enlarged rather than diminished the dominance of technique. By the closing years of the twentieth century technique in many aspects of life has become the determinant of purpose, notably in communications, an outcome implied in Marshall McLuhan's (1964) judgement on the technology of television – the medium has become the message. For the managerial and entrepreneurial classes the practical question has been: 'What can be done with present or emergent technology?' For environmentalists the right question is 'What should be done?'

The technological imperative has not been a determinant of priorities for the environmental movement. This observation does not depreciate the value of technology; it raises the question of its proper role in the implementation of societal priorities. Obviously there are important public purposes for which technique is not a driving force. Concern for the environment is one of them. Yet the power of technique is sufficient to deflect or distort environmental policies, even though it does not determine or effectively dominate them. Technique has been a source of controversy over the ways in which governments and nongovernmental organizations have addressed such major environmental issues as agriculture pro-duction, pollution control, forest and wildlife management, soil con-servation, and flood prevention.

Especially in the free market liberal democracies, technique is now regarded as if it were a natural force. It has become a conceptual successor to 'progress' which people once argued could not be stopped. The immense advantage of technique in influencing priorities is its apparent freedom from substantive content. Technique, being 'know how' rather than 'know what', appears to be an essentially procedural concept and its methods are characteristically invoked to serve procedural objectives. Thus it tends to avoid controversy over goals or outcomes. Technology can boost yields in agriculture, accelerate communications, reduce waste, and provide warning of impending hazards, natural and artificial. In effect, technique is much more than mere procedure.

A new technological era, with important environmental implications, is emerging with applied molecular biology and biotechnology (Sasson, 1988). Will humans attempt to remake the living world? Genetic engineering of new life forms and altered species has aroused concern and opposition among some members of the environmental movement. Threats to existing 'natural' genetic stocks are foreseen, and there is also fear of a 'Frankenstein effect' from new life forms escaping laboratory control. Although there has been an anti-technology element in the environmental movement, the advantages of technology preclude its unqualified rejection. There is a trend in society today to bring technology under control, to make it the servant rather than master of purpose, and, through technology assessment, to identify and prevent its harmful possibilities. But this trend is not yet dominant.

As powerful and subtle as the influence of technique has been on the selection and ordering of priorities, it has been only one of many forces at work. Reciprocal influences occur between economic, political, and military ends and technical means. In all such relationships technique provides the instrumental means through which financial and organizational power generates more advantageous technologies and puts them to work on the priorities for which they have been adapted. Priorities are thus structured by people who are in a position to set them and to control the deployment of available economic and technical resources. These persons have seldom placed protection of the biosphere very high in their structure of priorities. It is not a priority that leads to wealth and political power. But the unassessed potential of microbial and genetic biotechnology may alter this indifference.

This analysis of priorities would be incomplete without acknowledging the overriding priority of nearly all modern governments: military expenditures. It is of course true that war has been the primary business of the modern national state and the so-called defense budget has become the mainstay of many national economies. That this dependence is unnecessary is demonstrated by nations which, for various reasons, have little or no military establishment. But because a nation does not spend money on armed forces in no way indicates a preference for expenditures for environmental quality; Japan spends comparatively little on either. The inordinate expenditure on armaments in comparison with real social and environmental needs will surely be regarded in retrospect as one of the great irrationalities of modern history and a reproach to political leadership in the modern world.

Although budgets are indicators of comparative national priorities, they are not a wholly valid measure. Environmental protection often requires no more than abstinence from excessive or unsustainable development. In many national governments a comprehensive and adequate environmental policy would lead to budget reductions for expensive environmentally-impacting public works. It seems also reasonable to expect that insofar as a biospheric or planetary perspective spreads around the world, military expenditures will decline. Modern warfare is man's most environmentally destructive activity. Even to contemplate the use of atomic and biochemical weaponry may be regarded as equivalent to criminal ecocide against the Earth itself, tantamount in principle to murder compounded by suicide.

The environmental consequences of nuclear war have been extensively examined (Westing, 1979). A comprehensive two volume study has been published by the International Council of Scientific Unions' Scientific Committee on Problems of the Environment (ICSU, 1985–6; WMO, 1986). Unfortunately, as long as nuclear weapons exist, their use is not unthinkable (Kahn, 1960). Only their elimination could relieve the world from this threat of destruction.

INTERPRETATIONS OF EVENTS

The context in which people perceive events has greatly to do with how they interpret them. Even more, their span of attention may be too narrow or selective to include awareness of many events or trends that occur in their environments. Information is an important factor in determining what people see and what they understand. But information may be erroneous, incomplete and, if contrary to strongly held beliefs or hopes, may be rejected. Criteria for evaluation may differ among observers, leading to differing assessments of the importance or meaning of events (Buttel & Larson, 1980).

Efforts within the environmental movement to influence political choice have been handicapped by differing interpretations of the environmental problem. These differences in perception lead toward differing conclusions as to how the problem should be addressed. At least three levels of cognition and interpretation can be identified, although of course for many people these levels integrate. If fully understood, each level represents a valid though limited interpretation of mankind's environmental pre-

Table 1. *Perceptions of environmental impairment: levels of comprehension*

Perceived causes	Explanations	Remedies
I Incidental: harmful behaviors occurring in the normal course of human activities	Error or accident: dereliction, ignorance, and carelessness are causal factors	Exhortation: *ad hoc* corrections, clean-up campaigns, indoctrination and education
II Operational: errors in policy, program planning, and execution	Ineffective management: insufficient or flawed information; poor morale or operating procedures, avarice and corruption	Corrective laws: regulations, impact statements, technology assessment, review of planning proposals
III Systemic: impairment 'built into' technoeconomic systems (both capitalist and socialist)	Environmental damage inherent in design of our technoeconomic systems: most 'economically efficient' efforts may produce worst environmental results	Basic changes in technical and behavioral systems: redesigning of institutions and development of alternative methods, materials, and sources of energy

dicament. Table 1 represents these levels of cognition and interpretation. Such schematics help to clarify the implications of different social perspectives on environmental problems. They should not be taken as models of a more complex reality.

Level I perceptions interpret environmental impairments as largely isolated phenomena, incidental but inevitable in the course of life. Environmental disruptions are seen as accidents, miscalculations, or consequences of human ignorance, indifference, irresponsibility, or neglect. Policy implications are relatively few and not far-reaching. They include admonition, education, indoctrination, and a few legal sanctions such as anti-litter laws, prohibition of public nuisances, (such as fires in the open, or the causing of noise or noxious odors). Policy at Level I is essentially cosmetic. Its concern is characteristically expressed through community clean-up and paint-up campaigns, through planting trees, cultivating flowerboxes, establishing and improving public streets and parks, and enforcing municipal sanitary ordinances. These actions have been widely and traditionally accepted and are largely incidental to the environmental movement.

Level II perceptions similarly see environmental problems as largely inadvertent, but caused by inadequate or inappropriate organization and management of economic and public affairs – notably in relation to technology. Governmental intervention to prohibit environment-impairing behaviors, standard-setting for effluent discharges into the environment, automobile emission controls, and land use regulations identify this level of perception and interpretation. This is the level at which most governmental and intergovernmental environmental policy is developed and administered. It is exemplified in the environmental resolutions of the United Nations Conference on the Human Environment, in declarations by the European parliament and Council of Europe, in environmental directives of the Commission of the European Community, and in the environmental statutes of most modern governments. International treaties and comparable agreements are largely at this level of perception, as, for example, conventions for prevention of oil pollution at sea, prohibition of international trade in endangered wildlife, and regulation of the transport of hazardous materials. The objective at this level is to rectify behavior without attempting to alter prevailing economic or institutional arrangements.

At Level III a break point is reached between conventional and radical interpretations of environmental dereliction, its causes and cures. Radical, in this context, does not imply customary left-of-center positioning. 'Radical', as used here, implies an effort to uncover the roots of environmental degradation, and it seeks to remedy basic causes. As we shall see in the following chapter, Level III marks the major division within the environmental movement between people who believe that action sufficient to achieve sustainable environmental conditions is possible within the present socio-economic technological order (socialist and capitalist), and those who identify that order as itself the cause of deteriorating environmental conditions. Level III perception regards the attrition of environmental quality and the degradation of the biosphere as inherent in the assumptions, goals, and values of modern technological society and its economistic priorities. Remedial measures attempted by conservationists and preservationists are seen from the perspective of 'deep ecology' as superficial and temporizing, ultimately to be overwhelmed by the combined pressures of population growth, indiscriminate economic development, and technological determinism.

The denominator common to various Level III interpretations of mankind's environmental predicament is the systemic character of the problem. Within the environmental movement there is greater agreement that the modern industrial-techno-economic order is inherently environ- mentally degrading, than over what kind of system should replace it. Opinions range widely from anarchist to authoritarian solutions. Some opinions call for a one-world political order superceding national sovereignty (Falk, 1971). Others see environmental policy as integral to a world-wide egalitarian redistribution of wealth, technology, and political power (Myers, 1985). Still others perceive the ultimate possibility of an authoritarian world system of 'iron governments' compensating for the inability of people, unaided, to avoid degradation of their environments

(Heilbronner, 1980). From a more pragmatic and conservative point of view, however, the remedy is sought in progressive adaptation and innovation in institutional arrangements. The preferred approach to the problem from this perspective is a flexible, open-ended arrangement, which encompasses the present diversity of nations in readiness to deal with environmental problems, and brings them progressively into a world-wide transnational system for critical specified purposes (Dorfman, 1987).

At Level III one encounters the 'deep ecology' aspect of the environmental movement. The deep ecology perspective is not self-explanatory, and is not amenable to precise definition (Naess, 1973; Devall & Sessions, 1985; Sessions, 1987). Not all who profess deep ecology agree on its implications although most would agree on its major premise, which is that conventional interpretations of relationships between man and nature are erroneously anthropocentric, unsustainably self-serving, and inconsistent with the natural order of the biosphere. In brief, modern society has entrained on a wrong track, destined to end in the wrecking of the planetary life support system, disintegration of the biosphere, and the consequent degradation or extinction of humanity.

This apocalyptic assessment of the tendencies of modern society is moralistic in both tone and content. It draws heavily upon scientific findings and theory, but its rationale is more religious than scientific. Yet in relation to religious orthodoxy, adherents to deep ecology disagree. To some, the roots of our environmental crises lie in certain dominant tendencies of Judeo-Christian theology (Lynn White, Jr. 1967). The biblical admonition to be fruitful, multiply, and have dominion over every living thing is alleged to legitimize the arrogance of man toward nature and the separation of man from the planetary biosphere. Man-environment relationships as conceived in religious traditions prevailing in southern and eastern Asia and in parts of pre-Columbian America have been regarded by many deep ecologists as more consistent with the true status of humanity in the biosphere. Among persons most strongly persuaded of the moral imperative of deep ecology some see need for a new religion, consistent with the cosmic and evolutionary findings of science. This ultimate expression of deep ecology places man among other evolved species, occupying the planet as a fellow tenant and, by virtue of superior intellect, a responsible caretaker, but not an owner or master.

A less radical perspective sees the Christian religion and religious ecumenicalism evolving from Franciscan or Cistercian traditions toward an ecologically-sensitive relationship between man and the rest of nature. Man no longer stands outside of nature, but bears a responsibility for stewardship within it. The intellectual endowments that make possible man's discovery of the principles governing the natural world make wisdom and prudence a condition for their rational application to the opportunities inherent in the biosphere.

This concern for a reunification of man with nature within religious tradition has found ecumenical expression in the New Alliance movement, initiated at Assisi, Italy on the 25th anniversary of the World Wildlife Fund for Nature (WWF 1986/87). Representatives from major world religions were present and formed an International Network on Conservation and Religion under WWF sponsorship. A sudden transformation of traditional theologies is not to be expected, but the leaders of the New Alliance may work progressively to reorient religious perspectives. Beyond this interfaith effort various forms of neo-paganism have arisen which ought not to be regarded as nature worship in a primitive sense, but are instead sophisticated efforts to develop an ethic of respect for the biosphere in the spirit of Albert Schweitzer's reverence for life. Natural religion (not dependent upon supernatural explanations) is already incipient in our changing world (Dubos, 1982; Toulmin, 1982; Webb, 1915). Should it gain wide acceptance among thoughtful people the human prospect for a more national and harmonious relation of man to Earth might be improved.

POLITICAL MEDIATION AMONG PRIORITIES

In modern society the diverse and often conflicting interests of organized groups are commonly mediated through political parties rather than through religion. Out of this process emerges the priorities that government will pursue and the position of environmental values in the policies of the day. Mediation and priority setting are carried on differently in one-party, two-party and multi-party political systems and obviously differently in authoritarian as contrasted with democratic states. But categorical generalizations regarding their environmental policies are fraught with risk. Political parties provide the governments-of-the-day with the directive heads of the executive departments who oversee the work of adminis-tration. That work is undertaken by bureaucracies whose memberships are relatively permanent and upon whom the political authorities rely to carry out their policies. The responsiveness of bureaucracies to the priorities of the government varies with circumstances and the political systems in which they function. Where their own institutional prerogatives are concerned, bureaucracies tend to be conservative, and to rationalize self-serving policies as in the public interest.

The most reliable indicators of the policies of governments toward environmental problems are, (1) how governments are organized to deal with them, and (2) how money is allocated. The actual significance of these criteria are not always apparent on the surface; appearance may be deceptive. If a national government has a department of environment, its location in the bureaucratic hierarchy may indicate its status and influence. If environment occupies a cabinet or ministerial level position one may surmize that its mission is of higher priority than a department subordinate to a ministry of agriculture, development, or tourism. But structural arrangements alone may not indicate the real status of an agency. For example, in the United States, the Council on Environmental Quality is located in the Executive Office of the President by statutory law, but has been unable to exercise the authority that its statutory status would suggest. Uninterested in environmental issues but unable to abolish the Council, President Ronald Reagan ignored it for eight years, providing only enough money to keep it alive. And so the funds allocated to environmental programs must also be considered in assessing the extent of a government's commitment.

No individual range of perception is likely to encompass all attitudes toward man-environment relationships; the psychological variability of humans precludes this. Given the numbers and conditions of humans around the world it is possible that the majority of mankind sees no environmental problem for humanity in a general sense. For many people surely the environment is a 'given', an ambience assumed and responded to under the compulsion of needs, innate or cultural motivations, or hazards of external forces. In this perspective there is no generalized environmental problem; there are only particular problems of food, shelter, health, and safety with which humans as individuals must cope in order to survive.

A more sophisticated and reasoned but less informed perspective denies any great or general significance to man-environment relationships *per se*. The assumption common to this point of view is the belief that there is no problem in mankind's environmental relationships that science, technology, or economics cannot solve. In this perspective mankind's proper role is not to preserve a wild, unmanaged (hence wasteful) natural environment, but to domesticate the Earth and turn its resources to economic productivity. This point of view is more often tacitly accepted than argued at the higher levels of economic planning, economic enterprise, and government. Among the more articulate advocates of this viewpoint have been Wilfred Beckerman (1972) in Great Britain, Julian Simon (1981) in the United States, and economic planners in the USSR. More moderate adherents to this perspective concede that specific environmental problems do arise, but that allegations of techno-economic causes of an environmental crisis are greatly overdrawn. In political mediation of environmental controversies economic values weigh heavily.

For many major events or phenomena, the significance of environmental factors may receive widely differing interpretations depending, as has been noted, on the perspective of the viewer. For example 'world hunger' or famine may be interpreted as too little food or too many mouths. However, it may also have political explanations, as in the disruption of farming through civil disorder, and in purposeful witholding of seeds or food supplies. Or it may be attributed to natural causes such as drought or floods. Political and journalistic interpretations seldom consider basic causes. As with many other disasters, alleviation of the immediate situation is the customary focus of attention and the object of political priority to the neglect of preventive measures.

That human disasters associated with crop failures, floods, dust storms, landslides, land subsidence, salinization, waterlogging of soils, siltation, destruction by earthquakes and volcanoes, among other catastrophes, have often followed from the ways in which people have related to their environments have not been preferred explanations. Acts of God or nature are credited for what should often be charged to human ignorance or lack of foresight. Some natural catastrophes cannot be prevented, but humans need not place themselves in the way of avoidable disaster. Science is able to inform people why building in flood plains, over earthquake faults, or on unstable terrain is unwise. But economic, political, technological, even sentimental considerations may out-weigh geological and ecological information, and people will incur risks fatalistically or assume that society will somehow provide compensation for predictable losses (Burton, Kates & White, 1978).

The context in which environmental issues and events are perceived has therefore much to do with where they are placed on the scale of political priorities. The interpretation of events in the environment may be as much a matter of economic and political interests as of the environmental facts per se. But environmental events, when fully analysed and understood, may stand out too clearly to be dissembled or dismissed. Not all environmental events are amenable to unequivocal scientific explanation and evaluation. Some are, however, and to the extent that these explanations are accepted as real and important they may add incrementally to the mental images that people hold regarding the way the world works.

Paradigms seldom spring into existence full-blown and suddenly. Rather they are usually assembled piece by piece as prevailing understandings regarding events and relationships fail to provide satisfactory explanations. At some stage in a progression of events and unsatisfactory explanations a new cognitive configuration takes form. People see the world and Earth differently than they did before. It is a thesis of this book that the environmental movement may be understood as a social process leading toward the formation of a new perceptual planetary configuration. This is happening because threatening events in the environment now discernible on a planetary scale cannot be dealt with effectively under the paradigm that has dominated modern times. A reorientation of expectations has become necessary. Such a refocusing of perspectives and revision of priorities occurs at Level III perception. Its emergence signifies a social response to a growing recognition of environmental hazards with which the modern world finds itself unprepared to cope. Being a practical necessity if degraded social conditions are to be avoided, a reactive response seems likely in the long run to emerge. The outcome of this reaction, if it persisted, would be a comprehensive reordering of priorities at both national and international levels.

EVALUATION OF ALTERNATIVES

In the choosing of policy preferences, assumptions and values are obvious factors; less obvious are the ways they interrelate in the making of actual decisions. Values may conflict and the means for achieving a mediated choice may be unavailable or unacceptable. In society and government the choices that are made are not always those preferred by the majority. Close knit, focused, aggressive minorities often prevail over unorganized, indifferent, underinformed majorities. Public officials often become skilled at appearing to profess one policy while in fact pursuing another. Many people, even majorities, may hold basic values for which they are unable to obtain implementation through political choice.

Emergent social movements that challenge the prevailing norms of a society are likely to encounter incomprehension, conflict, and frustration. From its inception the environmental movement has been on a collision course with dominant economic assumptions and priorities. It has not always appeared to be compatible with religious orthodoxy, political liberalism, or economic conservatism, and it challenges anthropocentric assumptions regarded as axiomatic in modern society. The legacy of institutional structures and the priorities that they serve have been generally inconsistent with the goals and the priorities of dedicated participants in the environmental movement.

These considerations help to explain the apparent paradox of environmental values, placed high on the publics' scale of priorities in principle, yet hitherto relatively low among the priorities in practice of their elected representatives and public administrators. Some of the apparent discrepancy may be explained by emphasis in policy accorded to ends as contrasted with means. Members of the general public, but especially environmentalists, tend to emphasize ends. Their primary concern is to see their values realized in society. Politicians, however, must be concerned especially with means – with 'the art of the possible'. It is no coincidence that the most powerful committees in the legislatures of many states of the United States are named Ways and Means. Politicians and administrators are more likely to be aware of obstacles and opposition to any policy proposal than is the general public. The elected official's future depends upon avoidance of stirring up militant opposition that a sympathetic but politically inactive public will not offset.

Social movements focused upon a single issue risk failure to take account of the milieu of influence and institutional commitment into which they propose to inject innovations or reforms. The larger and more complex the issues, the more likelihood for collision with established interests and institutions. Institutional structures tend to lag behind changing social circumstances and priorities, and this is especially true in government where the legal basis for policy and action can seldom be altered rapidly. A major task for the environmental movement (hardly yet begun) has been to redirect and where possible to restructure public agencies that were designed for developmental rather than for environmental objectives. Where missions and structures are beyond direct change, environmental objectives have been sought through procedural reform, as in environmental impact analysis.

Because of institutional resistance and lag, the means needed to achieve environmental ends are seldom initially available. In most modern states, environmental ministries or departments have been established to implement policies which could not be allocated to other agencies of government. Their effectiveness varies among countries, but in many governments their role is largely an ineffectual formality. The traditional behavior of ministries of economics, agriculture, forestry, and public works has been to pursue their separate agendas with minimal regard for environmental policies to which their governments have rhetorically professed commitment.

Examination of the alternatives for implementation of environmental policies affords insight into the forces that shape governments and the policies they administer. The logic of organization in modern democratic governments is a reflection of interest group competition, rather than an indication of the tasks that society, in its broader interests, needs to address. Of the various ways to provide for the administration of environmental affairs, those chosen are possibly, but not certainly, indicators of the true state of environmental policy. Indicators of how governments really work are more often found in their budgets than in their formal structures.

Heads of state like to cite decrees, laws, and official pronouncements as indicative of their environmental concern. But their budgets speak with greater authority regarding their actual priorities. The budget is not the final indicator of commitment; action taken, or not taken, tells more. Yet without budgetary support there will be no action. Moreover, the relative amount of funds allocated to environmental protection is not fully informative. One must know what else the government is doing that may have an environmental impact. For example, a massive road-building program into a tropical rain forest raises a major question regarding the government's environmental priorities. To the unsophisticated observer a substantial allocation of funds for environmental research might appear to signify governmental intent. But that intent might be to delay, perhaps indefinitely, action on a 'troublesome' environmental issue on the argument that 'more research is needed'.

In most governments today, possibly in all, environmental considerations are subordinate to other policy areas, notably agriculture, health, economic development, energy, public works, justice, and foreign and military affairs. Because environmental issues cross conventional categorical jurisdictions, the implementation of environmental policies is difficult to impossible without the cooperation of various administrative agencies, each with its own mission and priorities. Frequently, environmental measures would require a modification or abandonment of a program or policy favored by one or more administrative agencies having influential political constituencies. Departments of agriculture, forestry, public works or highways, energy and land development are very often ill-disposed to environmental protection measures or to allocation of funds for mitigation of environmental damage.

The administrative structures of most modern governments exhibit an *ad hoc* political rationality that is poorly adapted to the ecological circumstances and challenges of the present world. The policies and programs of these governments are frequently counteractive – governments are actually working against themselves. Coordination of policies consistent with ecological realities is needed if constructive results are to be obtained. In attempting to trace the overall impact of its activities in selected countries UNEP was frustrated by the diverse and disjunctive structure of national agencies concerned with environmental issues. In its Evaluation Report, 1987 (UNEP/RE. 87/s, p. 78) the following findings were reported:

A serious problem however, was the difficulty of locating and identifying the departments and personnel responsible for the implementation of specific programmes and projects. This was probably due to lack of continuity in national institutions and personnel, lack of systematic records of activities in the national department and diffuse responsibilities....

At the national level, sectoral bodies, even those that do work with marked environmental implications, are for the most part not directly linked with the national and environmental body. Therefore in many cases communication between UNEP and these bodies flows through a wide variety of centralized channels such as the ministry of foreign affairs or the environment body that do not always have direct contacts at the working level with sectoral and technical bodies. Hence technical UNEP information does not yet systematically reach national technical bodies such as the ministry of agriculture.

The search for a coordinative concept or mechanism has been a major task for environmental policymakers. The National Environmental Policy Act of the United States is a comprehensive and ingenious effort to establish a non-structural coordinative mechanism to bring the policies and programs of all federal agencies into line with a set of principles enacted into law. The environmental analysis and impact statement requirement was intended to be interpreted against a background of substantive requirements specified in the Act. This intent has not been fully realized, but the requirement to 'utilize a systematic, interdisciplinary approach which will ensure the integrated use of the natural and social sciences and the environmental design arts in planning and decision making which may have an impact on man's environment' undertakes to give environmental science a coordinative role in policy. To give effect to the procedural requirements of the statute, departments and agencies must consult with one another regarding the implications of environment-affecting proposals.

In democracies seeking balance among competing interests, the idea of a high level coordinative agency in government is widely suspect among representatives of those interests and the administrators of programs to be 'coordinated.' Coordination implies an encompassing order of some kind. Bureaucrats marching to the beat of their respective drummers may be asked to step to a common rhythm rather than one to which they have been accustomed and which they prefer. Beyond the bureaucracies are public interests concerned to know what premises, principles, and policies will govern the new co-order. Alternatives proposed for the coordination of environmental and resource development policies often reflect differing assumptions and values regarding priorities, and relationships between citizens and their governments.

For example in France the High Committee for the Environment is a large citizen body (55 members in 1987) presided over by the Minister of the Environment for purposes of consultation and advice. It does not have coordinative powers. An effort toward limited coordination however is provided by the Interministerial Committee for the Quality of Life representing the ministries with major environmental concerns. The French example is more characteristic than exceptional. Coordination is difficult in pluralistic societies with diverse values.

Proposals in the United States to establish a department of natural resources have not only been opposed by developers, by managers of forests, minerals, land, water, and wildlife and by the existing bureaucratic agencies, but also by many advocates of environmental concern. Their objections differ. Economic interest groups fear political controls by environmentalists; the environmentally concerned see in 'natural resources' a bias toward economism. Conversely a department of the environment with real coordinative power would certainly be seen as threatening the interests of farmers, commercial foresters, miners, developers and speculators, numerous manufacturers, building contractors, outdoor advertisers and many more. Agencies such as Environment Canada, the Department of the Environment in the UK or the Ministry of the Environment in France have very limited coordinative authority, and the Council on Environmental Quality in the United States has never been allowed to exercise more than a modicum of the responsibility given it by law. Science, and the broad and long term public welfare, have little to do with the way in which economic and societal interests are balanced in the structure of government and in its programs and services.

We have noted that budgets of governmental expenditures may be the most informative indicators of values to be implemented and priorities to be served. But no less than with structures, surface appearances (in this case aggregated statistics) may tell little about what is intended and what will be done. For example, general allocation of funds for scientific research (where not intended to delay action) may be less significant than allocations *among* the sciences and particular areas of inquiry. Dissection of the science budgets of many countries would show a heavy concentration on research directly related to military and industrial purposes. Allocations for research in the biomedical and health sciences reveal differing assumptions regarding relationships between health and environment, notably in how choices between prevention or treatment are viewed. People generally know the risks of contagion from people or other animals but are less aware of the health effects of the inanimate environment – for example of temperature, humidity, noise, toxicity, and radiation. The paradigm that takes man out of nature offers only a weak connection between health, illness, and predisposing influences in the exterior environment. Findings of medical ecology are now strengthening that connection in relation to a growing number of diseases.

In social welfare democracies, strongly committed to health care for the public, the principal concern of politicians has characteristically been with delivery of services rather than with research toward prevention of disease. The fruits of research are often long in ripening, and productive harvest cannot be guaranteed. Health care delivery services bring tangible benefits to the electorate even when these benefits may be of short term duration. A science-based perspective on disease of the lungs, heart, kidneys and nervous system might argue a greater public benefit for basic research into causes and preventions than on expenditures, for example, on artificial hearts and dialysis machines. But the larger and longer-term public interests do not vote nor organize promotional drives, nor contribute to election campaigns. The life of any human is now, not in general, and not in some indefinite future, and this is surely axiomatic in practical politics. Moreover, susceptibility to environmental impacts often varies among individuals, although knowledge regarding environmental influences on health and disease has been increasing. Laws and regulations have been adopted to protect the public from known health hazards – tobacco smoke now being recognized as an environmental hazard. Thus many environmental risks to health are preventable only through changes in the behaviors and lifestyles of people, but it is politically easier to provide medical treatment for the sick than to persuade or compel people to avoid health-threatening activities or to pay the costs of sanative environments.

COMPETITION AMONG VALUES

The environmental movement has not yet achieved unanimity on how best to elevate its priorities in competition with other issues. Going against it is the inevitable predominance of the immediate personal interests of individuals and groups, often perceived to be economic, but also involving personal lifestyles that are environmentally damaging. For example, some forms of outdoor recreation cause excessive stress to the environment; among these are mass tourism, mechanised recreation (e.g. off-road vehicles), indiscriminate hunting and collecting, and recreational housing in natural areas. Organized recreationists assert their rights against so-called 'preservationists' whom they accuse of trying to deprive ordinary people of their preferred ways of enjoying the natural environment (Tucker, 1982). Perceptions of self-interest, economic or otherwise, are susceptible to error and may lead to policy choices that may not be the more generally advantageous among possible alternatives. Nonetheless, they may be the choices that prevail in the competition of practical politics.

An advantage possessed by the environmental movement to a greater degree than many of its political competitors is the openly demonstrable character of its principal ecological concerns. Environmental trends and conditions can often be analyzed, measured, and evaluated by scientific methods. Moreover, through science, now reinforced by computer simulation, likely consequences of policies and actions can be more accurately estimated than formerly. The reliability of forecasts depends, of course, upon the adequacy of the data to be projected, the power of theoretical knowledge and methodology, and the possible incidence of new or unforeseen factors. Nevertheless, the art and science of forecasting is certain to be extended and refined because of the obvious advantages that it confers. To the extent that its reliability is established, it gains credibility in the political world.

It may be that ability to project and influence trends affecting the biosphere will, in time, confer upon the environmental movement a degree of persuasiveness and political influence implausible under present circumstances. A dramatic intimation of what might be possible is provided by the Montreal protocol of 1987 in which 24 industrial and developing countries agreed to limit the manufacture and use of chemical products (CFCs) believed to impair the atmospheric layer of ozone that shields the Earth from dangerous amounts of ultraviolet solar radiation. In this international policy action, economic interests were subordinated to ecological probabilities; but in light of the risks involved, the choice was consistent with ultimate socio-economic interests. An irreversible destruction of the ozone layer would entail serious economic costs as well as threats to health in the ascertainable future.

A lesson to be learnt from the ozone protocol is that it is often a misconception to regard environmental values as invariably competitive with those that are regarded as essentially economic. Economics, however defined, is much more susceptible to varied interpretations than are the natural sciences, not excluding the relatively young science of ecology. The compatibility of economic and ecological values depends greatly on what kinds of economics and what kind of ecology are being compared. The variants of economic interest and reasoning almost always exceed the differences of interpretation that are possible in the findings of the sciences, but there are no value-free methods for assessing the relative merits of alternative economic or ecological propositions.

Relationships between health and environment revealed through scientific investigation ought surely to cause these areas of policy to be regarded as complementary rather than as competitive. The primary health care emphasis, which has been adopted of necessity in many developing countries, depends heavily for its effectiveness on the prevention of environment-related diseases, often associated with housing conditions, personal habits, water quality, and food supplies. The strength of the movement for reduction of air and water pollution in industrialized countries has been an alliance between social movements for public health and environmental quality. These efforts have been reinforced by those human interests, rural as well as urban, that are burdened with risks, costs, and damages because of exposure to contaminants in air, soil, water, and food. Labor organizations have often been active in these efforts, especially on behalf of safety in the workplace.

Questions of political choice among alternative policies are too often posed upon the basis of assumptions that fail to account for the full measure of relevant considerations. Priorities in public policy are customarily set upon the basis of compromise among interests competing over relatively short-term advantages. There is nothing new about this, but there is something new in the prospect that the longer term consequence of trends may, within acceptable margins for error, be predictable. Lengthened perspective thus becomes a more feasible and reliable factor in political choice than heretofore.

Most of what can be said about perspectives and priorities in relation to environmental policy rests upon inference. Empirical data is very limited, chiefly to Western Europe and North America. The funders of research have not regarded comprehensive studies of environmental policymaking a useful way to spend their money. Consequently the information that is available falls short of what there is to be known.

Science now has a significant role in shaping perspectives and priorities on life and the biosphere. The influence of science is often indirect and its movement throughout the various sectors of society and throughout the world has historically been slow and uneven. There are indications, however, that response to scientific findings has been accelerating; the atmospheric ozone issue is a case in point, reaction against cigarette smoking is another. When perspectives change, priority changes may follow among persons who see their environment from new points of view. To change political priorities more is required; institutions must also become responsive to the new insights. To accomplish this, politicians and bureaucrats must somehow be persuaded to adopt the new priorities. This objective is the principle *raison d'etre* for the environmental movement.

5
Politics of environmentalism

'It is entirely possible that when the history of the twentieth century is finally written, the single most important social movement of the period will be judged to be environmentalism.'[1] Understood in the context of man's changing relationship to Earth, this evaluation by sociologist Robert Nisbet (1982), seems probably accurate. But Nisbet has not described the movement in its true scope and complexity. Apparently focusing on environmentalism in the United States and on its more widely publicized fringe expressions, he has not offered a persuasive case for its being 'the single most important social movement of the period.'

He declares that 'environmentalism has become, without losing its eliteness of temper, a mass socialist movement of, not fools, but sun worshippers, macrobiotics, forest druids, and nature freaks generally, committed by course if not by fully shared intent to the destruction of capitalism.'[2] This assessment complements his argument that environmentalism is essentially utopian, that it aims toward a pristine world in which nature is understood as wholly innocent and benign. This commentary in his *Prejudices: A Philosophical Dictionary* entertains but misinterprets. How then should environmentalism be defined?

Environmentalism is the most strongly committed and concerned position in a more comprehensive environmental movement. In its most pronounced expression, environmentalism is to environmental concerns as economism is to economic values. In each case extraordinary importance is imputed respectively to environmental and to economic values, to which all other values ought to yield. Environmentalism in this sense does not characterize the environmental movement as a whole, although it has the greater visibility and assumes the role of vanguard (Milbrath, 1984; O'Riordan, 1981; Pepper, 1984; Petulla, 1980).

85

In the more general environmental movement, the relationship between man and environment is regarded as of high importance, but not necessarily above or beyond all other values. In conventional usage, the term 'environmentalist' indiscriminately includes this larger group. In the general environmental movement the environmental paradigm is regarded as the context within which other values exist, but the validity and under some circumstances the primacy of other values is conceded. The movement is life-centered, distinguished by a sense of moral imperative regarding human behavior in relation to other life forms within the biosphere (Anglemyer & Seagraves, 1984; Schrader-Frechette, 1981; Taylor, 1986). But this attitude is not necessarily utopian and is seldom sentimental; environmentalists, broadly speaking, regard their perspective as reflective of the 'real world' and that of their opponents as 'anthropocentric fantasy'.

The premises of the environmental movement are drawn heavily from science. Its tendencies are neither capitalist nor socialist although social or political intervention is widely favored when necessary to protect the integrity of the biosphere. Governments are perceived to have often been major despoilers of the environment. Environmentalist values are species-oriented and transgenerational, emphasizing personal and social responsibility but not consistent with 'rugged individualism'. This comprehensive and long-range orientation and its implication for public planning has caused some critics to regard environmentalist objectives as 'socialist'. This is largely an over-reactive perception; non-governmental strategies have been advocated and employed as, for example, in voluntary nature conservation efforts and governments, including those allegedly 'socialist' have been among the worst environmental despoilers.

To summarize, 'the environmental movement' identifies a broadly based, complex effort of international character; its adherents cut across social and economic sectors of population, but concentrate among the young and better educated. It is not an elitist movement in an excluding sense nor is it a mass movement comparable to those seeking economic or political reforms (Morrision & Dunlap, 1986). It comprises a diversity of organizations with common orientations but with differing emphases and strategies. A thesis common to the movement is that the undefined endless growth assumptions that now dominate governmental and economic policies are impossible of realization in the long-run and destructive in the short-run. All goals of the environmental movement have not been clearly defined, but among them the attainment of a sustainable economy of high environmental quality is a widely shared objective.

A POLITICAL PARADOX

We find in the world today a wide spectrum of agreement-disagreement over the incidence, significance, urgency, and implications of an environmental crisis. To students of policy choice, interest in this spectrum is focused upon changes it displays in the movement and direction of popular beliefs and values concerning the environment. Although there is much yet to be learnt regarding popular attitudes toward environmental relationships, leading analysts of opinion (Morrison & Dunlap, 1986; Milbrath, 1984; Mitchell, 1984), are in general agreement regarding trends. During the years since the mid-1960s there has been consistent evidence of public concern over the quality of the environment and a willingness to be taxed and regulated on behalf of environmental quality, health, and safety. In competition with other public issues, this attitude has held relatively steady throughout North America and Western Europe. Changing priorities of governments of the day appear to have had little effect upon public opinion. Yet in comparing apparent public preferences with policies of particular governments, questions do arise.

If environmental quality is valued as highly as surveys in Britain, Germany, France, the Netherlands, Canada and the United States appears to indicate, why has it not generally been an issue on which candidates for public office are elected or defeated? In Europe, chiefly in West Germany, the Green parties appear to be exceptions as they have elected candidates on environmental issues. Environmental issues are often more vigorously contended in municipal elections in Europe and North America, perhaps because many environmental problems are confronted most directly at local levels.

In the United States, Ronald Reagan was twice elected to the presidency although his negative attitude toward the environmental movement was well known. Exit interviews at polling places indicated that substantial numbers of people who voted for him disapproved of his environmental policies. Objections to Reagan's environmental record were as often directed toward what he failed to do in enforcing and extending protective measures as toward policies that were regarded as positively destructive (Dunlap, 1987). In the 1988 federal elections in Canada and the United States 'the environment' did at last emerge as a major issue. In 1989 parliamentary elections, governments fell in the Netherlands and Norway, in part a consequence of popular dissatisfaction with official response to environmental concerns. Ironically the head of the defeated government in Norway chaired the UN Commission on Environment and Development. Any simple explanation of an apparent discrepancy between the

environmental beliefs and values prevailing in society and those held by
public officials is likely to be misleading.

The principal variable in public attitudes on environmental issues
appears to be salience – the relative importance of an issue at a particular
point in time. Distinctions here should be drawn between enduring basic
societal values, among which environment now belongs, and issues of
immediate personal concern. Economic issues bearing directly upon the
lives of people have an obvious salience where personal anxieties are
present. Where the spirit of nationalism prevails, foreign relations may
become paramount. Until recent years, environmental concerns tended to
be localized and to be issues in local rather than national politics. Broader
environmental issues have gained salience, however, when need for
protective measures coincides with regional economic interests. Examples
are the high priority given to the acidic deposition issue in Canada and
Sweden and to coastal oil spills in France and California. Environmental
concerns have become broader still when public awareness of planetary
risks from a diminishing ozone layer, an atmospheric greenhouse effect, or
radioactive fallout became imminent.

Elective politicians almost everywhere, have had difficulty in learning
how to respond to the more aggressive demands of environmentalists.
Three variables influencing the responsiveness of politicians are (1) the
price of election to office, (2) the effectiveness of organized pressure from
particular interests, and (3) the limits of choice available to the public
official or legislator within the institutional context in which the public
business is carried on.

In most democratic societies election to public office requires publicity;
unknown candidates are almost never elected. Publicity, especially in an
age of highly developed information technology, costs money – often a
great deal of money, and altruism is rarely a motive for contributions to
political campaign funds. Money need not directly buy legislative seats or
votes to have some effect upon the issues that a legislator will initiate or
endorse. Economic factors weigh heavily in most political decisionmaking.
Environmental protection organizations are seldom equipped or inclined to
assist political campaigns with direct financial contributions, although
they may develop their own publicity to help elect or defeat particular
candidates. The League of Conservation Voters assesses and publicizes the
voting records of candidates for reelection for public office in the United
States.

Constituent pressure need not be improper or excessive to influence
political policymakers. Politicians generally know whom they must regard
as important and whom they can afford to neglect. So-called opinion
leaders may not in fact represent a numerical majority of a politician's

constituency, but if they represent active and concerned citizens able to inflict political injury, they will probably get the politician's attention.

At least one sociological study (Miller *et al.*, 1970), and testimony from officials and their observers, indicate that office holders and civic leaders, at least at local levels, tend to respond to direct importunities from well-organized and influential constituencies. Purposive minority pressure can out-influence an apathetic, uninformed, and unfocused majority. Where environmental groups have combined effective organization and ability to deliver votes they have been sometimes able to defeat more heavily financed economic interests. Frequently, however, it is not opposition that defeats environmental concerns; it is the combined pressures of aggressive politics on other issues that crowd often more fundamental environmental items off the politician's priority agenda.

Politicians work within institutional constraints and opportunities that affect what they can or will do. Legal provisions, customary expectations, and numerous interactive relationships influence their roles in the politics of environmental concern. Two conditioning circumstances are major factors in the apparent mismatch between the priorities of the public and those of their political representatives on issues of environmental policy.

The first circumstance is the pluralist and diverse character of the environmental movement. Because membership in the movement is voluntary, is not primarily professional, nor subject to regimentation or discipline by hierarchical authorities, as for example in professional or trade associations or unions, it does not easily present a united front in political contests. The strategies and tactics of environmental groups vary widely, from direct action, even resorting (on rare occasions) to various forms of violence, to mediation of disputes, to dialogues with opponents, and sometimes to compromise agreements. Amidst a diversity of opinion on environmental issues, to what voices should the politician listen? Which, if any, are 'voices of the people?'

The second circumstance, neither audible or tangible, is the accelerated transitory character of the present era. Neither politicians nor environmentalists can be expected to appreciate its significance, yet its effects are visible in the tempo of multiple change. Present day transitions are more rapid and far-reaching than at any previous time. Assumptions and values, ideas and institutions, have been unable to keep pace with technological innovation and advances in scientific perceptions. People in and out of politics are at differing stages of adaptation and comprehension. Laws and institutions are not easily altered in such circumstances, and obsolescence and unresponsiveness often characterize the policies and procedures of governments whose leaders are not sure where events are tending. But paradoxically, aggressive political minorities may force adoption of unprecedented official policies that leave many people disaffected and alienated in relation to political authority.

DIMENSIONS OF ENVIRONMENTALISM

If, as some opinion analysts allege, environmentalists are the vanguard of the more generalized environmental movement and of the development of a new environmental paradigm, their beliefs and assumptions should have major social relevance. The following summary of the environmentalist paradigm should clarify the ways in which it engages the varied aspects of politics. We begin with its assumptions, turning thereafter to the range, style, and tactics of the movement.

The assumptions of the environmentalist are few, direct, and simple; their ramifications are numerous, indirect, and complex. In the environmentalist paradigm the world of humans is unequivocally dependent on the Earth and its biogeochemical systems which make life on Earth possible. Even in outer space man's life is tethered to the Earth. This Earth, whose biogeochemical systems we call 'nature', is neither malignant nor benign, just or unjust. Nature may be described as 'indifferent' to human affairs, which, in part, succeed or fail to the extent that they are consistent with natural forces (i.e. laws of nature).

The environmentalist thus sees the opportunities and limitations of human society as governed by possibilities inherent in nature. Through understanding the 'laws' of nature and the way the world of nature works, humans are able to turn natural forces and processes to their own advantage. But it is not true that humans can accomplish whatever they can imagine. There are natural limits that may preclude possibilities that humans seek and in which many fervently believe.

Among these, the belief that puts environmentalists most sharply at odds with the traditional modern paradigm is their insistence on the limits to expansive growth. The environmentalists' position is that the term 'growth,' to have rational meaning, must be used in a more qualified and specified sense than is usually encountered in the rhetoric of political economy. Environmentalists find no warrant for the belief that expansive growth can continue indefinitely within limited space. But the growth syndrome is so deeply ingrained in the assumptions and values of conventional modernity that its defenders will go to great lengths to make the concept appear rational and necessary. Growth may be defined to mean improvement, or non-material growth, as for example in knowledge or in resource-conserving technology. But these appear to be semantic evasions of the problem; they are clearly not what politicians, business leaders, and most economists have in mind when they measure growth by

quantitative increases in sales, in investment, in agriculture, in manufacturing, in building construction, in mining, in transportation, in
generation and use of energy, in growth of human populations, and in all
activities contributing to the gross national product. Growth in this
context means what most people assume it to mean – 'more and bigger'.

In the environmentalist paradigm, the rational concept of growth is
exemplified by the self-renewing but physically limiting processes of
nature. Self-controlling organic growth characterizes all living things,
except perhaps cancerous cells which ultimately kill their host. In human
society this steady state or homeostatic growth implies stabilization of
populations at numbers low enough to avoid attrition of the self-renewing
capabilities of the natural environment. Science-based technology may
raise the support capability of the environment, but not without risk that
increased capacity developed in one sector may entail impairment or losses
in others. Certain unintended side-effects of the Green Revolution are cases
in point (Dahlberg, 1979).

The no-growth slogans of some environmentalists are directed to the
conventional use of the term which the public-at-large generally
understands to imply 'more and bigger'. In the paradigm of environmentalism the only economy sustainable in the long run will function in
a homeostatic self-renewing state. This state of affairs need not be static,
but it cannot be indefinitely expansive beyond limits set by nature,
including human nature (Hirsch, 1976). The danger now being incurred
by modern growth economies is overshoot beyond their support and
renewal capabilities, resulting in a crash from which recovery, if possible,
may long be delayed (Catton, 1980).

From these considerations it follows that environmentalism would place
restraints upon the political economies of both capitalism and socialism.
Environmental 'fundamentalists', more concerned over prevention than
remediation, would set the ground-rules under which enterprise operates
and are only secondarily concerned with the regulatory controls. This
emphasis does not imply an accommodating attitude toward currently
dominant practices in agriculture, manufacturing, merchandising or other
economic activities. In its most radical form, environmentalism would
require fundamental changes in the technoeconomic infrastructure of
society. The further modern society pushes population growth and
material consumption, and forces the productivity of natural systems, the
more radical the adjustment required to prevent ultimate failure of
planetary life-support systems.

The automobile is a case in point. The benefits of the automobile have
been seriously offset by environmental damage caused by its excessive use.
This damage is in large measure a consequence of numbers (i.e. of
growth). Toxic emissions from petro-fuels have created hazards to health

and comfort; accidents are a major cause of injury and death. The moderate, temporizing, but costly and questionably effective responses of modern governments have been emission controls and seat belts. Radical environmentalists would severely restrict the mass use of automobiles; a less radical polity would be to require a renewable non-polluting fuel as a condition for automotive manufacture. From an environmentalist perspective, such policies are prudent rather than radical inasmuch as the days of affordable fossil fuels are numbered. Other unwanted environmental effects of mass use of automobiles are their inordinate consumption of non-fuel natural resources, and the disposal problems presented by used tires, batteries, and hard-to-recycle metals and plastics, the space sacrificed to highways and parking facilities, and the uneconomic dispersal of residential and commercial facilities.

With automobiles as with people, the world faces a problem of numbers. That human populations are almost everywhere excessive by some criterion is an opinion widely shared among environmentalists. Nearly all of the factors that contribute to the attrition of environmental quality and the self-renewing capabilities of the Earth are exacerbated by numbers and densities of human populations. The issue of population policy is even more sensitive and contentious than that of growth, to which it is obviously related. From the environmental perspective there is no reason to assume a human right of unlimited reproduction.

It is possible that, as between the environmentalist paradigm and conventional modern catalog of human rights the number of items would be about the same, but the rights would be different. The 'rights' issue becomes problematic for the environmental movement because, although science has nothing to say about it, the concept of 'natural rights' is deeply embedded in modern Western culture. The natural rights concept is philosophical and its relationship to environmentalism will be considered in chapter 6, to follow. The relevant point here is that 'rights' are an issue upon which there are politically significant differences within the environmental movement. Are 'rights' exclusively human or, for example, do trees have rights (Stone, 1975, 1987)? On the matter of 'rights' there does not appear to be an environmentalist consensus.

The environmental movement is a manifestation of the transition from conventional modernity to a yet to be defined post-modern state. Its influence is more accurately attributable to the status of members than to their numbers. It incorporates principles of ethical conduct, social priorities, and laws that are not easily compromised with presently dominant assumptions. As with people generally, environmentalists may hold contradictory positions, and their opinions on non-environmental issues, especially on social and moral questions are diverse. They nevertheless exhibit a general preference for a stable, predictable world in which respect for the natural (cosmic) order of things is fundamental.

Clearly the environmental movement has attained international dimensions; from its origins in the so-called developed or industrialized countries it has spread to the less developed nations of the world. Non-governmental environmental organizations have grown in size in the developed countries and numbers in the less developed world. Contrary to its critics, it is demonstrably not a class-bound movement. Its elite tendencies stem not from privileges but from knowledge that some environmentalists regard as superior to that commonly held. There is within the movement a strong emphasis on popular education and information; environmentalists are more than ready to share their knowledge and perspectives widely. The movement has characteristics of a proselytising religion.

CRITICS OF ENVIRONMENTALISM

It should not be difficult to see why the environmental movement, especially in its more advanced forms, should arouse hostility among people whose values it threatens. A movement that contradicts people's beliefs about how the world works and should work and which simultaneously appears to threaten their personal economic interests is certain to invite opposition. Among the ways in which the environmental movement is inimical to the dominant conventional paradigm are these:

(a) it undermines the satisfaction of people in traditional beliefs and behaviors, contradicting the assumption that the world was made for man and hence rejecting the traditional theologies of creation;

(b) it threatens certain economic theories, interests, and objectives, especially those placing material growth above most other values;

(c) it exposes the short-term expedience that often characterizes politics and personal economic transactions;

(d) it accepts, where necessary, authoritative restriction of individual choice and conduct, often substituting politics for market allocation of values.

As of the end of the 1980s, outspoken critics of the environmental movement were relatively few, although some have been conspicuous. Skeptics have been more numerous, some professing sympathy with environmentalism but others questioning its sincerity (Tucker, 1982), or its priority among human social values (Neuhaus, 1971). These adversaries tend to group into two distinguishable categories – philosophic and materialistic.

Philosophic objections to environmentalism are voiced by *laissez-faire* libertarians and by some public choice political economists who see in environmentalist goals and strategies the imposition of a particular set of values on society. Libertarians not only oppose governmental interference with the free choices of people in their use of property and environment, some object no less to the more passive role of government in maintaining national parks, wilderness areas, and wildlife sanctuaries which, in their view, are involuntary subsidies from the entire public for particular values allegedly enjoyed by a relative minority of the population.

At the opposite end of the philosophical spectrum are those critics who see in environmentalism competition for funds and attention that they believe should be allocated to causes of social justice and welfare, health care delivery services, child-care centers, and education for the culturally disadvantaged, among the whole litany of liberal reforms. The libertarians see socialism in the environmentalist agenda whereas the liberal left often find it elitist, self-serving of upper middle-class interests at the expense of ordinary working people. Neither liberals nor libertarians are inhibited from borrowing objections from each other's list of criticisms.

The most widely held and influential philosophic attitude rejecting or discounting environmentalist perspectives is economism, a belief in primacy of economic forces and values in human affairs. Economism is surely one of the more important and pervasive elements in the foundation of modern society and government. Economic rationality postulates a theory of human behavior that owes little to science and much to a deductive logic that interprets events on the basis of philosophical assumptions regarding human motivation and rationality.

Economism is a dominating philosophical assumption in both capitalism and Marxist socialism. Its premises underlie a wide range of national and international policies and the failure of many of them to produce desired results has not noticeably lessened the faith of people in their veracity. It is important to distinguish the analytic capabilities of economists, essential to sound policy development, and too often under-utilized or distorted in politics, from the prescriptive opinions of political economists. The prescriptions of economists sometimes work, but so also do nostrums of witch doctors in whom primitive societies similarly retain an unquestioning faith. Not all economists, of course, endorse economistic assumptions; some few argue that valid economic theory should be consistent with ecological and sociological realities insofar as the latter offer demonstrably reliable explanations of human behavior (Daly, 1977; Boulding, 1981; Rhoades, 1985).

The fault in economism lies not in economics as a field of study; rather in the unwarranted confidence sometimes carried to the point of arrogance by some economists, but perhaps more often by economically unsophisticated persons among the general public. To inject ecological rationality into economic analysis has been an objective within the environmental movement that appears to be having some slight success. For example, there has been an effort by environmental organizations to bring genuine ecological analysis into the investment policies of the World Bank. But economistic thinking, although under challenge, is still deeply entrenched in the culture of modern industrial society.

Hardly philosophic in outlook is the penchant of a few individuals to attack the environmental movement and its objectives with the smirking enthusiasm of rebellious young boys itching to throw a brick through a shiny plate glass window. Such reaction is not criticism in any rational sense (although it has often claimed to be) and may be rooted in various causes in which environmental values are viewed as competitive. Anti-environmental polemics may also be instigated by the prospects of well-paying audiences, for example at conventions of industrial and trade associations. Attacking the environmental movement by ridiculing alleged absurdities has been a popular technique combining humor with moral indignation and invective. In the United States, books such as Cy Adler's *Ecological Fantasies . . . Falling Watermelons* (1973) and Grayson and Shepard's *The Disaster Lobby* (1973) struck a responsive note among journalists and business executives disconcerted by the onset of aggressive environmentalism. In the United Kingdom, John Maddox's *The Doomsday Syndrome* (1972) offered a more decorous rebuttal of environmentalist exaggerations.

Materialistic objections to environmentalism are less complicated and more obvious. Money, power, and mission are the motives that cause land developers and speculators, mining, lumbering, and industrial farming interests, manufacturers, and public works promoters, to damn environmentalism and regard it as a conspiracy against human progress. Still, not all representatives of these interests are hostile to all aspects of the environmental movement. Many important achievements in environmental protection have been assisted by corporate enterprise, which, of course, encompasses a wide range of diversity.

Criticisms of environmentalism from material interests tend to be directed to specific policies or actions that bear directly upon their operations or profits rather than against the environmental movement in principle. Some economic activities, however, are in chronic conflict with environmentalism. Transportation, land development, industrial agriculture, economistic forestry and the production and distribution of energy are activities in more general conflict with the objectives of environmentalists. These activities occupy sectors of the economy that the long range objectives of the environmental movement would substantially transform (Lovins, 1975).

Less consistent adversaries of environmentalism are 'blue collar' workers and labor union leaders to whom jobs are a major consideration. The allegation that working people reject environmental priorities is based largely on misinformation regarding the diversity of attitudes among them and by a distorted interpretation of environmentalism that identifies it as concerned almost wholly with environmental aesthetics. Among laborers as among managers a range and diversity of opinion can be found regarding environmental priorities.

Industrial employers have sometimes used threats of job losses or pay cuts to rally worker support against environmental controls imposed by government. The effectiveness of this tactic has proved dubious, especially when analysis of the alleged burdens of environmental controls shows them to be false or greatly exaggerated. Many unions have carried on educational and political campaigns on behalf of health and safety in the workplace. Some have extended their concern to worker communities, and have included on their political agendas issues such as safe housing, clean air, and provisions for parks and outdoor recreation.

A sign of changing times is that the smoking stacks of factories are no longer acceptable symbols of prosperity. In industrially advanced countries, quality of life considerations have penetrated working class ethos. Dangerous or degraded conditions in the environment are no longer tacitly accepted as 'the price of progress.' Farm workers exposed to toxic pesticides and industrial workers endangered by a long list of carcinogens and mutagens have resorted to legislation and to litigation in the courts for relief and compensation. In these efforts they have frequently been joined by environmental groups and through these associations have become open to the broader perspectives of the environmental movement.

As noted in chapter 1, the environmental movement has been a target of criticism and condescension among some scientists. Distinction should be drawn between idiosyncrastic prejudices, often based on misconception, and legitimate criticism of erroneous beliefs and propositions that are found in environmentalism as in all social movements. In the main, the criticism of scientists has been constructive, even sympathetic, to objectives of the environmental movement. Although there are many aspects of the environmentalist paradigm that are not scientific, science remains the most solid and durable element in its intellectual foundation.

ENVIRONMENTAL CONFLICT RESOLUTION

Politics implies conflict; were everyone to agree on everything, nothing would remain but implementation. Politics also concerns the problems that people perceive, whether real or imaginary, and for which public solutions are sought. The business of politics is to find ways to bring these problems to some sort of resolution. Where goals and values differ, answers to a policy problem cannot help but create winners and losers unless a transcending encompassing principle of agreement can be found. As we have noted, environmental policies in today's world create hostility among those interests who see themselves as losers and who often possess economic, and political, and journalistic means of defense.

Because the environmental movement must in large measure look to social action to accomplish its objectives, and because that action must frequently occur through government, environmentalism is unavoidably political. But because of the wide diversity of its adherents it seldom presents a wholly united front, especially in relation to the strategy and tactics of political action. Outside the arena of controversy, as well as within it, are efforts to inform and educate. However, when these measures become overt efforts to achieve a contested objective, policy questions arise over the wisdom or legitimacy of alternative forms of advocacy and action.

In the more advanced democratic societies the most widely used methods of resolving conflicts over environmental policies have been: (1) legislation, (2) litigation, and (3) mediation. In each of these approaches science plays a role, as of course it does in more passive methods of information, education, negotiation, and attempted persuasion.

A strategy common to the environmental movement everywhere is to revise the ground rules under which society operates. This objective is attained in a formal sense through written law: ordinances at municipal levels, statutes and constitutional provisions at provincial-national levels, and treaties or comparable agreements at international levels. Since mid-twentieth century a matrix of environmental legislation has been developed encompassing all political levels. Discussion of this substance of the body of law will be deferred to chapters 7 and 8. The forms and substance of environmental legislation and international agreements are the subject matter of books (Schneider, 1979; Caldwell, 1984) and we can do no more here than indicate their relationship to the environmental movement.

In the placing of environmental issues on the agendas of political parties and presenting scientific information to law-making bodies, the roles of non-governmental organizations, especially those with science-related missions, have been prominent. The proliferation of non-governmental policy-oriented organizations has been a phenomenon of the decades since mid-century (Feld, 1972), and this growth has been especially marked recently in relation to environmental issues.

Scientific organizations have played a major part in providing the informational base needed for environmental laws and treaties. In this process of framing policies and rules, science plays several roles. First, scientific investigation has often discovered the existence of a problem or identified the cause of disturbing phenomena. For example, national and international law-making has followed scientific investigation of the disintegration of the ozone layer and the acidification of lakes, streams, soils, and forests. Legislation to control or prevent environmental pollution has depended heavily upon scientific information, although it should be acknowledged that laws written by lawyers and politicians often use science selectively to accommodate political preferences and sometimes interpret scientific evidence in ways that scientists generally regard as unsupported by the known facts.

Legislative enactment does not in itself resolve a controversy or implement a policy. The validity of a law or ordinance may be attacked in the judicial courts by those who oppose it, or by those who believe that it does not really address the problem that it is purported to resolve. Thus litigation becomes another method of dealing with environmental conflict in countries where there are courts of law open to the adjudication of such disputes. In many countries, environmental disputes which very often relate to action by governmental bodies are commonly adjudicated in administrative courts. In most modern states the first forum for the arraignment of an issue is a hearing tribunal within a governmental agency. Appeals may thereafter be taken to judicial courts and this is the case to an exceptionally large degree in the United States where perhaps, as nowhere else in the world, the judicial courts have become the dominant expositors of the law.

Environmental litigation turns frequently upon disputes over the validity of alleged scientific facts. Contending parties undertake to marshall scientific expertise in support of their positions. Because of the scope and complexity of environmental issues several sciences may be involved, and opponents seek to ground their case on the sciences most likely to support their contentions or to refute those of their adversaries. Judicial procedures, however, are seldom well suited to determine the validity of scientific facts, or the weights to be given them in relation to other facts. Few judges presiding in courts of law are trained in the sciences or in scientific reasoning. To compensate for this deficiency, proposals have been made to establish special courts to adjudicate disputes resting primarily on interpretations of scientific evidence, but this idea does not appear to have won acceptance anywhere (Nyhart, 1977; Leventhal, 1974).

In many countries and notably in Scandinavia, negotiation and conciliation have been preferred to battles in the judicial courts (Lundqvist, 1974). Resolution of environmental conflicts is characteristically negotiated among the parties directly concerned. This may or may not result in the environmentally best solution, if indeed there is one. It is usually less costly and protracted than court proceedings and is more easily implemented if the negotiations result in agreement among the parties.

In Canada and the United States mediation by third parties, external to the disputants, has become a professional enterprise at local and international levels (Amy, 1987; Cormick & Knaster, 1986). Short of actual mediation, consultation among potential adversaries has also been undertaken (Utton, 1973). These forms of conflict resolution may be regarded as non-political, yet some elements of political behavior are inherent in any process that seeks a policy commitment as an outcome. Mediation and consultation work best where there is present common ground regarding assumptions and values sufficient to support a consensus or capable of being enlarged to achieve this result (National Coal Policy Project, 1978). Here, mutual respect for scientific criteria and evidence contribute to the possibility of agreement in defining the problem under dispute and in the mutual acceptance of evidence agreed to be relevant.

Arbitration is a method half-way between mediation and adjudication. It involves agreement by disputants to place the decision regarding the merits of their claims in the hands of a panel of experts. This method has not often been used in the settlement of environmental disputes although it has potentially the advantages claimed for special science courts. Its more notable uses have been to settle controversies arising under international law. The Trail Smelter controversy between Canada and the United States is the principal international environmental arbitration case to date (Trail Smelter Arbitral Tribunal, 1935; Dinwoode, 1972).

Finally, one other approach toward environmental controversy should be recognized, although its strategy is to heighten and dramatize conflict as a step toward ultimate resolution. This approach has been variously described as direct action or ecological guerrilla warfare. It has been adopted by strongly motivated environmentalist groups when legal or other conventional means of averting environmental destruction appear to have failed. More moderate expressions of activist discontent take the form of paid advertisements in the newspaper press, street demonstrations, picketing and boycotts, and blocking access to offices, highways, or sites in controversy (e.g. nuclear plants or forests threatened by lumbering). These actions may or may not be regarded as non-violent. Actions at the margin are illustrated by efforts of the international environmental organizations (e.g. Greenpeace) to frustrate the slaughter of fur seal pups by spraying their fur with a paint that would ruin pelts for commercial purposes. Greenpeace has also sought to obstruct the maneuvers of Russian and Japanese whalers and the testing of nuclear weapons by the French. So called pirate whalers (i.e. those not conforming to quotas established by the International Whaling Commission) are fair game for a number of environmental groups that discover and publicize their activities.

Where damaging enterprise is undertaken outside of the law or manifestly contrary to law, some strongly dedicated environmental groups are prepared to resort to selective violence. This is especially true where irreversible destruction immediately threatens environmental ecosystems or species and more orthodox defensive measures are unavailable within the time required. In these confrontations violence is not always confined to the environmental activists. Private, corporate, and even governmental interests have resorted to sudden, unannounced, and definitive destruction or impairment of a disputed site, landscape, ecosystem, or even a living species to remove any argument for environmental protection. This effort to create a *fait accompli*, thus leaving the environmentalists with nothing to preserve but regrets, has been called 'ecocide' or 'ecotage' and has been used with relish, albeit infrequently, by the more sturdy opponents of environmentalism. The guerrilla response is to fill the radiators of bulldozers with cooking rice, to pour sand in lubricating oil and to drive spikes into trees in forests threatened by chain saws. These acts have been taken less in expectation of stopping environmental destruction than in hope of drawing public attention to the issue. Especially where exploiters of the environment are acting illegally, the activists use these measures to embarrass indifferent or collusive bureaucrats into enforcement of the law. Science generally has little to contribute to the resolution of these disputes. Its appropriate role is to examine public policies governing the issues in which these controversies arise.

THE POLITICAL FUTURE

The environment has now become a regular and continuing political concern in all major industrial countries and in many of the so-called developing countries. This status has only been achieved during the past two decades, but will be a permanent addition to political agendas throughout the world if humanity is to safeguard its own future. It has become an international and even transnational issue and has already been the cause of important additions to international law and organization.

The circumstances that insure a continuing future for the politics of environmentalism are everywhere evident. Not only are people becoming aware of environmental problems, present but not hitherto fully perceived or evaluated, new problems are arising, the ozone issue being a case-in-point. Chapters 7 and 8 describe issues that either cannot or will not be ignored and that now demand national and international attention. Matters which societies are only now beginning to see as problematic as, for example, the carbon dioxide-trace gas balance in the atmosphere or the depletion and contamination of ground water will require policy choices regardless of political preferences. Most people appear to place health and survival above other considerations and these will inevitably be factors in the environmental politics of the future.

That environmental issues will be high on political agendas in the future is more certain than how they will get there. Either or both of two developments may occur, and to some extent already have occurred. Existing political parties may redirect their priorities to give a place, or a higher place, to environmental issues. New parties may form to the extent that the old parties appear to be unable or unwilling to accommodate change that would give higher visibility to environmentalism. The way in which these choices are made will vary from country to country, but a few general conjectures are plausible.

The first of these reflects the progressive character of the environmental movement. Although in democratic elections environmentalists have sometimes been perceived as single-issue voters, the environment as a political issue is not isolated from other concerns. This book shares the more widely held thesis (Inglehart, 1987) that environmental politics is an indicator of a major value shift in modern society. It is one of a number of social issues that characterize the transition from modern to post-modern times. Social scientists differ over how this change should be described. Is it a movement from materialism to quality of life values, from authoritarian to libertarian social relationships or the reverse, or from centralized hierarchy to decentralized autonomy?

That a significant shift in social values has occurred during the latter decades of the twentieth century is empirically demonstrable (Capra, 1982). It is also clear that this change has occurred more rapidly, pervasively, and fundamentally than has characterized most social transitions in human history. The phenomenal increase in information-communication technologies may account for this. The number and diversity of change indicators and their differing tempo in different societies complicates reliable conjectures regarding the outcome of the changes for the environmental future. Conclusions regarding the larger significance of these trends must therefore move beyond the limits of hard evidence. Yet the cumulative weight of inference drawn from observed trends supports the proposition that the environmental movement is a major aspect of a major change in how people believe the world works. The transition from modern to post-modern assumptions, values, and lifestyles, is the visible manifestation of this paradigm shift, and the environmental movement appears to be in the main current in this river of perceptual change.

Environmentalism is thus a part of a bigger social transition and will carry on as an integral part of it. In this transition the primacy of economics as a determinant of political choice has been modified with rising levels of economic well-being and diminishing degrees of socio-economic inequality in developed industrial societies with advanced systems of social welfare. But trends toward quality of life values are also discernible in some of the less developed countries in which there is a politically influential middle class that is literate and aware of trends in Western Europe and North America and of the findings of the sciences. The environment is therefore not an isolated or ephemeral issue vulnerable to shifting popular enthusiasms. It forms a large part of new political alternatives that seeks to broaden the value base of political decision-making. New alternative movements will be enduring because the circumstances that have called them into being will not go away.

A logical response of established political parties would be to coopt the New Choice movements and to reorder priorities, programs, and rhetoric. But political leadership almost everywhere has been counter-intuitive. This is partly because the paradigm shift is to a large degree inter-generational. Titular political party leaders, especially those of the authoritarian left and right, tend to be older males who still see the world as it was during the first half of the twentieth century. Popular support for ideological parties of both left and right has diminished while their oldish leaders cling to dogmas no longer regarded as axiomatic by younger voters who seek a new set of priorities for political action. Decline in strength of the Communist party throughout Europe is one case-in-point; inability of conservatives in the United States to implement their agenda during eight years of the ostensibly conservative Reagan presidency is another. The Gorbachev reforms in the USSR appear to be a hopeful effort to free socialism from nineteenth century ideological rigidities and open the Communist party to new values and perspectives.

The general response of established parties, having been slow relative to changing values, has left an opening for new political parties. In Western Europe, the Green or Ecological parties have emerged to represent the new choice constituency of younger voters. Ronald Inglehart (1987) summarizes the 'spectacular growth of Ecological parties, having a distinct and still evolving ideology concerning the quality of the physical and social environment.'

They have grown from almost nothing in the mid-1970s, to being the largest component of the New Politics parties. In the last few years, Ecology parties have won representation in the national parliaments of Belgium, Luxembourg and West Germany, and in the delegations to the European Parliament elected in 1984 from Belgium, Germany, Italy, and the Netherlands. Their future potential may be more than meets the eye . . . .[3]

Depending somewhat on national circumstances and leadership, influence of the Ecology parties initially may be greater at local levels. This would appear to be true in France as well as in the rest of Western Europe. In the United States the apparent political indifference of an indeterminate but potentially significant number of younger potential voters may be in part explained by the irrelevance of the Republican and Democrat parties to their priority concerns. There appears to be a potential constituency among the younger electorate that the party leaders have been unable or unwilling to attract. In Europe some of the Social Democratic parties have tried to coopt the ecology vote. But to the extent that the older parties absorb the New Choice constituencies they take new goals and values, thus risking their own transformation.

More speculative, but not implausible, is the prospect of a new international political party (or federation). The communist internationale became the world's first international political party, although the political organization of the world into national states necessitated its operation as a federation of national parties. The formation of the Council of Europe, the European Community and the Parliament of Europe has made the idea of multinational or transnational parties more plausible. This plausibility is not confined to Europe. It is not an unreasonable prospect where nationalism is declining and issues of growing urgency are transnational in character. In North America, non-partisan binational citizen groups in Canada and the United States have worked together on common environmental issues, pressuring their respective governments for desired policies and actions; collaborating in opposition to contamination in the Great Lakes, to acidic deposition, and to the ecological hazards of the Garrison Diversion irrigation project in North Dakota.

But will not traditional alignments reappear as the younger cohorts of voters age to maturity? More likely not. The world has changed and the literate and informed youth may see it more nearly as it is. Youthful interpretation of the meaning of what they see may, however, be distorted by the inadequacies of present day educational systems to provide an ecologic or synthesizing view of the world in historical perspective, and by dogmatic ideological indoctrination. Yet in Western societies, a large part of the generation reaching voting age during the 1980s was never socialized into the assumptions and values of the old industrial order. Even in the Marxist-dominated societies where nineteenth century socialist assumptions persist, the orthodoxy of the far left is on the defensive and concessions to new realities are beginning to be made by Communist party leadership in Eastern Europe and the Soviet Union. The best contextual argument for the persistence of a politics of environmentalism that I have seen is Ronald Inglehart's conclusion that:

The old ideological paradigm no longer corresponds to reality. Neither the Marxist fundamentalists nor the laissez-faire fundamentalists have adequate answers for the problems of advanced industrial society. The goals of individuals and the challenges facing society are different from those of a generation ago.[4]

Twenty years ago I concluded the book *Environment: A Challenge to Modern Society* (1970), with a statement which, although it then seemed clear to me, is more strongly apparent today: 'The management of man's relationship with his environment is a practical expression of a system of ethics, it is an application of values, beliefs, and moralities not only between man and nature, but between man and man'.[5] The environment, being a context common to all mankind, inevitably becomes a subject for politics as its challenges can be met only through social consensus or social action. Ethical and political concepts have been changing very significantly as an indirect, unintended, and largely unforeseen consequence of advances in the sciences. The emerging planetary paradigm is being shaped by these influences and the environmental movement is a principal agent of this process of transformation. How thorough and how rapid this transformation may be is, of course, a matter of conjecture.

NOTES

1. R. Nisbet (1982). *Prejudices: A Philosophical Dictionary.* Cambridge, Massachusetts: Harvard University Press, p. 101.
2. Ibid., 107.
3. R. Inglehart (1987). Values change in industrial societies. *American Political Science Review* 81 (No. 4. December): 1299.
4. Ibid., 1303.
5. Chapter 9, 'Environmental Management as an Ethical System,' p. 232.

6
Social and economic implications

Basic to this book is its focus on a critical aspect of a large and fundamental transition in human society, of which the environmental movement is a major manifestation. The transition has not been abrupt nor its indicators self-explanatory, but its momentum appears to be accelerating. From one viewpoint, a basic and irreversible change in human circumstances may appear as a historical discontinuity, occurring more significantly in human attitudes and values than in the visible world. Although the change may extend beyond a single generation, it has been marked by a sudden social realization that a major situational change has been occurring. There comes a day in the life of each person when the loss of youth is realized and the conditions of maturity and age are confronted. So it may be with modern society at the close of the twentieth century.

With insight earlier than that of most observers, Eric Ashby placed the environmental movement in its historical perspective in lectures delivered at Stanford University in 1978. He said:

What we are experiencing is not a crisis; it is a climacteric. For the rest of man's history on earth, so far as one can foretell, he will have to live with problems of population, of resources, of pollution. And the seminarial problem remains unsolved: Can man adapt himself to *anticipate* environmental constraints?[1]

This is the question of policy addressed in this book. I share with Lord Ashby the cautious optimism that the answer can be 'Yes'. Yet I have no illusion that any answer is certain, or that a positive answer will be reached.

How this question of adaptation to environmental (i.e. cosmic) exegencies is answered depends greatly upon the ability of people to break down the question into decisionable propositions. Many of these propositions will determine the choices made regarding human uses of the environment (artificial as well as natural). Such propositions are intrinsically socio-economic even though they may also include technological, political, and ethical considerations. How these propositions are formulated in public discourse, in laws and policies, depends, moreover, upon the perceptions held by people regarding their present and prospective environmental situations. For example, perceptions of the prospective consequences of a depleting protective stratospheric ozone layer alarmed governments into cooperative action in 1986–7. Short-term economic costs were accepted as a price for arresting a threatening environmental trend having major long-term economic as well as ecological risks.

An emerging planetary paradigm is accompanied by a behavioral imperative which is beginning to have a discernible effect upon social and economic attitudes. An emergent although not fully developed philosophy of environmentalism expresses this imperative, which is to respect and protect the integrity of the biosphere. From this philosophy and its reliance on sciences may be derived criteria by which social and economic choices can be evaluated in the future. This environmentalist way of understanding the world expresses a science-based ethic which is influencing a much broader range of attitudes and behaviors (Anglemyer & Seagraves, 1984). It is contradictory to the prevailing social paradigm of modern times, and its ultimate rise to dominance, if that occurs, will be a distinguishing characteristic of post-modern times.

PHILOSOPHICAL ENVIRONMENTALISM

We have treated environmentalism as an expression of concern placing an extraordinarily high priority upon the quality of the human environment and, more, upon an integrative relationship between mankind and the rest of the living world. But may we regard environmentalists as vanguards of a new society (Milbrath, 1984); to what extent are they utopians and extremists whose views may safely be discounted by practical people? In the ultimate test of unfolding history will the environmentalists be found mostly on the succeeding or failing side of political choice? Will they have been more often right than wrong about the shape of things to come, and would a societal rejection of environmentalism become a choice of failure for society?

Answers to these questions are conjectural, yet the natural sciences provide a basis for strong inference that trends now measurable in the biosphere will force a general reconsideration of man's relationship to nature in the relatively near future. Lord Ashby questioned whether society would muster the foresight to adapt to the limitations of the environment before the painful days of forced reckoning were reached. Some people are already feeling the consequences of overextended demands upon the environment, but although adaptive response has been occurring, it has been slow compared to the acceleration of environmental attrition.

Societies and their intellectual and political leaders have psychic and material investments in the state of things as they are (or are perceived to be). Adaptive change is halting and incremental. The industrial world seeks recovery of its lost youth in adventures into outer space at costs that may be regarded as excessive when proposed for coping with problems of life on Earth. Yet if there *is* an environmental crisis it is not in the environment itself. It is rather a crisis of will and rationality; a test of readiness to mobilize the demonstrated human capacity for learning toward a resolute facing of the circumstances that darken prospects for the future. Ashby is right, it is not the climacteric in man's relationship to the planet that is the crisis. The climacteric is simply the existential condition; the crisis is in the human response. The 'crisis' should be understood as a time for decision, a time when action taken or not taken may be decisive, and when choice among policies will set a course toward the future.

If society through its leadership had a century or more to consider the choices that are now being made, our circumstance might be less critical. There would presumably be time for correction in course. But the acceleration of history has changed the conditions under which choices are made. Opportunities pass swiftly. The tropical moist forests may be gone and the CO_2 balance in the atmosphere increased to a point of irreversible climate change before social behaviors and institutions can grasp at fleeting opportunities. Have we time enough to make the choices that will safeguard the future?

We have noted the range of opinion among environmentally concerned persons. Even where there are agreements in principle, there are differences in degrees of feeling or perceptions of urgency. Nevertheless there *are* beliefs shared widely throughout the environmental movement. Few but fundamental, they distinguish environmentalist thinking from more conventional patterns of thought. Being generalizations, they are not universally true of all environmentally concerned individuals; yet these beliefs are pervasive enough to be described as the philosophy of environmentalism. They are in essence a set of science-based ethical propositions which open the way to an expanding view of man's place in the cosmos, and his responsibilities on Earth. To accept these propositions is to enter a current of thought that moves beyond the boundaries of conventional environmentalism – toward a theology of the Earth and of natural religion.

The essence of philosophical environmentalism may be reduced to five propositions, each with social and ethical implications. Distinguishable from its political tenets previously considered they are:

1. The living world is a unity derived from a common molecular origin, shared by all living things among which mankind is exceptional, but not an exception.

2. All life and its environment are subject to limits inherent in the cosmos. Not all that people might wish to do is possible and nothing that people do is done without cost.

3. Such 'rights' as people enjoy are mutually conceded. Rights are irrelevant in the cosmos; humanity has no inherent rights against nature.

4. Freedoms are conditional within the parameters of nature and the possibilities inherent in the circumstances of human society.

5. The determining principle of human survival is behavior consistent with cosmic realities (i.e. with nature). The spacesuit epitomizes the human condition of biospheric dependency.

These precepts are mutually consistent and mutually interrelated. They comprise a coherent view of the relationship between man and nature. They have the strength of consistency with what humans have learnt through science about the nature of the world and man. Where science is silent, the propositions are not inconsistent with what has been learnt through experience. Unlike the traditional religious creeds, their credibility is not contingent upon acceptance of inspired revelation. Supernatural revelation may be invoked in an effort to refute or reject environmentalist precepts, but it cannot falsify them by recourse to the facts or logic upon which they are based.

The philosophic breadth and depth of these precepts are more often implied than articulated in the rhetoric of environmentalism. Yet even when inarticulate, they are assumptions tacitly underlying the most advanced and coherent environmentalist thought.

SOCIO-ETHICAL IMPLICATIONS

Environmentalists have moved into a domain of thought and policy far greater than all but a few of them have foreseen. Like the early European settlers on the continents of America, they have not comprehended the dimensions of the terrain on which they have entered, nor the possible future on which they have entrained. And like those early colonists, some will seek a return psychologically to familiar shores and others will not survive as active participants in a transition to a social order in which many of the premises and expectations of former times no longer prevail.

Without intending to do so, environmentalists have initiated debate upon a very large question – among the largest that humans have ever asked: What future will mankind make for itself on Earth?

As yet, however, the debate has not been set in such cosmic terms. More modestly, it has been divided between two subordinate issues. One concerns relationship between human rights and rights in nature. The other is the issue of growth in human society. Both issues have basic social, economic, political and ultimately ethical implications. Depending upon the position taken on these issues there are differing implications also for the role of science in society, in public law, and in policy.

Few if any issues are asserted with greater passion nor defended with greater conviction than the nature and extent of human rights. The issue is both philosophical and political, and has as long a history as any concept in Western thought. To question the basis of the rights concept has often been to invite dismissal as facetious or mean-spirited. And yet the rights concept has been based upon abstract deductions rather than upon empirical evidence. Belief that human rights are inherent in nature and are known intuitively by all mankind has been a basic tenet of liberal democracy. But the belief rests upon an assumption, more often tacit than explicit, that the world was made for man and that human rights inherent in nature extend to dominion over the rest of nature. Thus man has rights over nature, but finds no rights in nature over man.

In past experience, to whatever origin they were attributed, rights were treated as familial, communal, or national. Whatever their rationales, rights were administered for what they were, mutual concessions among members of a communal or political order. Rights might be extensible beyond their community of origin, as rights of Roman citizenship were selectively extended throughout the Roman empire, or British passports to former subjects of the British empire. But the 'rights of man' proclaimed by the American and French revolutions were not in practice extended to all mankind or even to all people subject to the laws of the United States or of France.

In tradition-directed societies, rights were often linked to obligations, a linkage also characteristic of feudalism. Dissolution of reciprocal relationships between rights and obligations has been a tendency in modern society, exemplified by various 'liberation' movements. Critics of this tendency see in its progression a loosening of the bonds that hold societies together. Among some environmentalists, liberation ideology is viewed with apprehension that unlimited freedom to do as one pleases contravenes the need to recognize obligations in relation to nature (and through nature to other people) as conditions of moral conduct and ultimate survival.

Philosophical environmentalism unintentionally forces the issues of rights in human society through efforts to extend the rights concept to the rest of nature. If there is a basic fallacy in an idea, pushing it to a point of *reducto ad absurdum* may reveal it, or at least the limitations of the concept. In the ideology of liberal democracy, the concepts of rights, freedom, and equality have been customarily although illogically joined. Justifying their linkage in modern social thought has required elaborate rationalization, abstracted from the realities of everyday life. When the rights concept is applied to the non-human world, difficulties are compounded. Can there be rights in any meaningful sense without remedies? Can humans act as surrogates in defense of the rights of rivers, trees, and fur-bearing animals? Or would such action be, in fact, an inverse application of the human rights thesis, namely that humans have a natural right (or obligation?) to act in defense of and in the name of human values in nature otherwise defenseless against the rights of man?

During most of modern times the question of rights of nature was strictly philosophic. In practice, nature had no rights that humans need respect. Yet today the question of human rights over nature has become an economic, political, legal, and moral issue. Science, in the broad sense, has played an indirect although critical role in this development. The need to refine and redefine the 'rights' concept has gained recognition as more is understood through science regarding the origins of life and the consequences of human conduct in relation to the biosphere and the molecular basis of life.

Only during the time of people now living has science been able to put the stamp of empiricism on the age-old intuitive sense of the unity of man with all living nature. Molecular biology has confirmed what V. I. Vernadsky asserted, and what philosophy and religion could declare but never demonstrate, that all life was somehow linked in a great chain of being (Lovejoy, 1936). Yet theoretical confirmation of the unity of life had little political significance until its practical implication broke into awareness of the possibilities inherent in applied molecular biology. Mankind suddenly became involved with nature in a new and unforeseen way. The question of man's responsibility in relation to nature could no longer be dismissed as theoretical and without practical significance. Although early doubts and fears over the risks of molecular biotechnology have diminished, they have not wholly disappeared. An unprecedented and portentous possibility has emerged and has been catalysed into a policy issue – the broadly inclusive question of human rights in relation to the genetic manipulation of nature, and this issue is now inseparable from the question of human obligation.

The recombinant DNA controversy and genetic engineering have dramatized in principle a proposition widely ignored or resisted when applied to life other than human. It is simply stated: human rights toward nature are limited by obligations. The welfare and survival of humans now and in the future requires of humans that they refrain from action impairing or endangering the reflexive and self-renewing capabilities of the planetary life-support system. Irresponsible modification of the Earth's genetic legacy has been regarded as intolerable by people who envision the creation of monsters in scientific laboratories. At least in principle, the Frankenstein syndrome has passed from science fiction into a perceived possibility with the advent of genetic engineering. That the possibility is improbable has not cancelled out the principle involved – that man has no inherent right to manipulate nature and that society could lawfully determine which rights in relation to nature were permissible and which were not.

One has not far to look to see human interventions in nature far more widespread, destructive, and significant than anything likely to be developed in biotechnology laboratories. But a question of principle is now less easily evaded. If scientists have no right to jeopardize humanity through experiments with genetically altered lifeforms, by what right are more conventional modifications of the biosphere carried on to the detriment of society? Does the practice of agriculture carry a moral right to erode, deplete, or poison the soil on grounds of economic necessity? Do the ostensible 'owners' of forests have a right to alter or destroy them to the impoverishment of the biosphere, now and in the future? Does our technoeconomic society have a right, through action knowingly contributing to climate change, to diminish the quality of life of future generations? Has man a right to prejudice mankind's future?

Such questions could be extended to a very long list. The answers might not always be obvious or unqualified, but one large implication would follow from them all: economic man has no inherent rights against man-in-nature. There are opportunities in the natural world for human betterment, but all are conditional. Francis Bacon's precept that nature, to be commanded must be obeyed, extends much farther into relationships between man and nature than Bacon foresaw. Science has extended our knowledge of the multiple and indirect consequences of human interventions in the natural world. Through science, great opportunities have been opened, but concomitant obligations have been implied. The environmental movement has opened the way to a reconsideration of the meaning of rights in human society and has thus become involved in one of the fundamental questions of political philosophy and law.

SOCIO-ECONOMIC IMPLICATIONS

Implicit in the environmentalist view of reality is the belief that nature in its cosmic dynamics cannot be nullified by human fiat. Yet a worldly homocentric view of human affairs has narrowed human perspectives on important issues to a degree that isolates them from realistic assessment in relation to the biophysical realities of the Earth. Curiously, a persistent conflict between cosmic reality and cultural illusion is over the implications of economic growth. It is curious because the conflict is posed, in terms that are basically false, as a conflict between ecology and economics.

Whatever else it is, economics is a discipline of limits. Economics deals with the allocation of scarce resources. In a world of endless time, material, and energy there would be little occasion for the study of economics. Basic economic concepts concern limits. For example, *opportunity costs* imply that one cannot eat one's cake and have it too, *optimality* suggests that more is not necessarily better, *marginality* shows that unlimited effort will eventually encounter diminishing (i.e. limited) returns, *externalities* reveal that the costs and benefits of consumption may not be fully accounted for in conventional transaction prices. These concepts are consistent with the way the world works and can be illustrated by reference to its natural systems. There is an economics of nature (Ricklefs, 1976) that is congruent with the economics of man, and both are premised on the finite character of the Earth and all within and upon it.

If this be so, why then is the 'limits to growth' hypothesis, adopted by many environmentalists, rejected with such vehemence by so many professed economists? And why do self-described environmentalists call for a 'no growth' society when growth is an indispensible attribute of life? There is confusion here among words and meanings. The conflict must be semantic, for if our understanding of the workings of the natural world hold true for economics and ecology, the question of growth in human societies ought to be open to rational analysis.

To make a point that I regard as essential to resolution of the limits to growth debate, I will state a position that more cautious observers might qualify. In my view, the 'growth' issue is in principle psychological. It is a deep-seated 'gut' issue, clothed in the language of economics and with trimmings borrowed from politics in the generic sense. Its hold on the human psyche has been fixed during two million years of evolutionary 'growth' from a status hardly distinguishable from that of the higher primates to the higher civilizations of the last three millenia.

Growth has become a modern obsession. All governments, whether capitalist or socialist appear to seek it. Economists (there are exceptions) say that modern society (meaning the present industrial order) cannot survive without it. They may be right. Were the pursuit of undifferentiated growth to be replaced by goals more meaningful for the quality of life, a major transformation of societal assumptions and behaviors would have occurred. But the will to growth is deeply ingrained in the ethos of modern society and will not readily be abandoned. It will be given up only when it can no longer continue, as some models of the future predict, or when unselective growth will be seen to work no longer to human advantage.

Through the social learning that has occurred during the recent past, human society has achieved a degree of control over its material circumstances, notably in relation to food supply, pathogens, shelter, and mobility, that makes its future growth a subject for political choice. The direction or substance of this domain of choice has become a question of policy. The factual basis of the need for considered policy regarding preferred future would seem beyond debate; it is nevertheless debated.

The Earth and its resources are finite. Axiomatic as this may seem, many people prefer to act as if it were not so, and some professional optimists deny it (Kahn & Simon, 1984). In some measure, resource availability for human purposes may be enlarged through labor, and recycled by science-based technology; but earthly space and its elements are not infinitely expansible, and hence they pose an ultimate barrier to the infinite expansion of human populations and material assets. With possible exception of the cosmos, all forms of expansive growth appear to be finite – cannot continue forever. A political economy dependent upon expansive growth for its survival thus lives on borrowed time. Its duration may be unpredictable but its end is certain – as certain as any 'law' of physical science. Hence growth, undefined but infinite, is a symbol suitable only for specious political sloganeering.

A political convenience but conceptual weakness of the term 'growth' lies in its ambiguity; it is a word of many meanings. For example, growth and continuous expansion are not necessarily synonymous. A balloon may expand to a degree in space without material growth other than in the gases which it contains and the space which it occupies. A population may expand its occupancy of space without increasing its numbers. A living forest grows, but beyond its climax may not expand. Trees continue to grow even when the size of a forest is diminished. No living thing grows infinitely; all reach a point at which growth ceases. Growth is best understood as a composite process of maturation, innovation, organization, and transformation. It cannot add matter to that which already exists. Consistent with the physical law of the conservation of energy, growth does not enlarge the material substance of the Earth, but may change its form and place. It therefore follows that *growth* – undefined and unspecified – is not a concept about which it is rational to be for or against.

That growth unspecified is ambiguous would seem obvious, yet intelligent people use the term as if they knew what it meant. Perhaps they know, but their concept may be an idol, an image created by the imagination rather than an existential reality. Until terms are specified, debate over an ambiguous concept will be unproductive of understanding or consensus. The subliminal emotional essence of the growth concept needs to be isolated from its material aspects if the concept is to be understood in relation to its rational significance for public policy.

Although not all occasions for growth are welcome – harmful things do grow – there appears to be an emotional predisposition among humans to favor growth. Healthy children grow, families grow, maturity is reached through growth, crops grow, great oaks from little acorns grow. Humans may grow in strength and knowledge – even in wisdom. Thus to challenge the concept of growth *per se* is to confront a very hard wall of psychological resistance. Deepening the commitment to growth is recognition that the natural control over growth is death followed by disintegration and transformation. Thus three different books promoting the growth concept bear identical main titles *Grow or Die* (Lockland, 1973; Weber, 1977; Wedderspoon, 1981). The titles mislead because they appear to misrepresent the true relationship between growth and death; their texts, however, take quite different points of view. In an organic world of physical limits, at least on Earth, death is a price paid for life. No organism lives forever. Life feeds on life, and forests continue to grow only because trees die. Had immortality been the rule of life, the Earth's surface would long since have been miles deep in dinosaurs.

Physical growth is thus a process of organization, development, and replacement; it has cyclical characteristics in a world in which expansion is limited. In a negative sense, death, transformation, and rebirth control the growth cycle even as they make it possible. Nature is constantly remodelling. Not only do the works of man decay over time, but the continents are ground down to sediment even as diastrophic forces create new land and raise new mountains.

To argue for or against growth in the abstract makes no sense. Therefore there must be some other sense implicit in the minds of participants in the growth debate. The term 'economic growth' narrows the field of definition, but helps little in identifying the ends toward which the growth process is directed. The growth concept is often used to imply increasing production of goods and services. Growth is measurable, and in modern political economies a statistical indicator of growth is the Gross National Product. The GNP is a measure of economic activity; it is a quantitative indicator telling us next to nothing about the qualitative aspects of economic production. To environmentalists who understand what it does and does not indicate it is an unsatisfactory measure of human or environmental welfare. Rise in the GNP may be, and has sometimes been, accompanied by the growth of poverty and deterioration of the environment. Of course it may also be accompanied by selective or even general improvement.

The most obvious way to increase the GNP is to expand the economy – to produce more. Increasing populations may equal more production and consumption (and also more residuals, i.e. wastes). To environmentalists, indiscriminate *more* is not necessarily better; increase, in effect, may be purchased at a price of decreasing quality of the environment and of the diversity and integrity of the biosphere.

As one penetrates the rhetoric of growth, it begins to appear that the environmentalists are primarily concerned with ends; and the pro-growth advocates with means. Environmentalists fear the possible consequences of indiscriminate growth, especially when equated with a homosphere, or human domain, ever expanding to the qualitative diminution of the biosphere. The economist is concerned with the often complex processes through which the material wants of humans are variously satisfied. Allocation of resources is an economic concern in a world in which human demands almost always exceed available supplies. In a world in which all things are not simultaneously possible, demand implies choice, choice implies preference, and preference is an indicator of values. Thus the issue of ends passes beyond the strict limits of economics into the realm of ethics and aesthetics. Economics can offer no more than a very partial answer to the question – what is good for human society?' Without becoming philosophers, economists are unable to address the question of what values humans ought to prefer and what goals societies should seek. Many prefer to argue that values are no more than arbitrary preferences, all entitled to be regarded as intrinsically equal. Economists are at home, however, when they consider how opportunities for realization of value preferences are allocated within and among societies. In a world where choice is limited, legitimate allocation is accomplished primarily in either of two ways, through authority or through markets. Fraud or theft may be regarded as illegitimate means inconsistent with the ethos of civil society.

To most economists the authoritative allocation of values is rejected because it lacks an automatic self-corrective mechanism. Authoritarianism *per se* has no inherent strategy for obtaining optimal results from minimal necessary inputs of materials, time, and labor. Thus the risks of suboptimization and waste are increased and potential productivity diminished. Free markets have the advantage of corrective tendencies. At least in principle, more than is wanted of anything will not be produced indefinitely, and incentives exist to encourage the production of that which is wanted. Markets are thus a widely preferred mechanism for economic growth and allocation of benefits. They evade the value choice problem in a pluralist non-consensual society and, when they work well, respond to many needs or wishes of individual men and women.

The principal beneficiaries of the rewards of market processes enjoy economic power that may be turned to their particular political advantage. Holders of political power, however, need not depend upon market forces for advancing favored economic interests; values may be allocated authoritatively with little regard to their economic implications for the society as a whole. An intermixing of political and economic power in government characterizes the process by which policies are determined and the course of society into the future is set.

As with many human arrangements, the mechanisms of the market work better in theory than in practice. Market response to demand is often distorted by arbitrary manipulation of prices and supplies. Subsidies and politically imposed restrictions distort the allocation of resources. Prices generally fail to reflect externalized or residual costs of production and consumption. The market is an imperfect arbiter among values. Market forces, especially when perverted by politics, are poor at making ecologically rational allocations of natural and common property resources such as air and water. Thus one implication of an ecological or environmentalist paradigm is that the appropriate use of market mechanisms in public policy implementation be carefully studied and defined.

Persons holding to a libertarian or public choice perspective on political economy see the interplay of market forces as generally the safest and most equitable means to realizing the substantive ends that most people prefer. Yet, as noted, markets often function imperfectly and there are common goals and values in society that markets alone cannot serve effectively.

Environmentalists might prefer an authoritarian allocation of values if ecological rationality governed policy choices, but many human choices do not involve ecological values in any significant way. In the world today, the firmest foundation for authoritarian allocation of resources among values, or the political modification of market choices, would be public consensus based upon tested knowledge of costs and consequences. A major achievement of public policy would be to obtain the benefits respectively of economic markets and political authority while simultaneously avoiding or compensating for their weaknesses and dangers. The descriptor for this feat is the unfashionable word 'wisdom'. Its implementation, however, requires institutional arrangements.

These considerations lead back to growth as a goal of policy. Primary reliance on economic growth through market processes restricts the scope of policy for determination of ends. The interplay of market forces shapes the future, reducing opportunities for planning toward specified goals. Growth directed through market processes alone holds no assurance of any particular outcome. Policies that seek outcomes that are both economically and ecologically sustainable must be based upon more than process. Growth in itself cannot be an adequate purpose or end of policy. Until the ends of growth are specified, rational determination of the means to growth cannot be made.

We need a new vocabulary for political economy, one that will take us out of the semantic labyrinth in which the environment-economy debate has been largely carried on. Reasonable and informed people should be able to discover where markets work to social advantage and where they do not. It might be more difficult to discover how and to what extent societies can really guide their futures. This task would be less difficult if people could agree upon their terms of discourse – on what those terms do, and do not, mean.

Agreement on the general character of the preferred environmental future would obviously assist the process of tactical negotiation. A supplementary alternative to social choice through market processes is through public planning. Even though the concept may not be popular, the practice is widespread, expressed in a high percentage of public laws and budgetary appropriations at all levels of government. Historical experience with public planning has revealed its risks and limitations but has not, in principle, established it as an impractical approach to policymaking. We know, or can learn, how *not* to attempt to shape the future. We are developing tools and methods of analysis, forecasting, and evaluation that narrow or bring into focus many areas of uncertainty. Our ability to discover causes and consequences has grown and is an aspect of growth that may have no limits beyond those inherent in the human mind. Our greatest need today may be for ways to think and talk more rationally about our problems and our prospects.

A NEW LEVEL OF DISCOURSE

The politics of environment and of economy are presently stuck at an elementary level of discourse at which minds do not meet and arguments by-pass, leaving attitudes and beliefs unengaged and unchanged. But how valid is this assessment in view of the promises of some leaders in the economy to be environmentally good citizens, and of other leaders in the conservation and environmental movement to accept growth and development if ecologically sustainable – which presumably means not self-destructive with incidental destruction to the biosphere? There is reason for encouragement in this apparent rapprochement, but there is also reason to inquire into its reality. Is the environment–economy dichotomy being dissolved in a new eco-economic accord, or is what we hear and see primarily rhetorical accommodation? A bit of both may be present.

The environmental movement and a wider general concern has persuaded many of the more conspicuous contributors to environmental degradation that it would be good public relations to show regard for environmental quality. In some countries, environmental laws and lawsuits have stimulated corporate awareness that overt disregard for environmental concerns is not good business and predisposes people to favor punitive legislation. Attrition of environmental quality occurs primarily in the course of satisfying consumer demand, but the consumers (i.e. the general public) seldom connect the substance and volume of their mass consumption with its environmental consequences. Yet more than enlightened self-interest lies behind the assistance of some business firms to environmental conservation efforts. There are leaders in business who share the concerns of environmentalists and have made significant contributions in money, land, publicity, and business practice.

Representatives of agriculture and industrial labor appear to be less responsive to environmental considerations, although exceptions occur. There are of course, special sectoral interests seeking protection of workers from environmental hazards in factories, mines, forests, and farms. Another issue in which considerations of ecology, the environment, economics, and ethics are brought together is in policy regarding the treatment of society's wastes. Here, as in so many environmental issues, debate usually centers on specific and local situations – multiplied perhaps throughout a nation, but usually to the neglect of underlying causes and permanent solutions. Many of the larger problems of waste and pollution are beyond the ability of individual producers or consumers to manage. Waste management has now become a major public responsibility. This is the 'down side' of economic activity; it is not a prestige-conferring aspect of public service, and is seldom well performed.

Here the economic concept of externalities is relevant. Waste and pollution are residual products of production and consumption that have been externalized out of home and factory into the environment. They represent both economic and ecological problems, and science and technology have been invoked to find feasible solutions. Here also the significance of short-term and long-term or of tentative and permanent solutions to ecological–economic problems comes into focus. Treating residual materials as 'waste' may be a short-term convenience, but is a long-term diseconomy, very often with harmful ecological effects.

Our mundane, inelegant perspective on waste and pollution is in fact a consequence of a narrow time-space paradigm that makes no provisions for societal accounting. The business firm that makes no provision in its accounting for the internalizing of the cost of managing its residuals exemplifies what the entire society does on a much larger scale. When the recycling and recovery of resources from residuals is 'uneconomical' under short-term accounting, the waste problem, if society permits, can conveniently be externalized into the future. Thus accruing liabilities of the present are transferred to the accounting books of future generations. In this practice, as in many others, the projecting of opportunity costs into the future is sound economics only when evaluated by a contemporaneous morality that takes no account of costs beyond those accepted in the present (e.g. of costs deferrable or extensible into the future). The management of nuclear wastes is a notorious case in point.

Search for a rational, sustainable, balanced, or bettered relationship between individuals and society and between present and future have been severely handicapped by psychological distortions which lead to a misreading of reality. The dichotomizing of rights and responsibilities and of ecology and economics are the more salient indications of failure in the presently dominant paradigm of man and nature. Failure to insure that an accounting of the growth of material 'goods' reflects an adequate accounting of the possible growth of environmental 'bads', exposes a widespread inadequacy in contemporary conventional economic thinking. There are other illustrations, notably relating to the numbers and conditions of human populations.

Poverty as a human condition is another point at which ecological, environmental, social, economic, and ethical considerations converge. It is also an aspect of human sociality vulnerable to ill-informed opinion, to unconstructive moral indignation, and to crossed-purpose value judgments. At the United Nations Conference on the Human Environment in 1972, the then Prime Minister of India, Indira Ghandi, declared poverty to be the worst pollution. If accepted, would this assessment imply that other problems of the environment would have to wait until the problem of poverty was resolved? An argument could be advanced that neither could be solved unless both were solved together.

In reality, if not in concept, circumstances relating to poverty, human rights, economics, biology, and environment are complexly and tightly interrelated. We can more easily demonstrate this linkage than discover how to deal constructively with these interconnected relationships. To believe that 'our best minds' have addressed the causes and cures of poverty overlooks the conceptual roadblocks that many of those minds place in the course of their thought. Denial of the reality of overpopulation is the most resistant of these obstacles. Strengthened by a cultural bias for growth and against its repression, this denial is reinforced by a solicitude for contemporary individual human rights, and a disinclination to consider consequences for both individuals and society in the future. Our conventional moral and value judgments embody deep-seated unarticulated assumptions about life and the world that only under severe duress are we willing (perhaps able) to put to the test. The proper context for discourse on poverty must include a larger set of socioeconomic and ecological issues relating to the evolution of modern society and its conflicting tendencies.

Issues in conflict are real in the minds of the adversaries, but those minds see the world at a level at which reality is fractured, and related things are seldom perceived in their interconnectedness. Political and theological dogmas which science should have revealed as irrational, continue to be alleged causes of social war, defeating concerted efforts to correctly define and constructively attack mankind's fundamental problems. Humans have a demonstrated capacity to learn, but societies today have not been programmed to learn as rapidly and as comprehensively as requirements for survival may now necessitate. Is humanity then condemned, to be 'Swept with confused alarms of struggle and flight, where ignorant armies clash by night?'[2]

After several thousand years of failed experience and eloquent admonition by prophets, philosophers, and theologians, it would not be unreasonable to conclude that humans are in certain respects slow learners. Some things are learnt more readily than others, but social or political wisdom seems exceptionally difficult to acquire, even more so to apply. Technical learning has been swift relative to social learning. Sociobiology might, but has not yet, discovered innate incapacity among humans to exercise restraint based upon dispassionate evaluation of demonstrable causes and consequences. At present it seems reasonable to regard socio-ecological misconduct as rooted at least as much in culture as in biology, perhaps more significantly so if, through culture (i.e. science) biological deficiencies, where identified, may be corrected.

Returning to Eric Ashby's interpretation of mankind's environmental predicament as a climacteric, it is logical to ask whether the habits and expectations of mankind's youth are appropriate or realizable if civilized society is in effect approaching a state of middle age. If human society or some part of it approaches a climacteric, while human individuals in significant numbers remain in intellectual and ethical adolescence, it is hard to see an outcome to the time of troubles in which we are already immersed. If a cultural defect obstructs human learning, its identification and correction would be the surest course to follow toward establishing the premises and guidelines most likely to move mankind toward a sustainable future.

Early in the modern era, a tacit assumption of the necessity of adaptive responses to natural forces gave way to a pervasive sense of human omnipotence. Exhilarated by advances in science and technology, and by industrial and political revolutions, all things seemed possible given time and resources. The classical Greeks had a name for this exaggerated self-confidence. They called it *hubris* and believed it to be offensive to the gods. In a manner of speaking, the hubris which David Eherenfeld (1979) called the *Arrogance of Humanism* may offend nature, bringing retribution in the form of feedback effects from ecologically unwise behavior. Among these are environmental contamination, ecological impoverishment, climate change, and dimming of the luster of the natural world and man's artistic achievements. The facade crumbles on the Arc de Triomph in Paris, and the inhabitants of Mexico City can seldom see blue sky, or lift their sight to the snows of Popocatepetl or Ixtaccihuatl.

The extent of conceptual integration achieved thus far is clearly not enough to develop policies that will resolve or reduce the conflicts present and latent in mankind's relationships to the planet. If human behavior in relation to natural resources and the environment continues to be based on erroneous premises, there appears to be no permanent escape from conflict and retribution. Conflicts based on erroneous perceptions are nonetheless real in social and political affairs. When believed to be fundamental, they may be unreconcilable, unamenable to satisfactory compromise. Where nature is truly a 'party' to a conflict, uncomprehending adversaries face certain eventual frustration. For human conflicts that cannot be permanently won, compromised, or abandoned, the only way out is through transcendence. The level of discourse must be raised to a higher level of integration based upon a truer conception of the circumstances of man on Earth.

The evolution of social learning does seem to occur as a dialectical process. Social paradigms appear to progress through successive stages of integration and disintegration. An untenable social consensus regarding man-environment relationships gradually gives way before accumulating contradictory information derived from science and experience. A condition of conceptual disintegration follows, characterized by value-interest conflicts among persons holding differing views of reality. With further advances in knowledge and experience, these differences are reconciled or eliminated to a degree that permits a new synthesis or 'higher' level of integration. In time, the processes of change which permitted this level of reintegration may work throughout society to produce disintegration of this consensus, to be followed eventually by a new synthesis (Corning, 1983).

This oversimplified model of changing paradigms or successive levels of conceptual integration should be understood as only a very generalized description of numerous, uneven, and diverse changes in real society. Yet the process of integration-disintegration-reintegration occurs with a frequency sufficient to give it a heuristic or suggestive value. For example, it affords an explanation of failures in efforts to balance economic and environmental values. Absent has been a common basis for consensus, or discovery of an encompassing level of integration. Resolution of environmental-economic disputes through compromise alone can do little more than give each disputant part of what he wants and may fail to resolve the basic issue.

INTEGRATION VERSUS BALANCE

Does it nevertheless follow that ecology and economy form a dichotomy between which some balance must be struck? There is a widely held assumption that this is so, but in the preceding chapter we argued that their relationship should be viewed as complementary, forming a unity – an economy of nature or an ecologically rational economy – rather than two disparate and basically divisive value systems. Human existence requires the satisfaction of economic needs and also the maintenance of the ecological basis of life itself. Both are necessary, but are they dichotomous, requiring choice between them, or a balancing of the values that they represent? The answer largely depends upon how one understands the economy which, unlike ecology, is a human artifact. There are many economic theories and practices that are incompatible with the integrity of the environment, but there are also economic concepts and behaviors that are compatible with ecological principles and are not dichotomous in relation to them (Elkins, 1986).

When people speak of balance or compromise between economic and environmental or ecological values they very likely have a particular concept of economics in mind although they may be unaware of its particularity. To make sense of economic-environmental relationships it is necessary to specify what kind of economics and what kind of environment. If unity and not dichotomy is the order of nature, then the concept of an incompatibility between economy and ecology *per se* belongs to a lower level of comprehension.

The 'balance' argument is more often invoked by one side of a controversy to restrain the other than to resolve real differences. On these occasions advocates of 'balance' present themselves as representing moderate, reasonable viewpoints in contrast to their 'extremist' opponents. Under social conditions where no common paradigm exists, value-interest conflicts may be irreconcilable. Where differences cannot be resolved at a given level of discourse the task of resolution is to find a higher level of conceptualization, where additional values and insights permit a new level of integration. This process is not automatic and requires time and change among human actors. New information and technology may aid a new synthesis.

To the extent that relationships and expectations in a society are adversarial (as between persons, classes, or interests), the integrative process will be handicapped. The present era is characterized by socio-economic trends toward collectivization of the techno-economic structure, proceeding simultaneously with trends toward individuation of behavior emphasizing rights as against responsibilities. It is a period of paradox and conceptual disintegration. Yet the trends identified in the biophysical environment, threatening to human welfare, are assuming the character of imperatives that impel society toward facing choices among responsive policy alternatives. The social and economic implications of planetary environmental deterioration are pushing reluctant peoples and governments toward new levels of conceptual integration adequate to cope with unprecedented circumstances.

Here science has a role which has hitherto been played with little enthusiasm. There are discernible gaps of uncertain dimensions between the natural and social sciences and between them both and the humanities. To obtain a coherent planetary paradigm, these gaps need to be narrowed, if not filled. Awareness of our deficiencies in understanding and in a meaningful synthesis of what we already know, grows among us as we contemplate our failure to achieve even widely proclaimed objectives – beginning with world peace. Surely there must be some large deficiency in our interpretation of our time and place on Earth. But how do we find a way to discover what we must do to attain the enlightenment that we need?

It seems apparent that the integrity of the biosphere and mankind's ecological and economic safety on Earth will not be secured by incremental measures alone. A larger view of the human predicament is needed in setting a course toward the future. Short-range calculations of 'practical' strategy will fail if based on inadequate premises. A massive conversion to a new view of life on Earth may be necessary if mankind is to move much farther toward establishing a sustainable relationship with the Earth. It may be that such a transition is in fact occurring.

NOTES

1. E. Ashby (1978). *Reconciling Man with the Environment.* Stanford, California: Stanford University Press, p. 3.
2. M. Arnold (1903). 'Dover Beach.' *The Works of Matthew Arnold in Fifteen Volumes* II. London: Macmillan, p. 57.

PART III

An emerging planetary polity

Governance implies a process of decision, cooperation, direction, control, and arrangements to facilitate the process. A planetary structure for policy, coordination and oversight (i.e. a polity) could emerge that was less than a government but more than an assembly representing governments. There is already in existence of international legal order of the environment that has the rudimentary elements of a system for collective governance. An uncoordinated structure of treaties, resolutions, and cooperative arrangements has emerged, ad hoc, in response to problems which nations cannot solve individually. National governments and their subdivisions form the operational level at which most cooperative action occurs. But the larger issues affecting the biosphere require policy decisions and coordination corresponding to the regional or planetary scope of the phenomena. Regional administration is as yet very limited, but with possibilities illustrated by the Commission of the European Community.

Emergence of a planetary polity for the environment has not been intended, or foreseen. Its growth has been incidental and incremental. The principal forum for new international environmental law and institutions has been the United Nations system. But the impelling force behind intergovernmental action has been the growing strength of non-governmental environmental organizations, increasingly as a worldwide network. Major international conferences sponsored by the United Nations and the UN Specialized Agencies have raised levels of popular and political awareness of issues and have provided occasion for new commitments. Official conferences have been paralleled by nongovernmental forums through which ordinary citizens participate in agenda setting and policy development, and are thus better prepared to pressure their respective governments for new initiatives and for implementation of existing agreements.

The science basis for transnational policy has increasingly been provided by the International Council of Scientific Unions and the scientific programs of the Specialized Agencies. Regional multinational investigations have also been undertaken, and global reconnaissance by Earth-orbiting satellites adds cumulatively to a planetary perspective that leads toward a paradigm expressed through a planetary polity. That possibility, presaged by present trends, has yet to occur. The world today appears to be passing through a discontinuity during which attitudes, values and institutions have become unsettled. Amidst this confusion, the environmental movement offers direction toward a post-modern world. Out of the chaos of the transitional period there must surely emerge a more rational order if the human experiment with civilization is to continue.

7
Facing planetary realities

The growth of a planetary consciousness has not been caused by any single factor. Space exploration has been a contributory influence; more compelling, however, has been confrontation with transnational or global environmental realities that must be addressed if human life on Earth is not to be degraded or put in jeopardy. Science has, of course, played a major role in arousing an awareness of planetary realities. An uncounted but certainly large number of people are now tacitly assuming a planetary environment without doing so self-consciously. In ordinary discourse, 'world-wide' and 'global' indicate planetary dimensions, but have seldom been more than extensions of the historical concepts of man's world, and fall short of conveying a sense of the whole Earth, its geosphere, biosphere and their interactions. Yet, confronted by the realities of atmospheric CO_2-induced climate change, of disintegration of the protective ozone layer, of acidic deposition, and the internationalizing of environmental effects once believed to be localized, (e.g. desertifications and deforestation) people in growing numbers have begun to comprehend the world in planetary terms.

PLANETIZING THE ECONOMIC ORDER

During the twentieth century, communication, transportation, commerce, investment and communicable disease control have, in effect, been 'globalized'. And these developments, largely economic and technical, have been affected in various ways by advances in the sciences. These globalizing developments have also had major impacts upon the options of national governments. The growth of international banks, multinational corporations, global communications systems, global and regional scientific research programs, international airlines, and international assistance efforts have created a techno-economic network of human enterprise capable of extension into all parts of the natural and political worlds and of bringing the planet under the influence of a world techno-scientific-economic order (Brezezinski, 1970).

The global expansion of this anthropogenic system or technosphere has a direct relationship to changes in the geosphere and biosphere that are causing peoples and their governments to integrate a 'one world' with a 'one Earth' paradigm. Expansion of science-based technology in the service of economic objectives has unintentionally impelled this transition. Since 1950, a revolution in applied chemistry has literally flooded the world with artificial compounds – many beneficial, some also harmful to life. The pesticide DDT has been exported from industrial countries throughout the world and entered food chains and ecosystems everywhere – even in remote Antarctica. Chlorofluorocarbon aerosols, released into the atmosphere in all industrial countries, appear to be principal agents causing disintegration of the Earth's protective ozone layer. These events have stimulated growth of a planetary awareness that transcends political boundaries.

People are beginning to understand the connections between the planetizing of the techno-scientific-economic order and the emergence of transnational environmental problems. The inordinate demands of expanding human populations for food, fiber, timber, and space have led to the swift and massive destruction of tropical and subtropical forests. Demands of a populous industrialized world for energy have been the indirect cause of oil spills in coastal waters, increase in atmospheric carbon dioxide and trace gases, acid rain and snow, and radioactive fall-out such as occurred after the accident at a nuclear plant at Chernobyl, USSR, in 1986.

Adoption of a planetary perspective has enabled humans, if they will, to see the world within the context of the whole Earth. In this holistic comprehensive view of things, traditional assumptions are changed, priorities are rearranged, and the dimensions of time and space are perceived differently.

For example, destruction of the rainforests of Amazonia can no longer be regarded as the exclusive business of the countries in which they are situated; its effects are felt worldwide. Ramifying consequences also follow: (a) from failure of governments to enforce strict containment regulations on the chemical, atomic, and petroleum industries, (b) from construction of massive hydro-electric and irrigation systems on international rivers, (c) from legalized export of hazardous materials (especially when prohibited at home), and (d) from excessive and wasteful consumption of non-renewable, polluting sources of energy. It becomes ever more difficult for national political leaders to evade international responsibility by declaring that their countries have a sovereign right to manage their domestic economies as they please, and that their policies are nobody's business but their own.

Formerly such attitudes were almost universal among national governments. The international legal obligation to prevent the use of a nation's territory for actions harmful to its neighbor was poorly defined and seldom invoked, and was always contradicted by preparations for war, and acts of war. Yet the permeability of national borders to invisible agents of disease has never been remedied by declarations of national sovereignty. Closed borders and quarantines offer limited protection against invasive pathogens, but require costly vigilance; they did not keep out unrecognized and undetected microorganisms such as viruses that destroyed native elms in North America and vineyards in Southern Europe.

As the volume and speed of modern trade and transportation have increased, so also has the vulnerability of nations to pathogenic intruders. To protect public health and national economic interests in agriculture, horticulture, and forestry, systems of international cooperation and control have been established. For example, an International Plant Convention was signed in Rome in 1951. Subsequently, regional agreements for plant protection were negotiated for South East Asia and the Pacific Region in 1956, and plant protection commissions were established for the Near East and Caribbean regions. In 1959 the Warsaw Pact nations adopted their own agreement for Cooperation in the Quarantine of Plants and their Protection against Pests and Disease.

Such measures were intended to protect human interests from hazards originating in the environment. But the agent transmitting the hazard was usually human, and the global mobility of people and products was accompanied by risk of infection from fellow-travelling microorganisms. Measures of international reporting, quarantine, and certification of sanitation or freedom from the vectors of disease have never afforded wholly reliable means of protection. The surest way to safety is to eliminate the danger where it originates, and for this to happen more than reliance upon voluntary international cooperation becomes necessary. Through the United Nations system, the World Health Organization and the Food and Agriculture Organization have developed networks of international organizations and institutions to facilitate, coordinate, and even to administer programs of research as well as surveillance for protecting the health of humans, their domestic animals, and their plants. Nations do together what none could do for itself alone. Thus a confrontation with planetary realities leads not only toward protection of the biosphere from man; it also causes nations to collaborate in protecting man from dangers latent in the biosphere and to establish transnational arrangements for this purpose.

Commerce across the seas and through the airways required, for its own security and dependability, reliable knowledge of conditions to be expected in the oceans, the atmosphere and the electromagnetic environment of the geosphere. This knowledge requires geophysical research of planetary scope. The circulatory currents of oceans and atmosphere, dynamics of wind and waves, changes in weather, and variabilities in climate affect a broad spectrum of human activities. Less predictable are earthquakes and electromagnetic disturbances, but knowledge of their probability and effects enables humans to take anticipatory protective measures. In efforts to reckon with the geophysical environment, the context is ultimately planetary. Responsive measures must consider international or trans-national circumstances even when direct effects of earthquakes, severe storms or other violent forces of nature may be localized (Maybury, 1986).

Prominent among agents in efforts to understand geophysical phenom-ena are members and committees of the International Council of Scientific Unions, the World Meterological Organization, several divisions of UNESCO, and the United Nations Environment Programme. Scientific organizations at national levels are major elements in international scientific research networks that now encompass the Earth. Orbiting surveillance satellites, corporate and governmental, also contribute to planetization. They see the Earth whole and not as a patchwork of national territories on a political map. Long range and more accurate weather forecasting necessitates a planetary system of surveillance and analysis and a transnational system for this purpose has been created in the World Weather Watch. In brief, national boundaries are being overarched in certain particulars by the world techno-scientific-economy, and this development is significant for the emergence of a world order of environmental protection. The *ad hoc* builders of the world economy had no intention, no intimation, that their achievements would induce, necessitate, and at least make possible, a world order of the environment.

One example of the ways in which international economic integration may induce international environmental policies is provided by the European Community, established by the Treaty of Rome (1957) to integrate the economies of Europe through a common market. In order to remove obstacles to trade between member states it became necessary to harmonize their environmental laws (Rehbinder & Stewart, 1988). Gradually (after further integration adopted in Brussels in 1965) the Community began to pursue environmental goals for their own merit without direct reference to economic considerations. But it was the structure established to facilitate transnational commerce that opened the way to transnational environmental policies.

ENVIRONMENTAL TRENDS AND PLANETARY ISSUES

In sum, until very recently, planetary issues were largely confined to those few global phenomena that were of concern to international commerce, and to the health of humans and their domesticated animals and plants. Except for health, economic considerations were the prime movers of international and transnational world-wide cooperation. The planetization of economic affairs continues and expands, but it is now being overtaken by an awareness of ecological problems of planetary dimensions, which extend beyond health and economy to considerations of natural resources, quality of life, of ethics, aesthetics, and prospects for survival of the human species and the biosphere. Yet all these issues, and others to be considered, interrelate in ways that are numerous, complex, often not readily apparent, and less often generally understood.

At present, no science or discipline analyses or describes these interrelationships although modelers of systems dynamics have begun to undertake the task. Jay Forrester in his World Dynamics model (1971) broke a path toward global modeling and simulation that others have followed and extended (Meadows, 1972; Barney, 1980; OTA, 1982; Bremer, 1987; Toth, Hizsnyik & Clark, 1989). The development of powerful computers and the assemblage of vast amounts of computer-readable data enable scientists today to undertake measurements, correlations and projections on a scale unapproachable a generation ago. Here we can see how science-based technology changes our perception of things. The computer enabled the coordination of the complex calculations necessary to place a man on the moon. Via moon-space, people everywhere could see the whole Earth in orbit – a visual and emotional impression. The computer also enables scientists to analyze complex data regarding the dynamics of that Earth so that we can begin to understand how the world works – a cerebral or conceptual process.

The earlier responses of people and governments to international environmental hazards (risks to plant and animal health) were largely issue-specific. They did not translate readily into a political planetary perspective; nor did the initial findings of scientists explicitly do so. Science was specialized and reductionist; no science alone offering a holistic perspective on planetary realities. But as more was learnt about how natural systems work, about the interrelationships between oceans and atmosphere, between plants, soil, and water, and the complex interrelationships among organisms, the idea of a unity in the subject matter of science began to be more than intuition. The significance of that unity lay beyond certainty, but its expression in nature was a reality demonstrated by empirical evidence.

Within the past quarter century a growing number of large and serious trends of planetary significance have with relative rapidity become subjects of widespread and international concern. Three of these trends are so patently transnational and multi-national in character and effect that international action on them either has occurred or seems certain to occur in the near future. They are, in brief: (1) the CO_2 greenhouse global warming trend, (2) the disintegration of the protective stratospheric ozone layer, and (3) acidic precipitation. Yet there are other harmful trends, of which five will presently be reviewed that, although planetary realities, have not yet become subjects of effective transnational action. That they have not yet become so may be explained by two considerations: first, nationalism and the concept of national sovereignty, regardless of their limitations, retain a tenacious hold on governments, and second, the world as yet has no institutional strategy to sort out relative risks and priorities and to implement in practice policies agreed to in principle.

That the legalistic concept of absolute national sovereignty is a political fiction does not prevent its obstructing international and transnational action, even where the concept is irrelevant and unrealistic (Kloppenburg, 1988). In coping with environmental problems of planetary significance the institutional choice is not solely between absolute national sovereignty *or* world government, neither of which are feasible in today's world. An alternative concept of national autonomy *and* collective responsibility is needed that would provide a better definition of the rights and obligations of nations, and be workable in a world in which national governments are major determinants of public action.

Political realities influence the way in which environmental problems are defined as public issues. Criteria for definition differ as between scientists and politicians. For a politician to act upon issues they must be stated as propositions that are decisionable; they must be amenable to policy choice – to answers of yes or no – to specific lines of action – and they must have an identifiable constituency. The public official can do very little about biogeochemical cycles, but given sufficient popular support, might be able to shape a policy to abate acid rain. To the scientists, understanding the fundamental cause-effect interrelationships that explain how the biosphere works afford the information needed for the choices that people must make to safeguard its environmental future. But scientific propositions may not easily be translated into discrete policies and may not take account of non-scientific social impediments and priorities.

Thus there is not just one interpretation of environmental issues to consider. How the issues are classified depends substantially on the purpose for which one seeks to understand them. Scientific investigation might require a different classification of issues from that considered here (El Hinnawi & Hashmi, 1982). Moreover, our concern is with perceptions of environmental hazard that may lead to political initiatives rather than with the range of possible responsive actions subsequently made through policy, law, technology, and behavior. Our focus is on public recognition of environmental problems of planetary scope which are believed to be solvable through processes set in motion through political action. How political choice is made is important, but is not an immediate consideration here.

Six large issues, presently described, encompass major anthropogenic threats to the integrity and renewability of the biosphere. Laws, treaties, and technology, all other things unchanged, will be insufficient to arrest their destructive effects – much more will be necessary, not less than a new set of human behaviors in relation to human life on Earth. The following comprehensive trends lead to environmental issues that are basic to choices for the future of man and the biosphere.

1.   Loss of topsoil through erosion and qualitative deterioration.
2.   Depletion and degradation of fresh water.
3.   Contamination of the biosphere: of air, water, soil, and living things.
4.   Devegetation of the land by:
     (a)   deforestation, especially of the equatorial rainforests, and by
     (b)   desertification, especially of grasslands in semi-arid regions.
5.   Destruction of natural habitats caused by all of the foregoing and, in addition, by the damming and channelizing of rivers, filling or draining of lakes, estuaries, and marshes, and by expanding urbanization and agriculture.
6.   Loss of biological variety and diversity – species' extinctions.

INTERRELATING PLANETARY ISSUES

Following are summaries of these six environmental trends. They are, in fact, aggregates of more specific losses and impairments. Each may be segregated for purposes of policy and decisionmaking into more specific issues. But the interconnectedness, directly, and through biogeochemical cycles, needs to be understood in arriving at political choices that are ecologically sound, economically feasible, and sociologically acceptable (Bolin & Cook, 1983).

Loss of topsoil through erosion and qualitative deterioration must be regarded as a planetary issue because it has become pervasive around the globe and because its consequences affect people everywhere (Kovda & Rozanov, 1987; Carter & Dale, 1974). As human populations have been expanding, the natural capacity of the soil to provide nourishment through the green plants has been declining. National policies for land use, agriculture, and conservation have therefore become matters of international concern because neither the soil loss nor its consequences are contained within national boundaries. Soils unprotected by vegetation are vulnerable to erosion by wind and water. Fine-grained topsoils may be transported by wind, reducing fertility in one place, sometimes depositing fertile layers of loess in another. But a large part of air-borne soil is carried out to sea and lost in the Earth's oceans. Erosion by water results in siltation of streams and lakes, changing their life support capabilities, contributing to flooding, and causing impoundments behind dams to lose their storage capacity. If or when the great dams built during the twentieth century are filled with silt, what will be the consequences for the regions that they now serve?

Topsoil is also lost by being paved over in the course of urbanization and road construction. It is also rendered unavailable through contamination by toxic spills or where land is set aside for storage of hazardous substances. Some of this soil may be retrievable, but often at considerable cost.

Soils vary greatly in fertility, productivity, and in susceptibility to deterioration. Soil exhaustion is not unique to modern times, having also occurred in earlier civilizations (Hughes, 1975). Failure to conserve soil fertility has been a conjectured explanation for the decline or collapse of social orders in North Africa, Southeast Asia, and Central America (Marsh, 1864; Murphy, 1951; Thomas, 1956). Many tropical soils, when exposed to sun and weather, laterize; an iron-like crust forming on their surface rendering them uncultivatable except at excessive cost. Soils that are naturally acidic may be rendered less viable by additional acidification through atmospheric deposition. Soils may also be contaminated by leaching from toxic dumps and by salinization of irrigated soils in areas of high evaporation. Subsidence of land caused especially by depletion of groundwater has been described as a worldwide environmental hazard (Maybury, 1986).

Agricultural technology has been invoked to offset losses caused by deforestation, overgrazing, compaction, and improvident use of soil and water, but invoked more often to increase yields and profitability. Large scale application of science and technology to commercial crop production has become a planetary phenomenon. Its research and development are carried on in technologically advanced countries; its Green Revolution applications have taken place there also, but especially in the developing countries of the Third World. Although conventional thinking has been slow to comprehend it, transnational dependencies upon international commerce in food is making agriculture and the topsoil upon which it depends a concern common to all mankind.

Green Revolution inputs of artificial fertilizers, water, herbicides and pesticides have increased the output of hybridized strains of rice, maize and wheat, but often at costs that may prove unacceptable ecologically and socially (Dahlberg, 1979; Doyle, 1985). This relatively expensive, although productive, form of agriculture requires large capital outlay, large tracts of land and sophisticated production management and marketing. Thus it tends to displace small land owners or to incorporate them into collective systems. Social and economic differences among people tend to be accentuated, leading to political and international disorders. In addition, qualitative changes resulting from excessive use of inorganic fertilizers, herbicides, and pesticides, can be observed in a majority of the world's agricultural countries. Science has made possible higher agricultural yields on less land, but this process has ultimate limits.

Threats to the life-support capabilities of topsoil have been accentuated by ever increasing demands for more production. More mouths to feed and bodies to clothe require more to be extracted from the environment and more wastes returned to the environment. Economic pressures cause agricultural producers to 'mine' the soil, transforming its minerals into food and fiber. Mechanization of agriculture greatly reduces the numbers of people needed to produce crops, and replaces hard labor by men, women, children and domestic animals with chemical and mechanical technology. But it also displaces the rural people of the world, too often forcing them, without an intention to do so, into the slums of the world's greatest cities.

The soils of the world vary greatly in their response to this industrialized agriculture. The emergence of molecular biotechnology offers promise of developing plants that may not require the heavy chemical dosages prescribed for Green Revolution agriculture. But this new agricultural technology carries certain risk along with its benefits and it does not remove all of the causes of soil loss and deterioration. More importantly, however, it holds great, although uncertain promise for improving the quality of life, especially in presently poorer countries (Ahmed, 1988; Sasson, 1988; Wolf, 1986).

Soil conservation entails immediate costs for deferred benefits. In the long term, no nation can afford to lose its topsoil or any major part of it. In the short term, today, few agriculturalists, farmers, land owners, or investors can afford to conserve it for the benefit of others. In theory, a sustainable agriculture is possible; in fact, in an ever-expanding economy, it is improbable.

In an interconnected world economy, the fate of topsoil cannot rationally be regarded as the exclusive concern of each nation. All nations may ultimately be affected by failure of food production anywhere. Nations that cannot adequately feed themselves – and their number has been increasing – depend upon surpluses in other states. Argentina, Australia, Canada and the United States have been major sources of food exports. Should soil loss (or climate change) reduce agricultural production in these countries, the effect upon dependent peoples could be famine. Inability of the soil to sustain human occupancy has already caused mass migrations of people out of impoverished areas into neighboring lands and into the industrialized world. But remedial measures are not simple; the loss of soil and decline in its natural productivity are linked with other trends and cannot be countered without taking many other factors into account. Clearly, ecologically informed national policies for soil should be adopted in any realistic international efforts to establish a sustainable planetary economy. Conservation of world resources in topsoil is inevitably becoming a subject of international environmental policy.

Depletion and degradation of freshwater, especially of sub-surface water, is one of those factors which diminish the productivity of the soil. The quantity, quality, and availability of fresh water are affected by geophysical factors, by human demand, and by technology (Chorley, 1969; Powledge, 1982). Human impacts upon sources of fresh water have increasingly become perilous as demand has grown prodigiously, and technology for interbasin diversion, for deep well drilling, and for irrigation through mechanical systems has advanced.

The consequences of the depletion and degradation of fresh water are felt at all levels of society and government (Barberis, 1981; Caponera, 1980; Cano, 1975; Matthews, 1984; Teclaff & Utton, 1981). It has been a localized issue for many years, but has now taken on worldwide dimensions. Downstream states are at a natural disadvantage in access to water of desirable quality and quantity and are dependent on international actions to obtain equitable treatment. For example, in 1953 Syria appealed to the UN Security Council to stop Israel from diverting Jordan River waters in the transboundary demilitarized zone. The United States has been obligated to construct a costly multimillion dollar desalinization plant on the lower Colorado River in order to deliver an acceptable quality of water to downstream Mexico. The Netherlands has been at issue with its upstream neighbors over contamination of the Rhine. In 1983 an International Water Tribunal was held at Rotterdam by non-governmental organizations to consider the problems of pollution of the Rhine and the difficulties of obtaining compliance with international agreements. The catastrophic chemical spill from the Sandoz plant in Switzerland in 1986 dramatized an intolerable situation (Wright, 1986).

A large number of the world's leading rivers form or transect international boundaries. To manage the use and allocation of these waters numerous international agreements (more than 200) and institutional arrangements have been consumated; enforcement of agreements is another matter (Caponera, 1980; Cano, 1975; Matthews, 1984). In 1966 the International Law Association meeting in Helsinki adopted the so-called *Helsinki Rules on the Uses of International Rivers*. Since 1967 an International Water Resources Law Committee of the Association has investigated a large number of international water problems and recommended legal bases for solutions (International Law Association (1980/1983). Paralleling these generalized efforts, environmental issues have led to elaboration of the North American Boundary Waters Treaty of 1909 by the Great Lakes Water Quality Agreements of 1972, 1978, and Protocol of 1987. But clearly governments profess better than they perform.

Interbasin transfers of water have become political issues. In the United States, agitation has begun to obtain water from the Great Lakes to permit continuation of irrigation farming and for controlling water levels. In the summer of 1988 the Governor of Illinois and a number of United States congressmen sought an increase of the authorized diversion of Great Lakes water to augment the flow of the Mississippi River, then at record low level. But designs on the Great Lakes must reckon with the fact that jurisdiction over the Lakes is divided between the United States and Canada. Any transfer affecting the quantity or quality of the waters of the Great Lakes would require a binational consensus and could be inconsistent with the Great Lakes Water Quality Agreements of 1978 and 1987 (Caldwell, 1987). Similarly, the North American Water and Power Alliance (NAWAPA) proposal in the 1950s to construct a vast network of pipelines to tap water from the Canadian Rocky Mountains for distribution over large areas of the United States became a binational issue which failed to find support in Canada.

In the Soviet Union, proposals to reverse the flow of several great Siberian rivers to replenish water supplies in Central Asia appear to have been defeated (at least for the time being) because of economic costs and possible ecological consequences, including changes in the Arctic Ocean. In South America, cost and ecological consequences appear also to have deterred a proposal to divert Amazonian waters into the Chaco region of Bolivia and Paraguay.

What these and other massive water transfer schemes appear to demonstrate is that humans have often been ambitious, wasteful and improvident water users. There may sometimes be ecologically and economically justifiable reasons for transfer from areas having a superabundance of water to areas having insufficient fresh water to achieve their optimal developmental potential. But the greater reasons for the proposed transfers have been to compensate for excessive use, to replenish unnecessarily depleting sources, to meet the demands of politically stimulated population growth, and to benefit politicians and promoters.

Protection of groundwater has become a significant environmental concern in many parts of the world (Bowen, 1986; Cano, 1980, Raghunath, 1987; Van Der Leeden, 1987). Groundwater depletion and its associated effects impose economic and social costs. As springs on the surface of the land run dry they no longer feed streams, whose flow is diminished and plant and animal life dependent upon the water is adversely affected. Humans and their domestic animals are deprived of readily available sources of water, which must then be supplied either by drilling even deeper wells or importing water through irrigation systems. In either case economic costs are imposed. Depending upon sub-surface rock formations, the draw-down of groundwater may be accompanied by a loss of water quality and surface subsidence. Aquifers, formerly fresh, may become brackish as their water pressure diminishes through excessive pumping, and adjacent saline water under higher pressure intrudes.

The quality of both groundwater and surface water is also affected by chemical contamination resulting from direct discharge, or leaching of toxic substances. In Central Europe and Eastern North America municipal and domestic water supplies have in many places become contaminated, necessitating costly alternative sources. As previously noted, irrigated agriculture in semi-arid regions frequently results in salinization and other chemical contamination (e.g. selenium) of the surface soil through osmosis from below, and from return flows from irrigated fields channeled into drainage systems and thence into rivers. Heavy dosages of artificial fertilizers, pesticides, and herbicides on the land similarly contaminate soil and water and are flushed into rivers and lakes where they may be absorbed into the aquatic food chain ending with man.

Freshwater is essential to human health and survival, and degraded, contaminated water has been a major cause of illness and an economic liability. Obtaining an adequate supply of water is only part of the remedy. Protection of water quality may be as great a problem. Engineering may provide water, but conserving and sanative lifestyles and behaviors are necessary to protect it. That the problem has been world-wide and of political concern is evidenced by adoption by the General Assembly of the United Nations of an International Drinking Water Supply and Sanitation Decade (1981–90) with the slogan 'Clean Water and Sanitation for All by 1990'. Achievement of this goal would be extraordinary considering the political, economic, and behavioral changes required. Success is compromised by the belief that sanitary engineering can solve the problem, whereas a technological solution alone would be insufficient. Human behavior is at the root of drinking water problems, and any permanent solution must address its social and economic aspects as well as its physical dimensions.

Contamination of air, water, soil and living things by chemical and radioactive agents is a third trend already identified as a transnational threat to the quality of environment. This trend escalated in scope and magnitude after 1950 and rapidly became a multi-media phenomenon regardless of where the contamination originated. The volatility and solubility of chemical compounds facilitates their movement from one medium to another: from emission point to air, air to land and water, from land and water into air and vegetation, and into the food chains of animals, ultimately to ingestion or inhalation by humans.

The health of humans, other animals, and plants, including the microorganisms of the sea, are principal concerns in the poisoning of the biosphere. But there is also damage to the inanimate environment of human artifacts: buildings, statuary, metals, and fabrics (especially paper). Air pollution on the Acropolis of Athens has become so intense that the caryatids on the facade of the Erechtheum, having survived the natural elements for 2000 years, have now been removed to a museum and replaced by copies. Statuary on the fronts of the great medieval churches of Europe have suffered premature decay and require replacement at modern day costs.

Radioactive and electromagnetic radiation at higher than natural levels may also be regarded from the human perspective as environmental contaminants. They are unintended effects of human technological ingenuity and have accompanied advantages which humans are not likely to relinquish willingly. The incident at Chernobyl in 1987 underscored the transnational dimension of the dangers of atomic radiation, which had already been recognized in international diplomacy, law, and institutional arrangements. The United Nations Partial Nuclear Test Ban Treaty (1963), adhered to by 110 nations recognized the inability of any nation to control the fallout of radioactive material in the atmosphere. Carried by air currents, atomic debris could encircle the planet. The obvious transnational character of atmospheric contamination led to negotiation of the Convention on Long-range Transboundary Air Pollution (1979) and of treaties to protect the atmospheric ozone layer (Vienna, 1986 and Montreal, 1987). In 1986 following the Chernobyl nuclear accident two international treaties were negotiated and consumated regarding International Atomic Energy Agency notification and assistance in the event of a nuclear accident (Adede, 1987). One need hardly be prophetic to predict that these agreements are incremental first steps toward a far more comprehensive system of atmospheric protection (Flinterman, et al., 1986). The UN Convention on the Law of the Sea may afford a model for a consolidated international code of law for the atmosphere. Addressing the United Nations General Assembly on 19 October 1987, Tom McMillan, Canadian Minister of the Environment declared that the 'Earth's atmosphere, like its seas, is a global commons. Ultimately, critical atmospheric problems need to be addressed through international law – a Law of the Air' (MacMillan, 1987). Adverse effects of sulphur dioxide, nitrous oxides, and certain other gasses emitted by modern industrial activities, have raised the acid precipitation issue. Of less immediate but more portentous concern, an increasing carbon dioxide concentration in the atmosphere threatens to cause a global warming 'greenhouse' effect. Protective measures against these hazards have been stalled largely for relatively short-term but powerful economic reasons, but international action seems certain in the relatively near future.

As we have emphasized, issues planetary in scope may also be localized in incidence. Contamination by toxic and other hazardous materials has become a major international issue. International incidents have been common. The 1986 spill of toxic chemicals in the Rhine from the Sandoz plant in Switzerland is a dramatic instance. Spills from oil tankers in coastal waters have been numerous. Chronic contamination of the Niagara River and of Lake Ontario from chemical waste dumps near Buffalo, New York affects binational waters of Canada and the United States. Transportation of hazardous materials has become a critical topic of intergovernmental concern in North America and Europe.

Even more localized are the walls and roofs of man-made structures that fail to afford reliable protection against chemical and radioactive contamination. Some building materials have inadvertently incorporated radioactive or volatile elements, and houses constructed on contaminated sites have been penetrated by emissions from uranium and radon gas. The occurrence of this form of contamination may be exceptional, but the contamination of indoor atmosphere by cigarette smoke is common and only recently has come to be recognized as a form of environmental contamination.

In several countries public laws have been enacted to restrict smoking in confined public places. The ceasing of cigarette smoking would be a major achievable advance in environmental health everywhere. Unfortunately there are large behavioral and economic obstacles to this end. There is also a conceptual difficulty because many people, failing to understand environmental relationships, perceive pollution as something external to their own behavior. They may urge governments to prohibit smokestack pollution but oppose restriction of their personal habits. Tobacco is, of course, an article of international commerce, tax revenue, and in some regions an important cash crop. Science and clinical medicine have thoroughly confirmed the adverse health effects of tobacco and, in time, will surely overcome the resistance of habituation and industrial profitability. With some people, the physical and social costs of this form of contamination are already beginning to exceed the limits of toleration.

One less recognized form of contamination of air and water, particulate matter, chiefly dust, has reached planetary proportions. This phenomenon is not new, but has been greatly augmented by human activity notably in cultivated agriculture, overgrazing of grasslands, and urbanization. Desertification increases the incidence of airborne particulates. Measurable deposition of dust from the Sahara has been reported in North America, and in Japan from the Gobi Desert (Pewe, 1981). Atmospheric dust, attributable perhaps to agricultural malpractice, may account for the presence and expansion of the desert in Rajastan and Pakistan in South Asia (Bryson, 1971). The socio-ecological-economic disaster of the North American 'dust bowl' of the 1930s was largely the consequence of agricultural error exacerbated by drought. Atmospheric dust from volcanoes has encircled the globe, and falling ash has smothered biota in localized areas – but these events are relatively uncommon whereas the dust resulting from human activity has become continuous.

Flowing streams may carry a burden of contaminants adhering to sediments which, when excessive, may adversely affect aquatic life. Chemical contaminants, often airborne, are deposited on the surface of land and water and accumulate in bottom sediments of lakes, bays, and estuaries, becoming chronic sources of active or latent contamination. Point sources of contamination may be identified and contained; non-point sources, notably in agriculture, are very difficult to control.

The complexity of the contamination issue precludes any simple solution. Substances may be toxic in differing ways, in varying degrees and under particular circumstances. Analysis of relative risks and of alternative methods of control and development of safe substitutes for toxic products, are now essential elements of national policy; and global realities make environmental contamination an issue of relevance for all nations. Elimination of the toxic compounds may be the only feasible method of protection. Discovery of non-toxic substitutes is a major challenge for science.

Devegetation through deforestation involves all of the afore-described adverse environmental trends and has, in addition, been caused by chemical warfare (Westing, 1984). It is a major cause of the erosion and degradation of topsoils, the disruption of stream flow and groundwater levels, the sedimentation of rivers and lakes, and of the loss of wildlife habitat. Forests and fields are also the unintended or inadvertent victims of chemical contamination. The 'death' of forests in Central Europe has been attributed to severe air pollution. Chemical devegetation has also been employed by some governments in their 'war' on narcotic drugs.

The accelerating destruction of the tropical forests, especially the rainforests of South America, Central Africa, and Southeast Asia, have aroused world-wide concern among informed people who are relatively powerless to stop this horrendous ecocide driven by political ambition, explosive population growth, and inordinate demand for timber and agricultural expansion. Efforts both public and private are now underway to conserve these tropical forest ecosystems, but the demographic and economic forces that impel national politics and international commerce and investment to deforestation are extremely difficult to arrest. Were some modest percentage of the world's expenditures on armaments diverted to this task, the prospects for success could be greatly improved. Efforts by several environmental NGOs to buy foreign debts of developing countries in exchange for agreements to conserve the forests hold some promise of retarding deforestation and conserving tropical forest ecosystems.

Devegetation causing desertification may be induced by climatic variations (Hare, 1985) but is more often a result of overgrazing or exposure of topsoil through 'clean' cultivation. Deforestation without regeneration has also been a causal factor; deserts are now found in places once forested and where climatic conditions alone do not appear to account for the change. Continuous cutting of trees and browsing by cattle, sheep, and goats has removed the vegetative cover from the Earth and enabled wind, rain, and sunlight to so change the character of the surface soil that regeneration of plant life does not occur. As noted in our description of topsoil deterioration, laterization and loss of fertility may follow removal of the tropical forest cover. Once clear cut, even the partial regeneration of a tropical moist forest would require centuries. Restoration of a sub-tropical dry forest would require a protective vigilance, especially during early decades, that would be very exceptional for humans to provide.

An environmental threat not widely perceived or understood may be called the 'desertification of the sea.' Deserts need not necessarily be dry, but true deserts are largely devoid of life. A major form and source of life in the biosphere are microscopic plants on the surface of the seas. The phytoplankton are not only near the beginning of the oceanic food chain; they are also believed to be a major source of atmospheric oxygen. Their importance as oxygen regenerators grows as the tropical forests shrink and the burning of carboniferous fuels raise the level of carbon dioxide in the Earth's atmosphere. Chemical contamination appears to be the principal danger to the phytoplankton, although greatly elevated surface temperatures or levels of ultraviolet radiation might also affect their vitality. On this aspect of devegetation scientific evidence appears inconclusive, but the theoretical possibilities are sufficient to justify careful monitoring.

Destruction of natural habitat has been caused by all of the trends just described and by other human impacts upon the environment. The indifferent destruction of the living space of plants and animals not domesticated by man and condescendingly termed 'wild' exemplifies the arrogance of humans (Ehrenfeld, 1978). Ecosystem degradation or elimination has resulted from the damming and channelizing of rivers, the draining and filling of wetlands and lakes and the dredging, dyking, and filling of estuaries and embayments. Expanding agriculture and urbanization have also preempted wildlife habitat, and military action has had a generally but not wholly destructive effect. Modern warfare devastates the environment, but preparations for war have caused military reservations to be established from which the public and development activities are excluded but the natural environment is often left relatively undisturbed.

Loss of habitat is a major cause of the diminution and extinction of species. Loss of species is loss of genetic variety and diversity and a loss also of opportunity for scientific research and development, especially in molecular biotechnology. There is of course an aesthetic loss in the homogenization of landscapes and the disappearance of plants and animals that add interest and liveliness to the environment.

In many parts of the world today industrialized agriculture has turned once pleasant rural landscapes into outdoor factories. Farmers have been advised by agricultural economists to plow from fence line to fence line. Bulldozers have flattened terrains and felled trees, hedgerows have been uprooted and fields greatly expanded to accommodate large machinery. This extended monotonous acreage is doused with pesticides, herbicides, and inorganic fertilizers to produce a green miracle of prodigious yields – frequently supported by government subsidies. Vestigial remnants of native shrubs and wildflowers are to be found only in isolated patches, inaccessible to cultivation. In many places the birds and fur-bearing animals of the former groves and hedgerows are gone, displaced by biologically impoverishing large scale technology which, in addition to its destruction of wildlife, has lowered water tables through deep well pumping, often drying up the shallower wells of nearby smaller farmers who could not afford the costly equipment to drill as deeply and to irrigate as widely.

As earlier noted, this form of homogenizing agriculture, developed initially in the United States, has been exported or adopted in many parts of the world – in Australia, Brazil, Canada, India, Sudan, and also in

Western Europe – even in Britain where sentiment for countryside aesthetics has been historically strong. People have been fed and clothed, but at a high ecological cost.

The progressive extension of traditional agriculture to all available land has been no less destructive of natural environment. No area of habitat on land or sea is immune to human intrusion. The destruction of the moist tropical forest accounts for the greatest loss of habitat and species. But areas as remote as Antarctica and its surrounding seas are not secure as long as economic pressure for resource development and harvest of marine life persists.

Loss of biological variety and diversity is a consequence of all of the foregoing trends. This trend is not new, and is believed to have begun in prehistoric times (Martin & Wright, 1967; Erhlich & Erhlich, 1981). In modern times, however, and especially in the 20th century, the rate of extinctions has been accelerating. Many species have been eliminated over large areas of their former ranges – notably the larger mammals, e.g. elephants, bison and larger predators. Many marine mammals, e.g. whales, dugongs, and sea otters, have been greatly reduced in number, and species of birds, reptiles, insects and plants have been eliminated. The extent of species loss is difficult to ascertain in as much as the total number of species extant is not known with accuracy.

Any significant loss in bio-diversity represents a corresponding impoverishment of the biosphere and a limitation of options in the future. Human utility is one, but only one, among reasons for the prevention of genetic attrition (US Dept of State, 1981; Wilson, 1988). Through selective breeding and genetic engineering humans have added to the varieties of evolved species. But the options for applied molecular biology and biotechnology could be reduced through losses of natural genetic materials. Opportunities in natural materials chemistry and in applied agronomy would also be reduced by species' extinctions.

Loss of bio-diversity has now become a matter of both scientific and policy concern. The issue of species loss is intertwined with questions of ecology, economics, and equity growing out of the expanding field of applied plant genetics (Kloppenburg Jr, 1988; Sasson, 1984). Efforts to protect and preserve genetic diversity in plants have been undertaken within the United Nations system notably by the Food and Agriculture Organization, the International Board for Plant Genetic Resources (IBPGR), and the Consultative Group for International Agricultural Research (CGIAR). The Convention on International Trade in Endangered Species (CITES) undertakes a more general approach to species protection, but offers no protection for species within national boundaries.

The extinction issue is obviously linked to issues of contamination, devegetation, and habitat destruction. Destruction of tropical forest ecosystems is the greatest and most immediate threat to bio-diversity in all its forms. The rapid extension and commercialization of biotechnology has further internationalized the issues (Caldwell, 1988) and led to a new 'geopolitics of germplasm' (Kloppenburg Jr, 1988).

FACING THE REALITIES

These destructive trends and the anthropogenic forces that drive them form sequential and interrelating processes. The linkages are sometimes indirect (as in extended chains) but are nonetheless present if not always evident. Professed efforts toward remediation, however, are not always wholly serious and are widely compromised by other and often conflicting objectives. These deleterious processes share two consequences following from two causes which must be considered in a serious effort to arrest or reverse their destructive effects.

The consequences, as we have seen are *first*, the breaking of the biogeochemical cycles revolving through air, land, and water, and organisms that keep the biosphere in homeostatic balance and permit its self-renewal, and *second*, as previously noted, the impoverishment of the biosphere through loss of species and ecosystems. The extinction of plants and animals caused by human preemption of the Earth is comparable in magnitude to those losses caused by the diastrophic forces that raised the mountains, and climatic changes that have moved the mile thick continental glaciers that have periodically advanced over large areas of the Earth. These consequences, of course, lead to others – secondary and tertiary effects – that in the end could leave the Earth a poorer and less hospitable place than we know today.

The causes are disputed, even as the significance of the trends is denied by those for whom acceptance of their reality would threaten deep values and ideological commitments. Two causes seem beyond question, yet they are today rejected or evaded by many, perhaps most, people. *First* is the inordinate increase and concentration of human populations, *second* is the ill-considered use of technology in exploiting the resources of the Earth. The two causes are linked by the concept of *growth* (critiqued in the preceding chapters) which, undefined, undifferentiated, and vigorously asserted, has become a talisman of modern political economy.

Thus the attrition and degradation of the biosphere is a planetary reality which confronts humans, but which modern society has not as yet forthrightly confronted. Reluctance to face unpleasant realities is a common trait of human character. Still, some environmental developments may become too threatening and pervasive to be ignored. Three, involving the planetary atmospheric and interactive with all of the five trends previously reviewed, are now on the agenda of international concern. Repeating their previous identification they are: (1) the CO_2 greenhouse global warming trend, (2) disintegration of the protective stratosphere ozone layer, and (3) acidic precipitation. The destruction of tropical forests appears to be emerging as a fourth major international concern. Serious deleterious consequences have been projected for each of these developments, harmful to economic and ecologic values and to the quality of human life. Despite popular reluctance to accept the remedies required to overcome these hazards, the issues they raise will not be suppressed (Kates, Ausubel & Berberian, 1985).

Beyond indication of their policy implications, it seems unnecessary to discuss these concerns at length in view of extensive coverage in other publications (e.g. Polunin, 1971, 1977; Malone & Roederer, 1985; Clark & Munn, 1986). Their obvious transnational impacts and threatening consequences have given them a salience unavailable to the more inclusive, less dramatic but hardly less serious trends reviewed earlier in this chapter. The policy implications and political resistances relating to these trends may be considered national or regional in the short term. Yet all presage globally destructive ecological and economic consequences in the long term which will affect people and their welfare everywhere regardless of nationality. The United Nations Conference on Water (1977 Mar del Plata), and on Desertification (1977 Nairobi), raised international awareness of growing threats to the biosphere. The UNEP program to combat desertification has made some headway against this menace (UNEP, 1984), but in the aggregate the desert appears to be gaining.

If, as it seems, the measured increase in atmospheric carbon dioxide will, if continued, cause a massive and irreversible change in the Earth's climates, a social response to the trend will become unavoidable (Nanda, 1983; Bolin, 1986). The probable economic, ecological, and political consequences of global warming are estimated to be sufficiently severe that timely prevention would seem to be preferable to adaptation. To arrest the trend, a shift in energy sources from fossil fuels (coal, oil, natural gas) to non-carbon alternatives would be required. Because of the non-renewable character of fossil fuels, this strategy is logical, but would require massive change in present day industrial society.

An international cooperative effort toward adoption of alternative energy sources would be the most rational policy response to the 'greenhouse' issue. United Nations conferences on New Sources of Energy (Rome, 1961) and on New and Renewable Sources of Energy (Nairobi, 1981) considered the alternative issue, but with equivocal results. Representatives of the developed nations kept questions relating to oil, atomic energy, and conservation off the agenda. Thus, the nations most responsible for creating the CO_2 problem seemed least inclined to address it, and this remained the situation at the end of 1990.

As the scientific evidence of impending climate change has grown, both the scientific community and governments have shown increased concern. In 1985 a joint UNEP/WMO/ICSU conference was convened at Villach in Austria in which scientists from twenty-nine countries assessed the role of CO_2 and other 'greenhouse' gases and aerosols in prospective climate change and its associated impacts (Bolin, 1986; WMO, 1986). Subsequent workshops at Villach (28 September 1987) and Bellagio, Italy (1–13 November 1987) developed policies for responding to climate change (WMO, 1988). The first three recommendations based upon the Villach conference clearly underscore the consequences of expanding populations, economies and technologies for man's changing relationship to Earth:

1.   Governments and regional intergovernmental organizations should take account of the results of this assessment (Villach, 1985) in their policies on social and economic development, environmental programmes and control of emission of radiatively active gases.

2.   Public information efforts by international agencies and governments should be stepped up on the issues of greenhouse gases, climatic change, and sea-level; the documents of this conference (Villach, 1985) should be given wide distribution.

3.   Major uncertainties remain in predictions of changes in global and regional precipitation and temperature patterns. Ecosystem responses are also imperfectly known. Nevertheless, the understanding of the greenhouse question is sufficiently developed for scientists and policy-makers to begin an active collaboration in exploring the effectiveness of alternative policies and adjustments. Efforts should be made to design modalities for such collaboration.

A consequence of these efforts was the establishment of the Intergovernmental Panel on Climate Change (IPCC) which first met in November 1988. The Panel is assisted by a secretariat in Geneva staffed by UNEP and WMO, and is organized in three sections dealing respectively with (1) impacts, (2) science, and (3) response strategies. Further indication of changing political attitudes toward climate change was a resolution by the General Assembly of the United Nations (Item No 148) on 30 November 1988 relating to 'Conservation of Climate as Part of the Common Heritage of Mankind' (UNDoc A/63/905). This resolution, entitled 'Protection of Global Climate for Present and Future Generations of Mankind', indicates as have the scientific meetings that national policies today may originate at the international level.

National action has begun to follow. Examples include the conferences on The Changing Atmospheric Implications for Global Security sponsored by the government of Canada and held in Toronto (27–29 June 1988),

Senate Resolution 2667 in the Congress of the United States 'to establish a national energy policy to reduce global warming, (28 July 1988) and hearings in 1988 by the Senate Committee on Energy and National Resources on 'Greenhouse Effect and Global Climate Change.' The climate issue was clearly on national political agendas.

The ozone layer problem, in contrast, has met with relatively more response, expressed in a multinational treaty and protocol. The explanation is that the threat of exposure to a harmful increase in ultraviolet radiation shielded by stratospheric ozone was more immediate than the 'greenhouse' effect, and the means of prevention much simpler and less costly. The principal corrective appears to be a phase-out of chlorofluorocarbon (CFC) emissions, a process now begun within the manufacturing industry. The ozone agreements are an international response to a generally conceded adverse planetary trend, and strengthen precedents for future planetary legislation.

The effects of acidic precipitation have been widely recognized for many years. Its causes, although complex, are sufficiently established to justify corrective action. The problem is most acute in Eastern North America and Western Europe and the remedy lies in the sources and uses of energy in those countries, chiefly in electricity generation, manufacturing, and automotive transportation. Acidic by-products of fossil fuel combustion appear to be the principal causes of the death of inland lakes and forests and the contamination of seas and coastal waters. The prevalence of short term, economistic priorities in the more heavily industrialized countries has slowed corrective action. The deliberate delay of abatement measures is an example of the unreadiness of policymakers in the problem-making countries to acknowledge planetary (or ecological) responsibilities.

MAN-MADE ENTROPY

It may seem perverse to regard humans as promoters of entropy (i.e. randomized disorder) on Earth. Mankind is preeminently an organizing species, and an argument for human domination of nature has been to bring civilized order to the 'chaotic' prodigiality of nature. Insofar as human order has not fundamentally disturbed the order of nature, humans have often improved and enriched the biosphere for their own purposes (Dubos, 1980). In this respect, the quality and diversity of plant and animal life have been increased without loss to natural systems. The constructive interventions of man in nature have not necessarily been purchased at the cost of destruction to habitat and species. Rather, the negative impacts of human intervention have been caused by inadvertence, ignorance, indifference, avarice, and perceived necessity. These impacts, many of which have just been described, have broken biogeochemical cycles, disrupted ecosystemic relationships, caused crashes and explosions of populations, invasions and extinctions of plant and animal species, and created unstable and unsustainable conditions in the natural environment where formerly there was ordered homeostatic stability.

Mankind discovered, but did not invent, the Second Law of Thermodynamics. Yet few humans seem aware of its implications (Geogescu-Rogegen, 1971). In the historical record of humanity there is abundant evidence of man's disordering and randomizing the elements that comprise the biosphere. Man, to the best of our knowledge, is the only animal to adopt an unecological way of life and get away with it – at least in the short-run as planetary time is measured. The greater part of man's disordering impact on nature has occurred in scarcely more than a century – a short interval even in human history. The science-based technology that has enabled humans to flourish while impairing the planetary life-support system might help avoid further jeopardy to their future in the biosphere – but for that to happen more than science and technology will be required.

The human mind is especially good at evading unacceptable realities. It is also good at learning from investigation and experience in pursuit of desired outcomes. Unfortunately for future prospects and rational policies, modern society is reluctant to accept the reality of planetary limitations that contravene long-standing assumptions and strongly held aspirations. When faced with intractable natural phenomena the modern inclination is to try to conquer and subdue. Within the modern ethos, the costs of working against nature have been systematically preferred to the concessions necessary to obtain the benefits of working with nature (Mishan, 1967; Murphy, 1967). The environmental movement represents an effort to change this perverse calculus of costs and benefits. But if this objective is to be obtained, the institutions of public education, of public information, and of public administration will need to be mobilized on its behalf. This task has only recently been attempted and its successes are as yet only marginal.

If the trends that we have outlined are permitted to continue indefinitely, even though partially moderated, they will eventually turn back upon their progenitors. More likely the excesses of population and expansive material growth will diminish the quality of life of their descendents. History, however, appears to be accelerating, and who can be sure that the future may not arrive well in advance of expectations? Processes of disintegration and ecological disorder are today plainly visible. They are being measured by the most reliable of our mathematical and scientific methods and their consequences are being projected by sophisticated computer technologies. Denial of their significance does not change their reality, but may weaken the public will to take the actions necessary to arrest or reverse the destructive trends. For such will be to asserted on a planetary scale, a change in social beliefs, attitudes and priorities would be necessary with a speed and fervor for which only the outbreak of great war offers a partial precedent. That humans have the innate ability to make so dramatic a transformation seems plausible; that they will do so is uncertain.

8

Shaping world institutions

By this time, experience should have taught us that a complex planetary biosphere cannot be addressed effectively for protection or for rational management by a fragmented and uncoordinated political order. This lesson is being learnt, but it is not easily applied. During the past quarter century an international structure for environmental protection has begun to take form, but it is as yet uneven in coverage and effectiveness. The emergent process has been incremental, in response to particular issues and alarms. The structure for policy has been international and incorporates the reservations, exceptions, and exclusions that characterize the international relations of national states.

There is a fundamental contradiction between the "Only One Earth" of the Declaration of the United Nations Conference on the Human Environment (1972), precepts of the World Charter for Nature adopted by the General Assembly of the United Nations (1982), and the behavior of national governments. The unity of the planetary biosphere is declared in principle, but denied in practice. To put the problem simply, many informed people throughout the world sympathize with the goals declared by these documents, but they do not know how to achieve them or are unable to move their governments to action. Relationships among national states are not ones of trust or altruism. Governments seek their 'national interests' which are seldom the interests of all their people, and often not even of a majority of them. National sovereignty is involved to protect those interests that national governments wish to shield from external intrusion. Even when nations cooperate through international organizations or programs, they customarily seek their own interests through obtaining key positions for their nationals or through blocking or qualifying resolutions or conventions that they believe threaten their interests or autonomy. The world is not now and may never be ready for world government, but it cannot resolve mankind's planetary predicament through the existing order of sovereign national states. Have we then a problem without a solution?

In national politics, strategic military, economic, and political interests invariably take precedence over environmental considerations with the rare exception of a catastrophy of Chernobyl proportions. Yet the increasing involvement of scientific information and investigation in almost every field of policy has been changing the sources and contents of inputs into policy-making. Nowhere is this growing role of science more marked than in environmental policy. As noted in Part I of this book, science influences policy indirectly as well as directly. When science, outside of government, reveals the existence of an environmental problem such as the death of forests, the impending extinction of species, or breaking of the protective shield of atmospheric ozone, governments, reflecting popular concern, invoke science to help formulate an appropriate response. Then science is brought officially into the policy and planning process.

As emphasized throughout this volume, science is increasingly a critical input to policy, but seldom a determinant. That input, as we have seen, is injected in a variety of ways and at different stages in the policy process. We have also noted that science as it has evolved to the present, has not been well adapted to address environmental issues, which are almost invariably cross-disciplinary. The structure of modern science has been disciplinary and reductionist; environmental problems are, in substance, interdisciplinary and their solutions synthesizing and syncretic. In consequence some of the anomalies and inconsistencies of environmental laws may be attributed to their being written with insufficient regard to their ramifications and interrelationships with other areas of policy.

There is now in place a juridical world order of the environment (Schneider, 1979) consisting of international agreements and institutions constituted to deal with those aspects of transnational environmental problems that are amenable to decisions by national governments. A structure of international cooperation has been assembled, piece by piece, to enable nations to accomplish together what no single nation can achieve independently. This process of institution building is inherently political and the persons who formalize its objectives and preside over its realization are national public officials. As architects of policy they are politicians, although many different skills are required in drafting acceptable agreements on complex issues.

The complexities of modern society exceed the informational or analytic capabilities of any single profession. International affairs were once the almost exclusive province of diplomats and their legal and military advisers. Politicians affixed their signatures to treaties and other international agreements, but the draft work was done by lawyers. This is still the formal process, but increasingly experts in science and technology are telling the lawyers what to say and advising the politicians what to sign. What the experts say is, of course, not always what the politicians sign. Lawyers and diplomats are there to see that scientists and other experts do not compromise national interests in shaping policies to resolve international problems. Agreements have been negotiated by officials having little understanding of science, with advice on technical matters by various scientists who were unable to integrate their special expertise into administrable policies. The special skills of legalist and scientist are necessary but insufficient to determine arrangements and policies capable of effectively addressing the problems of human relationships within the biosphere. Informed political leadership is also necessary.

WHAT WE HAVE

We presently have four types of institutional structures officially concerned with man-in-biosphere. With respect to planetary environmental policy, the most pervasive, oldest, and collectively least coherent are the national governments; they comprise aggregates of agencies, departments or ministries, collectively responsible for national environmental administration and sometimes for implementing obligations assumed under international treaties. Today, this latter function is more commonly performed by ministries of external relations or of special offices in departments of environmental affairs, although governmental organizations differ widely.

The second, third, and fourth arrangements are international in status. Of these the largest and most formalized is the United Nations system and especially the United Nations Environment Programme and the science policy and research units of the Specialized Agencies. A third unofficial structure is formed by the network of non-governmental organizations that has grown prodigiously during the years since the UN Conference on the Human Environment. These organizations, public in interest, but private in status exert pressures on both the international and national domestic fronts. Fourthly there are at least three organizations intermediate between public and private status. They are the International Council of Scientific Unions, the International Union for Conservation of Nature and Natural Resources, and possibly, the World Wildlife Fund for Nature. Not officially governmental, all have close relationships to governments and intergovernmental organizations and receive directly or indirectly financial support from governments.

In organizing to deal with environmental issues, governments face difficulties comparable to the complexities of the fields of action. All things in life are ultimately interrelated, but most problems may be reduced and defined to permit resolution without addressing indirect or remote relationships. Environmental relationships, however, are seldom easily decomposed. Coping with environmental pollution is an obvious example where abating a problem in one medium (e.g. water) may transfer it to another medium (e.g. air or land) from which it may reenter water. Environmental issues in agriculture, forestry, or mining invariably have numerous social and economic implications. Matters not generally regarded primarily as environmental (e.g. highway construction or port facilities) may have significant environmental aspects.

Given the diversity of assumptions regarding the appropriate functions of most governments, there is no generally accepted logic or criteria to guide the structuring of national responsibilities in relation to the environment. As noted in chapter 4, the place of environmental affairs in the structure of a government is one (unreliable) indicator of the importance which they are accorded. In most countries today, environmental ministries, departments, or environment-related agencies (e.g. for national parks, forests, wildlife, or pollution control) have been added to structures reflecting concepts of governmental responsibilities and priorities predating the environmental movement. Moreover, these traditional agencies are often linked to economic interests with strong but unobtrusive political connections. Then when environmental issues clash with special economic interests, the latter are likely to prevail unless the environmental value is widely shared, highly visible and has its own economic rationality.

These considerations help to clarify the problem of obtaining compliance with international treaty commitments. The external or foreign affairs office of a country, or perhaps an environmental ministry, may sign an international treaty and secure its proforma ratification. But it may have great difficulty in persuading or pressuring other agencies – co-equal or stronger – to honor the commitment. Presidents, premiers, and cabinets may be reluctant to push for compliance when prejudicial to their perceived political futures.

Where there is effective non-governmental national political support for the implementation of environmental policy and law, and for observance of international treaty obligations, international-minded administrators of environmental programs may prevail against more traditional competitors. This would be most likely where environmental values have been rising among politically active groups, and the heads of government and other political leaders find personal advantage in being seen as responsive. Even so, governments are organized primarily to deal with domestic issues; their external relations traditionally have been largely categorized as defence, diplomacy, and commerce and are seldom easily integrated with international environmental commitments. The international dimension of environmental policy is relatively new and governments have only begun to discover how to organize in relation to it.

This helps to explain why the extent of national fulfillment of international environmental treaty obligations may be dubious on matters which countervene the interest of politically influential groups – including the government bureaucracies – within a country. Practical international cooperation might be assisted by comparability of administrative structures from country to country, but this circumstance does not generally prevail. Military and foreign affairs departments are among the more generally comparable agencies of national states. Ministries of commerce, trade and finance have counterparts in all major governments. The environmental agencies of countries are not generally comparable in mission and status. Their relationships to other agencies of government differ, but are almost everywhere subordinate to more influential ministries or departments (Cutrera, 1987). In brief, there is not among nations generally a well established pattern of administrative authority and responsibility for environmental affairs comparable to that prevailing for the traditional functions of government.

This is partly a consequence of the relative newness of the environment as an issue and partly because there is no obvious way to organize in relation to those other functions of government with which most environmental issues interrelate. To deal effectively with problems of the environment, solutions are needed for organizational problems that may extend broadly to the general administrative structure of government. The scope and range of environmental relationships makes sectoral status a poor organizational choice, but public and political interests are not ready to confer a super-departmental status upon environmental affairs – at least not yet.

The diversity of international organizations dealing with environmental concerns precludes more than very general groupings by status and function. Within the United Nations system, the sector most specifically identified with the environment is UNEP, the United Nations Environment Programme. The great resources of personnel, money, and linkage with governments are, however, with the science and environmental-related programs of the Specialized Agencies, notably the World Meterological Organization (WMO), the Food and Agriculture Organization (FAO), the World Health Organization (WHO), the United Nations Education, Scientific and Cultural Organization (UNESCO), the International Maritime Organization (IMO), the United Nations Industrial Development Organization (UNIDO), and the associated International Atomic Energy Agency (IAEA). Within these agencies are bureaus and programs relevant to environmental concerns. Even a summary of their activities could fill a book (Caldwell, 1984). For our purposes here it is sufficient to note that collectively they constitute important elements of a structure of international environmental policy and cooperation. In theory UNEP provides a coordinate facility for their environment-related activities. In fact UNEP is unduly limited in this function by constraints of budget and status. Even so UNEP provides initiatives and coordination through joint programing with other agencies whose funds supplement those of UNEP.

Of present significance, but greater future potential is UNEP's role as a focus for the international activities and concerns of nongovernmental organizations (NGOs). The Environmental Liaison Centre at Nairobi facilitates communication between UNEP and, as of 1987, at least 252 volunteer environmental groups representing 65 countries. These and other non-governmental organizations have regularly held forums or unofficial meetings in conjunction with official United Nations conferences, thus linking informally, but possibly influentially, international, national, and domestic environment-related institutions.

Intermediary between the United Nations organizations and non-governmental organizations of scientists and other citizens are two federated organizations whose members are non-governmental, quasi-governmental and governmental. As previously noted, the International Council of Scientific Unions (ICSU), comprises representatives from international scientific associations and from national academies of science. In some countries the academies are non-governmental, but in others they are to be regarded realistically as within the government. The work of ICSU is carried on by international scientific committees, but often in association with scientific agencies within the United Nations system such as the World Meterological Organization. The International Union for Conservation of Nature and Natural Resources (IUCN), is a federation of national and international conservation and environmental organizations, but it also has members that are governments (e.g. France), or are governmental agencies (e.g. US National Parks Service). Like ICSU it maintains working relationships with UN Specialized Agencies especially with UNEP, FAO, and UNESCO.

Membership in both ICSU and IUCN may be traced back to the national level. There are, of course, many non-governmental environmentally concerned groups at the national level that are not affiliated with either of these 'umbrella' organizations. The increasing flow in information around the world and greater ease of personal communication makes possible greater coordination of international and national non-governmental political efforts than has been possible heretofore. Non-governmental organizations may pressure their own national governments to honor international commitments and introduce new initiatives. Thus the apparent growing strength of citizen participation in public affairs and especially in international issues increases the possibility of a coordinative structure of environmental action. What governments agree to rhetorically in international conferences, resolutions, and treaties, their citizens at home may require them to put into practice.

WHAT WE NEED

This book lays out no master plan for future world environmental institutions. Such an exercise might have a heuristic value, but is not the purpose here. Our aim is to interpret the environmental movement, broadly defined, in relation to the advancement of science and the changing (i.e. maturing) relationships of man to Earth. Institutional change is born from a convergence of knowledge, experience, perceived advantage, and perhaps necessity. Youthful humanity sought control over Earth on a trial and error basis. There have been some successes and many errors and only lately has science begun to discover more reliable and predictable ways of interacting with the planetary environment. The shaping of world institutions to resolve environmental problems will probably proceed with greater rapidity as the pressures of motivating forces increase.

In this process, the influences of expanding knowledge and of expanding transnational receptivity indicate a need for flexibility in institutional arrangements. The growth of social consciousness may be influenced but not programmed; the process is organic rather than mechanistic. We cannot predict the exact shape of world environmental institutions in the future, but we can foresee some of their probable characteristics. To some extent, the problems shape the form of effective response and the options for coping with the problems are not unlimited. One of the reasons for believing in the possibility of a world polity for the environment is the wide scope and growing vitality of the international environmental education movement. Environmental education is now organized through national and international associations and networks. The IUCN Commission on Education was an early organizer of regional associations, UNESCO and UNEP have been major sponsors of international communication, and the International Society for Environmental Education now provides additional linkage among educators around the world.

In the absence of political receptivity, no strategy for environmental protection is likely to succeed; but, of course, creating receptivity in society and government is a basic element in a strategy to extend and strengthen environmental protection. There is no *one* way to build receptivity. It follows not only from the experience and information that people acquire, but also from the institutional circumstances that may or may not facilitate the growth of new perceptions and understandings. A major force for spreading information and developing understanding is the growth of a transnational publication and telecommunication network (Horn, 1978/79). Largely serving different audiences, the UNESCO-UNEP Environmental Newsletter *Connect* and the UNEP service *INFOTERRA* provide institutional structures reaching many thousands of individuals. As of 1986 *INFOTERRA* assisted over 5,500 national institutions and 127 participating governments. Bulletins and other publications of UNEP, the IUCN, and the World Wildlife Fund for Nature are prominent among many whose messages are distributed throughout the world. The World Conservation Strategy may be regarded as an important vehicle for this dissemination (Allen, 1980; Talbot 1980).

Buckminister Fuller once remarked that humans, in effect, had been permitted to take command of Spaceship Earth, but had not been provided with an operating manual (Fuller, 1969). Only with poetic license could humans be said to be in command of Earth; and Earth differs in fundamental ways from any spaceship that humans can as yet construct. But Fuller was right in declaring that we humans would have to develop our own planetary operating manual to avoid cybernetic errors and overlooked opportunities. Environmental science has been assembling the data for such a 'manual' and some control mechanisms to guide our behaviors are in place. But we have yet to acquire the orientation and operational capabilities needed to make what we have achieved serve its intended purpose without impairing the natural systems upon which our existence depends.

Our operational capabilities are expressed through institutional arrangements. The ad hoc structure through which international environmental policy has emerged – national governments, the United Nations organizations, NGOs and scientific unions – do not provide a complete or coherent system for the development or implementation of policy. Operational responsibilities remain almost wholly at the national level. If humans are to establish a rational and sustainable relationship with the biosphere a more comprehensive and operational system will be necessary. The institutions that we have were never intended to deal with transnational global issues; the institutions that we need would compensate for the limitations of the national state system and strengthen the capabilities of the international legal system in relation to agreed upon policies.

With no pretensions toward a definitive assessment, I have identified five areas of policy development and implementation for which institutional innovation is needed. They are: (1) implementation of treaties, (2) high level representation of global environmental policy concerns, (3) adequate funding of environmental protection efforts, (4) a politically acceptable trusteeship capability, and (5) an international political federation for specified purposes. Speculative as the prospects for institutional development in these areas may be, they address real and recognized inadequacies in our efforts to carry out commitments already made for protection of the biosphere.

IMPLEMENTATION OF TREATIES

Our strategies of implementation for international environmental policies have relied heavily upon treaties. These formal political agreements or conventions are the closest approach that we have to transnational laws. They are, however, the laws of nations, not persons. They are administrated (if administered at all) by governments which have reserved to themselves determination of whether they have complied with their obligations under the agreements. There is an International Court of Justice (the World Court), but its jurisdiction is severely limited and it has no positive power of enforcing its decisions. There is now an elaborate matrix of environmental treaties in place (Rüster et al. 1975–83; Kiss, 1982). They offer unreliable assurance that the issues with which they deal are receiving public attention and that their prescriptions are being observed.

We cannot easily discover whether some treaties are being disregarded, or treated as legalistic facades behind which environmentally damaging activity goes on. In the world today there is no institutionalized authority to force governments to observe treaty obligations or even to reveal the extent to which they do or do not implement them. Persuasion will likely be ineffective where a national leadership perceives observance of a treaty obligation to be contrary to its interests. There are many forms of persuasion, however, and some may have the effect of coercion. Publicity can often be persuasive in public and governmental affairs. Public officials almost universally have a special sensitivity to embarrassment and to the opportunity it gives to rivals. Environmental NGOs are sometimes able to expose laxity in treaty compliance by their own governments. Through networks of NGOs, pressures may be brought simultaneously on numbers of governments.

A government that does implement a treaty has a legitimate concern that other parties also honor the commitment, especially where their non-compliance would be injurious to its national interests. Verification of compliance has been a critical issue in treaties, notably regarding limitations and reduction of armaments. On-site verification has been accepted by the US and the USSR with respect to intermediate-range nuclear missiles. For less sensitive issues, informal, unofficial observation of national compliance can, and has, been undertaken by volunteers. The IUCN has reported both official and unofficial observations in its publications and brought harmful non-compliance to the attention of the governments responsible. Other non-governmental environmental groups, such as Greenpeace, have sought overt confrontation to obtain maximum publicity regarding an issue in controversy. Governments may respond by declaring these investigations to be unwarranted and illegal intrusions into their domestic affairs. They may allege that the practice or events portrayed are exceptional or exaggerated; or they may ignore the criticisms. There is, of course, the possibility that critics may not have complete knowledge of circumstances and may misinterpret events. There is more often the probability that they may be right.

To activate where necessary and to assess the effectiveness of the international regime of environmental treaties, strengthened transnational institutional arrangements are needed. The idea is not novel, it having already been proposed in principle to the Legal Committee of the Organization of American States by Vice-President Victor H. Martinez of Argentina (1987). Whether a number of separate but related environmental treaty surveillance agencies or some form of comprehensive system, an effective arrangement would need to provide for some measure of mutual coercion mutually accepted. It would be premature today to suggest more than the very general character of such a system or agencies for treaty implementation. Clearly the arrangement would be international, most likely situated within the structure of the United Nations and with access across international borders accepted by participating states. An interdisciplinary staff would be needed, but use could be made of specialists from any of the sciences where needed. Very important would be the reporting functions for which adequate and dependable budgetary provisions should be made. An annual report to the General Assembly of the United Nations through its Secretary-General would be desirable. Such a system need not impose large costs relative to what governments spend on foreign affairs. In many countries use could be made of non-governmental environmental groups in alerting international monitors to problems of governmental compliance. Voluntary observers and reporters are presently active in many countries, especially in relation to natural phenomena such as severe storms.

Parts of this transnational institutional structure are already in place. They are the secretariats provided for the implementation of the relatively recent environmental treaties. A unique provision is the International Joint Commission of Canada and the United States, charged with oversight of the Boundary Waters Treaty of 1909 and subsequent environmental agreements between the two parties. To strengthen the regime of international treaties is therefore to build upon what we already have – not a radical departure from precedent.

HIGH LEVEL REPRESENTATION

A second strategy would be establishment of a top-level World Environment Council, supplementing or possibly replacing the present Governing Council of UNEP. An objective of this strategy would be to change the balance of attention in the United Nations organization, elevating environmental concerns from their present programmatic status to the level of the three major councils – Social and Economic, Trusteeship and Security. At the 1972 conference at Stockholm the dominant view was that attention was needed to world environment problems, but that these problems were secondary to the big issues of poverty, food, health, trade, security, and colonialism. The industrial powers had lost their enthusiasm for the United Nations, and the developing countries had not yet discovered the importance of environmental factors in their futures. Some participants in the conference understood the fundamental and interrelated character of economic and environmental problems; most regarded the problems as sectoral, each with its own causes and cures, and not requiring a grand strategy for the planet as a whole. Following 1972 the social and economic assumptions of pre-Stockholm years were left intact. Growth and development remained the dominant goals, but a change of perspective was beginning.

Today, recognition is growing that refining and refocusing the concepts of growth and development must be accomplished within a planetary environmental context. We are discovering, but only just beginning to act on the recognition that concern for the environment is not a sectoral or secondary consideration – another special interest. It is the reality within which growth and development occur. Our growing awareness of the ecological planetary context of our existence pushes us to question our objectives: to ask what kind of growth we seek, and development toward what kind of environment?

As always in human affairs, institutions lag behind social realities. Persons closest to the UN system and most conscious of its infirmities will be the most skeptical of prospects for its reformation. But who are the utopians? If the prognosis for the planetary future, deducible from accumulating scientific evidence is valid, is it realistic to believe that the policies and practices that have caused ecologically destructive trends will continue indefinitely to prevail, and that society will make no effort to reform them? Perhaps, but a human preference for survival makes the prospect for reform – even for systemic change – at least plausible.

The concept of a World Environmental Council, premature at Stockholm, may be acceptable before the twenty-first century. Evolving out of experience with the Governing Council of UNEP, the new body would not be a wholly untried experiment. Detailed speculation about the functions of this hypothetical council would not be useful here. There are, however, at least two ways in which an Environmental Council might move the world toward a planetary polity for the biosphere. It could be the authoritative and supervisory body for a system of treaty surveillance and implementation, and it could assist the extension and strengthening of connections between scientific investigation, environmental protection and reconstruction efforts, and national policy and performance.

The charter of the council should specify the scope of its functions and the limits of its authority; but with realistic appreciation of the magnitude and importance of its task. Its relationship to international science would require careful consideration. If effective, the council would be certain to influence priorities for scientific research and development. At the least it would doubtless review the status of scientific inquiry on environmental issues, extending a function already partially performed by UNEP and ICSU. Council recommendations could also promote the funding of large transnational research efforts which national governments might otherwise be disinclined to support. The scientific communities of the world would, however, need assurance that an Environmental Council with real power would not be a deterrent to independent scientific investigation. In particular, leadership in the International Council of Scientific Unions would need to be persuaded that the council would be an understanding patron and not a meddling preceptor.

The relationship of the Council to the international environmental NGOs would also be important. The rise of non-governmental organizations to prominence in policymaking has been a phenomenon of recent decades. Because the proposed Council would probably be smaller than the present Governing Council, a broader forum for expression of views would be desirable. Consummate political skill would be required to establish an ancillary non-governmental citizen assembly to review and advise without assuming powers of decision that it could not make effective. NGOs are already represented at UNEP through the Environment Liaison Center; what I propose is an extension and appropriate institutionalization of the NGO relationship consistent with the growing transnational character of environmental uses.

Relationships between the Environmental Council, the Social and Economic Council and the Specialized Agencies would also be major considerations whose outcome would depend heavily upon the political strength of an international environmental movement to which national governments felt compelled to respond. If the environmental NGOs possessed political strength sufficient to cause governments to establish the Environmental Council, they would have strength sufficient to form an international constituency for its functions.

There could be a challenge to rationality and constructive creativity in developing a relationship between an Environmental Council and the UN Trusteeship Council. History has progressively deprived the Trusteeship Council of its original role as an agent of decolonization. Its principal function now appears to be vocalizing of Third World resentments, but it might be reconstituted to serve more constructive and tangible needs, presently to be considered.

FUNDING BIOSPHERIC PROTECTION

Pursuant to recommendation by the United Nations Conference on the Human Environment a World Environment Fund was established on a voluntary basis. The initial goal of $100 million United States dollar equivalent over five years was pathetically small compared to the magnitude of the environmental tasks identified by the Conference, even though much of the Action Programme would be funded by national budgets and augmented through joint programming with Specialized Agencies. Still, given the disposition of national governments in 1972 and the absence of an international infrastructure to utilize more adequate funding, the action taken at Stockholm and subsequently by the UN General Assembly was as much as might reasonably be expected at the time. Today, although some governments may be no more responsive than they were at Stockholm, the need is evident for an international environmental financial institution with fiduciary (trust fund) capabilities. It is possible that the World Bank might assume a substantial part of such a role. This could hardly be undertaken without a revised concept of development (toward which the Bank may be moving) and perhaps a revision of its charter.

The World Environment Fund was intended to support the UN Environment Programme. This arrangement was necessary but insufficient. A comparison between the resources of the World Bank, the various regional development banks and the World Environmental Fund illustrate dramatically the relative priorities of national governments. Monetary commitment to development totals billions, funds for environmental programs are measured in uncertain millions. This comparison is not wholly valid because some (minor part) of the transactions of the banks serve environmental protection purposes. But historically, many of the investments and loans of the banks have had adverse environmental effects, notably in relation to deforestation in the tropics, large scale water engineering for hydropowers and irrigation, and industrialized agriculture.

In comparing international funding for environment and development, account should be taken of allocations by the UN Specialized Agencies and the UN Development Programme. There are moreover, national and non-governmental sources of funding for environment and development. To attempt a balance sheet of relative expenditures might be useful but cannot be attempted here. The sustainable development concept implies an integration of developmental and environmental expenditures. Yet if peoples and governments are seriously committed to environmental protection of the biosphere, their financial commitment will need to more adequately reflect their intentions. Discrepancy in the scientific, technical and financial capabilities of the more and less developed countries necessitates the availability of assistance where it is needed, both because of the importance of the environmental issue (e.g. protection of rainforest ecosystems) and because of the severely limited capabilities of poorer countries. More than transfer of economic and technical resources is required, however, because preparedness to use aid wisely is as important as willingness to extend it.

A new look should therefore be taken at the world's resources for environmental protection and consideration given to a possible restructuring of existing financial institutions including the possibility of a World Environment Trust with broad and flexible capabilities. This facility could have a major role to play in assisting the recovery and stabilization of nations that are approaching conditions of socio-ecological bankruptcy. In such an effort provision should be made for more than economic and monetary considerations. Resource transfers will be of little avail unless their provident use can be assured through preparatory education, training, popular receptivity, and governmental accounting.

During the past two decades we have witnessed worsening socio-ecological conditions in a growing number of 'Third World' countries. These developments were not unforeseen. In 1968 a conference on the ecological aspects of international development reviewed the all-too-frequent failure of international development efforts because environmental factors were discounted or ignored (Farvar and Milton, 1972). Near its close the conference also considered the problem of nations in which ecologically excessive population growth, severe attrition of environmental assets, and improvident economics were creating conditions of socio-economic-ecological bankruptcy. In addition to impoverishment of people and nature, life in these countries was characterized by hunger, disease and social disorder. They might be regarded as the political failures of this world, going nowhere in international development efforts.

These cases of national socio-ecological disaster appeared then to be beyond self-help alone and events since then have only confirmed this assessment. But the sovereignty syndrome, anti-colonial sensitivity, super-power rivalry, preference for philanthropy over reform, and failure to perceive the chain reaction effects of socio-ecological bankruptcy, have deterred consideration of fundamental corrective measures. On those infrequent occasions when international salvage measures are considered, strategies for the ultimate well-being of people and their environments are characteristically put aside in a focus on immediate exegencies. Basic cause-effect relationships are not considered, in part because of a need to deal with the immediate situation, but also because that line of inquiry would lead into socially and politically 'sensitive' matters. To many humanitarian-relief administrators, these reasons are sufficient to explain why nothing beyond immediate assistance and continuing relief can be contemplated.

Ideological and economic rivalry among the world's great powers may be the greatest barrier to an international trusteeship for socio-ecologically insolvent nations. Nevertheless a rational case can be made for an international rehabilitative effort that would be in the interest of all mankind. In a closing session of the conference on ecology and international development in 1968, I introduced the proposal which follows and which slightly modified, is as pertinent to conditions today as it was then:

International conferences and agencies must respect the conventional assumptions of the sovereignty of nations, and accordingly there are propositions, which, because they are inconsistent with national-state ideology, cannot easily be placed on their agendas. How, for example, would the community of nations deal with a national government that either threatened the viability of the biosphere through ecologically unwise action within its own territorial jurisdiction or mismanaged its environment to a point of collapse of its social and economic institutions? In such circumstances, which become less hypothetical daily, some generally acceptable means of international intervention would be advantageous. There is need for a legitimized and effective means through which international action may be interposed to prevent, or to take into receivership, cases of national ecological bankruptcy. At the very least, some means is needed whereby a national government, without loss of respect, could ask for and obtain temporary international administration of its natural resource base and its resource-based economy. Total collapse of a natural resource base in relation to human need is unlikely, but less unlikely now than in the past. Yet in many countries today, the life-support system of soil, water, air, minerals, and living things is being stressed to a degree that could result in the failure of one or more critical components. The most probable failures are the familiar ones of food or water supply... but the most wide-spread cause of 'ecological bankruptcy' is the gradual wearing-out of the environment – the stressing of natural systems beyond their capacity for regeneration. As the viability of the resource base diminishes in relation to the demands upon it, and the margin available to compensate for misfortune lessens, an unexpected failure at some critical point could conceivably trigger the collapse of the human socio-ecological system.

Advanced nations may be as vulnerable as underdeveloped ones to this type of catastrophe, but they might be better able to take unassisted remedial action. In any case, an international organization able to cope with large-scale environmental disasters is becoming an increasingly practical proposition in a closed-system, interdependent world. If the prospect of 'ecological bankruptcy' is seriously considered and timely action taken, catastrophe may be prevented. However, the uncertainty of the nature, scope and timing of ecological disaster makes difficult the development of an effective operational plan for coping with it. Nevertheless, the need for an international organization to mobilize and direct measures to remedy ecological disaster is sufficiently obvious to justify its consideration at an early date.[1]

AN INTERNATIONAL POLITICAL MOVEMENT?

None of these conjectured developments will become realities unless by force of positive political will or reluctant presumed necessity. There are such forces nascent in the world today, but scarcely discernible to those who do not look for them. There is present an embryonic political force that could change world politics and has already had visible effect. But because it has not yet achieved coherence or attained the dimensions necessary to its full effectiveness it is largely overlooked, dismissed, or discounted.

This force may be identified as an international environmental political movement and its implications are probably least perceived by those persons closest to the daily conduct of governmental and international relations. Inattention to unobtrusive trends, and close continuous concentration on day-to-day events combine to account for the consternation which people in authority experience when a predictable but unforeseen future suddenly, and with full force breaks in upon them unannounced. The advent of an international political movement is more likely to be gradual than dramatic. Even so, it would doubtless take many otherwise well-informed people by surprise.

Today we have tools of analysis and forecasting hitherto unavailable. Sufficient data have been assembled and analysed to give us credible evidence of the emergence of an ecological consciousness throughout the world (Milbrath, 1984). As yet a minor factor in world politics, this consciousness has assumed political form in countries in which 'green' parties have appeared. It should be possible today to develop a profile of environmental concern among the principal nations of the Earth. Enough has been done to obtain plausible indications of attitudes in the United States, Canada, Great Britain, France, West Germany and the Netherlands, but not enough to permit a reliable assessment of environmental attitudes worldwide. Nevertheless, we have sufficient evidence of attitudinal change to infer a significant increase in environmental awareness among literate people in a large number of countries (Inglehart, 1977, 1987).

Among the sources of this inference are increases in the number and activities of non-governmental environmental organizations, the establishment of environmental departments or ministries within national and provincial governments, ratification of international environmental treaties, treatment of the environment in the newspaper press, and public events such as conferences having an environmental or ecological character. International meetings such as the triennial assemblies of IUCN or the non-governmental forums associated with major United Nations conferences, and memberships in the Environment Liaison Centre at Nairobi provide positive, although indirect evidence of the international status of the environmental movement.

These various sources of information regarding environmental activity are not isolated. Growing ease of international communication and transportation facilitates the growth of the network phenomenon which has been noted. In countries heretofore outside of the main currents of science and intellectual movements, volunteer environmental groups are no longer isolated from world trends and from the flow of information around the world. In nearly all of the major scientifically advanced countries of the world there is demonstrable evidence of environmental concern and in most of them the visible presence of an organized environmental movement. This development is both political, intellectual, and ethical. It forms a nucleus needed for the emergence of a new phenomenon on Earth – the emergence of a coherent and coordinated transnational movement which, in effect, could become a world political party.

The concept of an international political party, introduced in chapter 5, is not new. The Communist Internationale may be regarded as the first worldwide political party, although organized in each state as a national party. The internationalization of the communist movement was induced and facilitated by the internationalizing of economic affairs, of commerce, trade, and manufacturing that followed the industrial revolution and colonial expansion. Problems common to people in similar circumstances may elicit similar responses if a format for their reactions is provided. Whatever the validity of its thesis and program, international Marxism provided an operational model which with national variations was widely adopted, and exercised a profound influence on the history of the twentieth century.

International Marxism may be said to have failed as a world political party even though its force is still significant. It failed in part at least because of what it was and what it was not. It was a movement based upon social warfare, upon an international class struggle that could be won only by the iron rule of force directed by an ideological priesthood. The classless society could not be achieved through democratic politics; removal of its governing 'class', 'the party' would put its goals and principles in jeopardy. Contrary to the claims of its ideologists it was not a movement based upon the reality of the world as revealed by science or experiences. There is today, no objective empirical referent for Marxist truth; it rests on political faith.

The international environmental movement differs fundamentally. Although it is also a consequence of the internationalizing of industrialism and economic affairs and a reaction against certain of its consequences, it is not by intent socially aggressive or divisive. Its attack is not on some people, nor even necessarily on institutions, but upon certain behaviors injurious to all people and to all living things. It is not dedicated to enmity toward religion and has, for example, become associated with the ecumenicalism of the New Alliance, an ethico-ecological religious movement initiated by the World Wildlife Fund for Nature at Assisi in September 1986 (World Wildlife Fund for Nature 1986/87).

Unlike Marxism, environmentalism finds support for its tenets in empirical science. yet there is much more than science in the environmental movement. Its currents contain ethical and aesthetic elements as old as classical antiquity, with analogies in all human cultures, giving it a universality that no other social movement appears to equal. The movement draws upon intimations bedded deeply in the human psyche. Thus there is great emotional power latent in this movement which already has a foundation in its 'scriptures' (i.e. the literature of environmental concern), but has not yet found its demiurgic prophet. To borrow a phrase from Jean-Francois Revel, environmentalism moves forward without a Marx or Jesus (Revel, 1971).

Where does it move? In many places and many ways. One sees it in local neighborhood improvement and protection groups, in municipal and provincial environmental organizations, and in the large national and increasingly international federated associations. Although their agendas are unavoidably political, these environmental organizations are in the main non-partisan in relation to conventional political parties. Their purpose has been to influence policy, not necessarily to take control of or to administer government. This strategy assumes at least a minimal receptivity by some or all of the regular political parties. But when those parties are perceived to be impervious to environmentalist values the alternative course of direct political action may be elected.

This route has been taken by Green parties in Western Europe (Capra & Spretnak, 1984). Are these parties transient phenomena, or are they forerunners of a new phase in world politics? The opportunity to elect members to the European Parliament provides incentive for transnational political collaboration. The practical necessity for transnational solutions to nearly all of Europe's environmental problems is another incentive for transnational Green politics. It is presently impossible to foresee what the future of the Green parties will be. It is possible, however, to conjecture an important role for them or their successors in the ultimate emergence of a worldwide political confederation of parties whose common purpose is the creation of a planetary polity.

Where the ultimate configuration is that of a world party with national or regional sectors, or a confederation of national parties, a consequence could be the establishment of a world polity for the environment. If one extrapolates the politics of the present into the future this conjecture might seem improbable. But whether people through their governments respond effectively to the trends threatening the biosphere, or whether they fail to do so, the future world will not be like the present. Throughout the world today there is great and visible popular disaffection for the present political parties, especially among youth. People have seldom been happy with their politicians, but there have been few eras in human history when as many people have found as much irrelevance in the slogans and postures of their would-be governors.

In one form or another it appears inevitable that a planetary policy in some form will eventually emerge. It is not likely to resemble any political system yet experienced or to become a general world government. It is more likely to emerge as a worldwide confederation of limited and specified powers, but sufficiently authoritative to coordinate and focus the efforts of the world's peoples and nations to resolve the complex and unavoidable problems of mankind's relationship to a finite Earth. This eventuality assumes a politics differing in fundamental respects from what we know today.

To argue that politics will never change is to imply that societies cannot or will not learn – that the possibility of a better politics is an illusion. Yet a case can be made for the proposition that, allowing for exceptions, more people today are better served by politics and government than at any previous time. Popular dissatisfaction, in part, expresses a conviction that improvement is possible. The environmental movement and the developments that brought it into existence provide persuasive reasons for believing in the possibility of a new politics that is more than rhetorical promises.

If a future politics is oriented more toward human relations with the Earth and less toward controversy among humans, there may be at least five ways in which this politics may differ from that which we accept as conventional today. Human relations with the Earth should, of course, be understood as broadly inclusive and not merely ecological in the narrower sense. These relationships inevitably include people-to-people issues, because human behavior in relation to the Earth is societal and involves those differences among people that are resolved through political choice and policy. One should also note that those differences are not new in the sense of never having been present in political life. They would be new in emphasis, and in the way in which they characterized political values and behaviors (e.g. in relation to human rights).

First among the characteristics of this 'new' politics is the influence of science or, more accurately, the influence of knowledge. This is clearly an enlarging of an influence that has been present and growing throughout modern times. Knowledge interpreted and disseminated through education and information services has been a decisive factor in many environmental policy questions. Growth of an environmental focus in the sciences had a powerful feedback effect on research and development. And we are now seeing what may be the early stages of the influence of psychology, influences of the sciences of the mind and behavior on politics in a more fundamental way than in hitherto largely manipulative uses. As the human brain discovers more about itself and the sociobiologists learn more about the interactive forces among humans in society, new understandings of human nature may emerge which we cannot presently foresee. It seems improbable that this new knowledge will fail to have political implications.

Second, at least in the more advanced societies, future politics will not necessarily be primarily class-based, will not be essentially a contest between poor and rich. Positive effects of economic growth have reduced poverty in many countries, and broadened the popular stake in the economic order, thereby weakening the argument for the Marxist class-struggle. As numerous economists and social scientists have observed, when basic economic needs are met, new levels of aspiration and dissatisfaction appear. Quality of life considerations become more important; the environmental movement is a conspicuous case in point.

Third, political differences are more likely to arise over the allocation of societal resources in relation to considered priorities rather than over redistribution of income. There may be a redistribution aspect in the funding of societal priorities, but the intended result is more likely to be a substantive objective (e.g. a public service or opportunity) than merely a transfer of income assets. Redistribution is therefore more likely to be a side-effect of policy than its explicit goal.

Fourth, the distinction between public and 'so-called' private affairs seems likely to diminish. The identification of *public* exclusively with *governmental* will probably diminish as the public character of many non-governmental activities and organizations becomes apparent. The use of non-governmental organizations for public functions was not uncommon in the past (e.g. for collecting certain taxes and the performance of welfare functions by religious institutions). During the twentieth century governmental bureaucracies assumed all or most of these formerly non-governmental public functions. But as government has grown in size, complexity, and bureaucratization, difficulties in holding governments to account for things done and not done, has become more difficult. Selective 'privatization' has been recommended by some theorists and political leaders to obtain more accountable and responsive government, and this raises a further distinguishing characteristic of the new politics.

Fifth, it seems plausible that the present heavy emphasis on individual rights will give way to greater concern with social responsibility. Both individuals and organizations are likely to be held accountable for acts harmful to the environment as well as to future generations. Changing evaluations of man's social and environmental relationships have led to changes in socially acceptable behaviors. Changes in public attitudes toward industrial pollution of the environment have stimulated the enactment of laws providing civil and criminal penalties for acts formerly regarded with complacency. Presently, direct harm to persons or property must be shown in order to invoke these penalties. In the future, however, a class of crimes against the environment seems plausible (Canada, 1985). Actions today regarded as legitimate and respectable, notably in relation to land and natural resources development, could be outlawed, not only as offenses against people, but as crimes against nature which are ultimately also crimes against humanity.

The principles and goals of the environmental movement cannot be attained without the cooperation and compliance of large numbers of people, and so an emphasis on responsible conduct and stewardship becomes necessary. Scientific establishment of cause-effect relationships will mean that innocence and inadvertence will less and less excuse violations of the environment. Depending upon findings in the science of human behavior and mentality, democratic theory may need to be further developed and refined. Some long-accepted assumptions may have to be modified, although some might also be reinforced.

I do not believe that this politics of the future can emerge without an ethical-religious content that modern political parties have largely rejected for historical reasons in particular, but which in principle must now be reintegrated into public life if humans, looking to the future, choose the road to survival. Religion, in the principle, is no barrier to a unifying view of relationships between humanity and Earth. Indeed an ethic and theology of the cosmos and the Earth, a natural religion, would seem to be the logical concomittant to a planetary perspective and polity. The intolerant monotheisms of historical religions have divided humanity. It may be that a new synthesis will arise that, retaining valuable elements of the traditional religions, will be consistent with what the human mind, aided by science, discovers to be the true nature of man in the biosphere. Thus the role of science in the environmental movement extends to the most fundamental consideration of the place and role of mankind in the cosmos.

IMPLICATIONS FOR SCIENCE

The thesis of this book attributes to science an influence and lays upon it a burden that some scientists will surely decline to accept. To many people science and politics seem poles apart – and so have they often been. And the direct services of science to politics have conspicuously been in the destructive weaponry of war, in public health, and in exploration of extra-terrestrial space. The science predominant today has served the hardware of technology far more effectively than it has served the software of social policy, and the indirect results of science as it has hitherto evolved have been a major force in bringing the world to its present danger. Can science now serve to protect mankind and the biosphere from the hazards to which it has inadvertently contributed? Many scientists and scientific organizations are engaged in this effort, but more than science alone will be necessary for it to fill this role. It will need the assistance of education, politics, and activated social concern.

NOTE

1. Lynton K. Caldwell (1972). 'An Ecological Approach to International Development: Problems of Policy and Administration', in *The Careless Technology: Ecology and International Development*. Ed., M. T. Farvar and J. P. Milton. Garden City, New York: Natural History Press 1972, pp. 941–2.

9
Attaining the attainable

The tenor of this book has been cautiously hopeful; there *are* reasons for hope that people can reverse the course of destruction that has been leading toward an impoverished and contaminated Earth. But hope implies uncertainty. The gap between the possible and the probable in surmounting our environmental predicament is so wide that an optimistic forecast is hardly realistic. Hopeful prospects are more likely to be attained, however, if approached with unrestricted recognition of what must be done to attain them.

Were Earth to be invaded by colonizing organisms from outer space it seems plausible that all humanity could be mobilized to repel the invaders. Similarly, if some identified inorganic agent threatened the Earth with environmental destruction as comprehensive and irreversible as humans have wrought, would not the nations of the world mobilize to avert this disaster? Such coordinated action in mutual interest seems probable. The ozone treaties suggest this possibility. But the prospect of worldwide cooperation to forestall a disaster of mankind's making seems far less likely where deeply entrenched economic and political interests are involved. Many contemporary values, attitudes, and institutions militate against international altruism. As widely interpreted today, human rights, economic interests, and national sovereignty would be factors in opposition. The cooperative task would require behavior that humans find most difficult: collective self-discipline in a common effort.

We have seen that belief in a human right to reproduce, and to exploit the environment have been the major obstacles to a prudent and conserving relationship between man and Earth. The concept of 'rights' evolved in an anthropocentric world, and has been applied almost exclusively to humans. Rights of non-human nature have gained attention recently, but as yet have very limited application. All rights, including those claimed for humans, are definable only in human society from whence these rights have been derived. They cannot be defended against the Earth, which concedes no rights – only opportunities and penalties.

There are ample opportunities for human societies to self-destruct. These possibilities need not be intended choices; they may follow as unforeseen consequences of social policy or they may occur as deliberate acts by a few individuals. Technoscientific innovations have made this latter possibility a reality that can no longer safely be disregarded. Biological, chemical, and atomic means are available for devastating inadvertent events, and the extent of their effects as well as the possibility of their instigation by malevolent groups or individuals is cause for concern. A greater danger to the future, however, lies in the disruptive and disorganizing effects upon the biosphere from the ways in which ordinary mundane human activities are being carried on.

Historically, human attitudes, values, purposes, and the available technology have been more or less in coincident phase. Purposes and consequences were often more visibly linked and humans were seldom able to undertake more activities than they could control – were less able to embark upon projects (e.g. nuclear energy), the outcome of which they could not foresee. The consequences of ignorance or destructive impulses were limited by the available technology; but unprecedented advances in science and the economy in the twentieth century have thrown technological and environmental relationships out of phase with one another. The beliefs and behaviors of people have been less than successfully adapted to the opportunities and risks of science-based technology.

In this mismatch between inherent or culturally inherited tendencies, and behavior necessary to protect and conserve the biosphere, we have seen that science plays a dual role. Rapid and radical transformation of the biosphere by people and technology has been possible because of advances in science. But science has also been the source of information about the effects of those transformations, and offers possibilities of preventive or remedial action. The practice of science requires objectivity and freedom from ideological prejudice, but science as knowledge is not a neutral presence in society. This book has delineated the critical role of science in the environmental movement in both a positive and negative sense. For an environment at high and sustainable levels of quality, a positive role of science will continue to be essential. And that role will necessarily be extended to inquiry in the biobehavioral and social sciences, and increasingly to interdisciplinary synthesis.

THE PENULTIMATE QUESTION

A proposition underlying the argument of this book is that we (meaning modern people in general) face frustration in efforts to cope with trends toward environmental deterioration to the extent that we have accepted a misconception of the task of environmental policy. Because we have often asked the wrong questions, we have obtained answers that are wrong in relation to what our chosen policies have been intended to accomplish. Our questions have misled us because they have been based on assumptions which certain of the sciences are calling into question, and on conclusions some of which may be demonstrated to be untrue.

The penultimate questions for our time is under what conditions can people draw upon the natural world for sustenance and a higher quality of life without causing the degradation or impoverishment of the biosphere? Beyond this question lies the fate of humankind on Earth. And as with many large and basic questions there are differing answers depending upon differing assumptions. The choices that people make in relating to their environment are expressed in their culture and implemented through their technologies. Bushmen of the Kalahari Desert, the Itruri Forest Pygmies, or the traditional Inuit of the Arctic have drawn upon their environments for centuries without environmental degradation, whereas agricultural and pastoral practices in traditional societies have under certain circumstances led to environmental deterioration (e.g. Marsh, 1865; Murphy, 1951; Thomas, 1956). The problem becomes acute and widespread in populous industrial countries and in those less developed societies imperfectly acculturated by modern medicine, technology, and economics. But unlike traditional cultures, science and technology provide modern society with the knowledge and means to choose a complex and expanding quality of life, sustainable by informed and prudent uses of the environment.

The presence of means toward a sustainable environment of high quality does not promise wise use of those means. Many environmental disorders of our times have been caused by the inappropriate and abusive use of scientific and technical knowledge which may be as readily applied to ill-conceived and destructive ends as toward a richer and more benign world. By the 1960s, efforts to satisfy the multiplying demands of rapidly expanding human populations in a world of exhaustible and finite possibilities reached a point of impact that persons aware of escalating damage to the biosphere could not ignore. From this awareness 'growth' became an issue, and the environmental movement emerged, with consequences recounted in previous chapter in this book.

An expression of this awareness was the formation of organized groups to address what one of them, the Club of Rome, described as 'the problematique': the predicament of mankind. Other efforts to address worsening environmental trends have been identified in previous chapters, but few have closed in upon the problem of social choice which can be phrased in the question: what kind of control over what kind of environment? The character of the environment as the relationship between people and their environing context is the critical factor in any answer. The question of control, or in its generic sense 'governance', is answerable rationally only in relation to a desired quality of the environmental relationship. That answer, if adequate, identifies what is required of means, measures, and behaviors needed to attain or to sustain that relationship. The identification or selection or invention of operational specifics may follow thereafter.

A question of environmental policy is then a question of choice. All choices are contextual, they are made within the limits of time, place and circumstances. The perception of that context occurs within the psychophysical human, which physiologist Claude Bernard called the *environnment interieur*, but also in relation to the environmental context in which humans exist, which Bernard termed the *environnment exterieur*. Beliefs and assumptions about that context are assumed to be largely cultural although psycho-physiological factors are also believed to be present – some of which are more surmized than understood.

The diverse cultural-psychological values that are present in the choices that people make in environmental questions complicate consensus-building regarding environmental quality and sustainability. As the state of the world environment has been seen by many to be rapidly worsening, with dangers of irretrievable losses, leaders in the environmental movement have sought an accommodating formula to reconcile the most pervasive of the apparent value differences which, in previous chapters, has been identified as economics vs. ecology. The fundamental relationship between these alleged polarities is critical to the thesis of this book to an extent that justifies repeated emphasis.

THE RHETORICAL TRAP OF SUSTAINABLE DEVELOPMENT

In principle, economics and ecology as differing interpretations of reality cannot be rightfully understood as dichotomies. They are interrelating concepts when understood generically rather than from particular and excluding points of view. They share the same linguistic roots in ancient Greek, and their present differences are explained by their particular usages in the modern paradigm. The complementarity of these conceptual domains has suggested their combination in the phrase 'Sustainable Development,' (Clark & Munn, 1986); Redclift, 1987; Tolba, 1987). Although the words ecology and economics do not appear, they are strongly implied when the phrase is used in relation to the environment. 'Development', which is the leading term, is commonly understood as economic development or at least a process in which economic considerations are among the driving motives. 'Sustainable' is generally interpreted as socio-ecological renewability or relative stability in a changing world. The idea to be conveyed by the phrase has been a socio-economic process of growth that did not undermine its own prospects through ecologically unsustainable enterprises and behaviors. Nothing in the following critique of the sustainable development concept should be regarded as denigrating constructive proposals and propositions advanced under its rubric. My argument instead addresses the inadequacy of the unqualified term for policy choice.

The sustainable development concept was preceded by the idea of ecodevelopment which is similar in many respects. But the antecedent 'eco' appears to restrict the scope of development and the term has failed to win wide acceptance. Sustainable development, however, is artfully adapted to convey whatever content one places (or wishes to find) in this otherwise uninformative rhetoric. The phrase 'sustainable development' offers a way toward preventing or mitigating environmentally destructive development of only short-term economic benefit. But it also has the effect of glossing over differences between particular economistic and ecologic values. Sustainable development as a concept or a catchphrase is sufficiently positive and sufficiently unspecific to become a motto for the international environmental movement. It also risks becoming what Martin Holdgate, Director General of IUCN and former Senior Scientist for the Department of the Environment in Great Britain, has warned could become the environmental cliché of the 1990s.

The sustainable development concept has been a limited positive step toward restraining the environmentally negative effects of technoeconomic proliferation. But we have noted its inadequacy as a guide to policy choice. First – its empty rhetoric: words open to being filled by various interpretations not necessarily conducive to maintaining high levels of environmental quality; second – its focus on means over ends (Barbier, 1987).

The word 'development' signifies a process. In contemporary international development policy the substantive goals of the process, as distinguished from statistical abstractions, are more often implicit than specified. Aggregate economic indicators, such as gross national product, are widely accepted as measurements of development trends. Specific estimates of productivity in agriculture, natural resources exploitation, manufacturing, and construction are compiled to indicate trends in economic activity, and by inference economic well-being. Yet observers have often noted that in many countries a fall in the quality of life and environment for the mass of people coincides with a rise in the level of economic activity. Economic growth (i.e. 'development'), regardless of sustainability, has not reliably served the general good or quality of life and environment. For economic growth to raise the quality of life without detriment to the environment, selectivity in goals and careful planning and follow-up implementation are necessary.

Sustainability may suggest to some people the maintenance of a preferred state of affairs, but the term does not identify what preferences are sustainable. The importance of sustainability from an ecologic perspective is in the adoption of policies and processes that protect the integrity and continuity of natural ecosystems. But other perspectives (e.g. economistic), may prevail. Before sustainable development can become a reliable guide for environmental policy, the goals of development require definition not solely in statistical terms, but more importantly in substantive outcomes (Theobald & Mills, 1973; Dasmann, Milton & Freeman, 1973). The goal of an improved environmental quality of life may be assumed to be a reason for which developmental efforts are undertaken. But this assumption is no more than a possibility.

Development, in the conventional sense, is driven by the need of so-called underdeveloped or Third World governments to cope with their often worsening problems of poverty, and by the need of First World financial institutions for investment opportunities. There is in addition, the heavy demand of First World industrialized countries for raw material resources from the Third World and for markets for manufactured products. There are, of course, claims of altruistic motives in development policy, but they are commonly expressed as giving or sharing, and may make no lasting contribution toward removing chronic causes of poverty and deprivation (Wilkinson, 1973).

Third World governments initially sought economic aid to stave off social unrest and to improve living conditions. The socio-economic circumstances and the mind-sets of their leadership were almost everywhere strongly influenced by the technoeconomistic thinking pervading the industrialized world – whether capitalist or socialist in orientation (Dworkin, 1974). Moreover, economic aid and development projects may be important props to political power. Development offers opportunity for politicians to dispense jobs, incomes, and access to resources; environmental conservation often is perceived to have the opposite effect. It is not difficult to see the direction of political advantage.

In the capitalist world, the development process, with no more than generalized economic goals, could be an ideal agent for market forces. In theory, the interplay of buyers and sellers would give people the environment that they demonstrably preferred. Democratic values would also be served, as no super-ordinate authorities would determine what environmental conditions or relationships were 'good' for people. Even so, markets do not adequately allocate uses of common property resources, e.g. water, air, sunlight; nor do they protect rare or endangered species.

In Marxist economies, 'development' has been an equally convenient concept, because its ends are already fixed by the ideology of dialectical materialism. Transformation of the natural world through human labor into material goods is inherent in the unfolding of Marxist history. Production goals thus become the ends served by development. Cultural or scientific advances are regarded as ancillary although importantly reinforcing to the primary political-economic objective.

Neither capitalist nor socialist ideologies provided an adequate interpretation of the place of humanity in the living world – Engels' *Dialectics of Nature* notwithstanding. Both perspectives are products of the techno-industrial revolution of the modern age; both project linear views of life in relation to the complexities of the whole living world. Under both systems of thought the environment, as distinguished from material resources, has been misconceived as no more than the physical setting within which the human drama occurs. For minds locked into the techno-industrial paradigm the 'right' questions about man–environment relationships have not been asked; they simply have not occurred because the relationships appeared to be little more than the placement of props and scenery for the human drama on stage. For persons who subscribe to economistic ideologies, the play is material production, and its proceeds are derived from its environment conceived as natural resources.

The pervasiveness and pertinence of this essentially techno-economistic mind-set for environmental and international policies can hardly be over-emphasized. The development horse, driven by political economists, has pulled the cart of the economy, and the environment has been widely perceived as the paint on the cart. The difficulty with this metaphor is that neither horse nor driver has had a clearly defined destination. The objective has been measurable progress. The prevailing assumption in both capitalist and socialist systems has been that the road toward material growth would lead to improved levels of human welfare. And so it might, were it not for the counteractive trends in population growth and environmental attrition that have too often accompanied development. The obsessive commitment of nations to military expenditures has also severely handicapped options and possibilities (Westing, 1986, 1988).

As previously noted, the initial response from the Third World was to deny the relevance of rapid exponential population growth to poverty. Anti-Malthusians in the developed world have argued that population growth is the road to prosperity (Simon, 1981; Wattenburg, 1987). At the 1972 Stockholm Conference, Third World representatives insisted that environmental protection measures sought by First World environmentalists be paid for by additional development aid and not through reallocation of existing funds. By the mid-1980s, failure and disappointment in the development process along with the demonstrable effects of environmental mismanagement upon the health and economic welfare of people, persuaded many governments that environmental factors in the broad socio-ecological sense (including population growth) ought to be considered. Thus, ecodevelopment and sustainable development metaphors emerged as policy options.

Under aegis of the United Nations two efforts in particular have been undertaken to deal with the development problems of the so-called Third World. Through the vehicle of the United Nations Conference on Trade and Development (UNCTAD) a group of 'unaligned nations' proposed a New International Economic Order and in 1975 formulated the Lima Declaration and Plan of Action. Subsequent action in the General Assembly failed to materially change economic relations among nations, but expressed an inconsistent attitude toward access to natural resources. Exclusive sovereign control was claimed for resource within each nation but claims were also laid to natural resources in the common spaces, notably in and beneath the high seas, as the heritage of mankind. Nevertheless, the Cocoyoc (Mexico) Declaration adopted in 1974 at UNEP/UNCTAD Symposium on Patterns of Resources Use, Environment and Development Strategies called for new approaches to development, including imaginative research in alternative consumption patterns, technological life styles, land-use strategies, with institutional and educational reinforcement (United Nations General Assembly, 1974).

Of greater significance for the definition and advancement of development that could be sustainable was the World Commission on Environment and Development established in 1984 by the United Nations General Assembly and chaired by Gro Harlem Bruntland, Prime Minister of Norway. In 1987 the Commission published its reported entitled *Our Common Future*. Its function was 'to examine the critical environmental and development problems on the planet and to formulate realistic proposals to solve them, and to ensure that human progress will be sustained through development without bankrupting the resources of future generations'. Membership on the Commission was largely representative of the Third World and socialist countries and its report evidenced compromise between objectives of the NIEO and a more positive ecologic orientation. There was, however, sufficient agreement about fundamentals to make *Our Common Future* the most explicit statement of sustainable development goals to be set forth thus far.

As yet, the driving assumptions of the development process have remained essentially economic, although now more often modified or informed by socioecological considerations (Lewis and Kallab, 1986). Sustainable development thus serves as a conceptual halfway-house between a narrow economistic and technocratic concept and a reformulation which would treat development as selective means toward specified socio-environmental goals. Instead of an environmentally neutral process, guided by the invisible hand of economic forces, development would be recast as a means toward a specified quality of life and environment. Development *per se* would no more be a major policy goal of government than would accounting. Both processes are needed but neither represents a primary purpose of government, nor a substantive goal of public policy.

BEYOND SUSTAINABLE DEVELOPMENT

Our policies follow from our purposes, from our assumptions, our perceived circumstances, and our beliefs about how the world works. Sustainable development as a policy derives from an assumption that economic values are the irreplaceable prime movers of human activity. True, they are often prime, but not always so, and never exclusively so. Other motives may at times and places outweigh economic considerations. Among these are physical survival, health, self-respect, love of others, patriotism, and religion. Sociobiologists find, in an instinct for genetic survival described as inclusive fitness, an aspect of altruism serving the continuity of a living species. The affairs of this world have never turned exclusively upon economic considerations, narrowly conceived. Self sacrifice or restraint for the good of the group has also appeared to be a moving force in cultural as well as biological evolution. Religion has been a powerful motivating force. Conditions for survival have been handed down in the economy of nature in which the differences that we call ecologic or economic are chiefly in the way we see them.

The development concept fails when, taking a very partial view of economic and ecological relationships, humans see them only as dichotomies or as modifiers of one another. Economic and ecologic relationships and processes are inherent in the way the world works. They are integral elements in the larger environment that is our Earth. We therefore need to understand their true relationship, and to answer this need, science may help. This is not to imply that science can today fully provide the answers we need to better manage our planetary relationships. Rather, we must look to further advances in the interdisciplinary uses of science and other relevant knowledge, and in opening of new avenues of inquiry to provide us with the understandings that will enable us to reorient our own individual, collective and institutional behaviors to safeguard, enlarge, and enrich the quality of life on Earth.

It should be a reproach to development economists generally that the views of a group of French economists writing in the 1960s did not receive greater attention. During the decade of the 1960s a broad ecological-sociological approach to development was taken by writers in the journals *Economie et Humanisme* and *Tier Monde*. Prominent among them were Raymond Aaron, Jacques Austruy, Louis-Joseph Lebret, Francois Perroux, René Dumont and Peter de Santoy (Caldwell, 1972). Their humanist perspective was shared in part by some American students of development, but mainstream economics continued to influence the policies of the World Bank and the United Nations Development Program. Only in the late 1980s did the Bank, under pressure from Environmental NGOs, the United States Congress, and under new management, begin to apply in practice the commitment to environmental values that it had earlier professed.

The major problem of reconciling development and environment is thus fundamentally the evaluative and the perceptual. The leadership of collective humanity has not been able to find an answer to the penultimate question of policy for the future of our species perhaps because it has not asked the right question. Our primary task today is finding out how to put the question right. What may appear to be small differences in the way we phrase our question may lead to very wide differences in the answers we obtain – and not all answers can be right.

Using science as a tool for manipulating the environment to the neglect of its use as a means for testing the validity of our assumptions and their implications, we have chosen the so-called development process to improve the human condition. Disappointed with its too-frequent tendency to yield only short-term benefits and to incur long-term costs or unredeemable losses, we have sought to ameliorate the development process through sustainability – by implication, development that does not negate its intended outcomes through environmentally destructive consequences. Following disillusion with the results of the UN Development Decades and the documented cases of development failure through destruction of its environmental support base, the logical question appears to be: How can we make ecologically desirable development sustainable? Environmentally concerned persons interpret this phraseology to imply ecological sustainability. In this context however, a literal explanation of the word sustainable, unmodified, tells nothing about what is sustained other than the process of development, and says nothing about the level of environmental conditions to be sustained for how long, or at what cost, and to whom.

We have believed that to arrive at desirable ends, whatever they might be, the logical course was to focus on the means. But putting means in the forefront of our policies is to risk losing sight of ends or, equally important, of the range of possible consequence. 'How to make development sustainable?' is the wrong first question. If sustaining a high level of quality of life and environment is our purpose, we should ask instead how to make development serve that purpose. Putting the question this way changes fundamentally what is needed for an answer. Our emphasis is now on substantive goals and less on a process. It now becomes necessary to be specific about levels and substance of environmental quality. Experience has shown that development, unguided by reliable estimates of possibility and probabilities, does not necessarily lead to a life-enhancing environment. The right first question for the 'predicament of mankind' today is: *What kind of environment is good for human life?* If humans are indeed a part of the biosphere, the answer can hardly be different fundamentally from an environment good for the living systems of the Earth (Iltis, Loucks & Andres, 1970).

Of course human society and human relationships are part of the equation if we accept the proposition that environment is a contextual relationship and not just those things that surround us. All of science has a role in finding an answer to the principal question. But beyond science, the humanities are also essential contributors to understanding. If this reasoning is correct, it follows that the question of mankind's environmental relationship is not a sectoral aspect of sociology, nor is environmental concern *in principle* a 'special interest'.

Environmental concern may be misused or misinterpreted, but fully understood it presents a mega-problem to human society. Mankind's relationship to its domicile on the planet Earth is now a basic problem for human society. A continuing relationship can no longer be taken for granted. Were this mega-problem solved in principle, a very large number of the socio-economic and political problems that perplex and distract us today would disappear or would be far less difficult to resolve.

TASK AND NECESSITIES

It is easier to know what is not good for human society than to arrive at consensus on what is good. The range of possibilities for social choice extends beyond those that lead to benign outcomes. Science and technology have extended the range of the possible and have provided methods for ascertaining which among possibilities are the more probable. Perhaps because there are more wrong answers than right answers to any question, science is better at warning us of the risks and dangers of our choice than of which choices are likely to prove predominantly beneficial.

René Dubos (1965), for example, has warned of the risks of adaptation as a choice for coping with environmental deterioration. Humans can and do survive at very low levels of environmental quality and this adaptability is often accompanied by low levels of human health, culture, and ethical conduct. Colin Turnbull's account of the African Ike (1972) is a notable case in point, and there are many other examples.

Today in intellectually advanced societies too much is known and too much is possible to leave the future to chance, presumed necessity, or the invisible hands of interacting perceived self-interests. Yet the probability of a critical mass of society anywhere breaking out of self-imposed barriers to a high level reintegration within the environmental or biospheric context seems presently to be unlikely. The options that in the long-run may be beneficial may not be those that most people now and in the short-run will prefer. A world environment improving incrementally here and there, but worsening in the aggregate, seems the more probable course of events. The gloomy conjectures of *Limits to Growth* (1972) or *Global* 2000 (1980) are not inevitable nor were they asserted to be. The brighter forecasts of *The Global Possible* (Repetto, 1985) are in theory attainable. But the probable depends upon a fundamental restructuring of dominant social beliefs about the nature of the world and man, and their interrelationships, a development not reliably predictable.

To make attainable futures probable, positive and unprecedented measures would be necessary. Given the mix of interactive forces in the world today it seems improbable that a durable balance of human values at rising levels of quality will be attained by chance. The possibilities for continuation of levels of environmental quality comparable to the higher of those presently existing seem dubious unless in the very near future there is a fundamental perceptual change among people who largely determine the policies and actions of nations. Our inherited ways of thinking and acting in relation to our environment have been rendered dysfunctional by developments of our own making. Overtaken by events, our policies and practices, developed under other circumstances, persist in the face of their failure to answer our needs. Our situation, as I see it, has never been better described than by Gail Stewart, who says that:

Our predominant intellectual depiction of our situation is thus at odds with the facts and reality of our current situation, in much the same way as was that of those who believed that the earth was flat after it had been discovered to be round, or those who continued to believe the sun was circling the earth in its rising and setting rather than that the earth was spinning on its axis in orbit around the sun. Thus have environmental concerns entered economic discussion as a component of economic decision-making, rather than as the context in which the economy and human life itself exist.

A Copernican revolution in our perception of our situation is thus called for ... and the problem lies not with the environment but with ourselves.[1]

The Copernican revolution removed the Earth from the center of the universe around which all extra-terrestrial spheres revolved. By implication, it undermined the assumption that the cosmos, including the Earth, was created for man's exclusive dominion. Yet although the traditional cosmological-geophysical paradigm ultimately changed, universal social acceptance of a new view of man and Earth has required centuries. Even the Mission Apollo photographs of the Earth in space failed to convince a small residue of science-illiterates who alleged that the photographs were faked. Nevertheless, the Copernican paradigm at last prevails as a basic assumption in our public policies.

The ecological revolution, where it has occurred, has completed the reorientation of mankind in nature by reintegrating man into the biosphere and demolishing the assumption that all Earth was created for mankind's convenience. This shift of paradigm is less easily accepted than was the astro-physical reorientation. Man's self-image and perceived self-interest are threatened. The power of modern science and technology to drastically alter conditions of life on Earth is unquestioned, but the wisdom and rightness of the exercise of this power emerges as a question that may be evaded, but cannot be eliminated. Through science we now understand how man's life and future are inextricably and complexly involved in the biosphere. Man may diminish the biosphere to degraded levels of quality that may yet be sustainable, but he thereby also diminishes the quality of his own life and reduces his options of achieving higher levels of existence.

To persist in acting upon assumptions demonstrated to be wrong and to base policies and priorities upon those erroneous assumptions must surely be to invite failure if not disaster. Persistence in the face of failure may be admirable if the cause is ethically right *and* the goal achievable were the right strategies to be employed. If, however, the effort is ill-conceived in relation to the way the world works, then perseverance is folly. The 'valor of ignorance' leads to almost certain defeat (Lea, 1942). To make the possible become probable, the major obstacles to the possible will need to be identified and overcome. For some policy objectives, the obstacles may prove insurmountable or may appear so initially – only to be found surmountable over a period of time with enlarged understanding.

As we approach the end of the twentieth century, the prospect of preserving the present diversity and quality of the human environment and the biosphere appears doubtful. Massive attrition of the biosphere over large areas of the Earth seems probable even though efforts are now underway to reduce or reverse destructive trends. The momentum of destructive transformation remains great, even though slowed in some countries and for some aspects of the environment. Timely application of scientific knowledge, technological capabilities and economic ingenuity could retard, even reverse, this process. The knowledge needed to put the world on a sustainable course toward a higher quality of life exists, but the commitment thus far has been largely superficial. The possible may be improbable not because the means are lacking, but because the political will is insufficient.

Given the way in which the membership and leadership of nearly all political parties see the world today, environmental relationships and policy, in principle, could not be placed high up on their real agendas. They could not easily be convinced, in relation to how they see the world, that they have their priorities reversed. Short-term success with misdirected economic policies delays the time at which repeated failure to solve problems based upon prevailing erroneous assumptions will open the way to new choices. At this point, the development process will be put in proper perspective as a means to the reorientation of man-environment relationships rather than, in effect, as an end in itself. International development agencies would be reorganized as environmental recon-struction and protection services. Economic development would be reoriented, not diminished, and would be integrated within a broader context of social-environmental objectives. The apparent antagonism of economic and environmental values would then be understood as an anomaly or contradiction inherent in an obsolete paradigm.

For the attainable to be attained, certain critical changes of policy would be necessary. Although changes would have to be accepted at the national level before they could be implemented internationally, policy initiatives may arise, as they often have, at the international level. Having considered these areas of policy earlier in this book I will do not more than reiterate them here. Four are critical; all are interrelated and all would require change in prevailing attitudes so as to free existing possibilities for practical realization.

First, the population question needs to be faced realistically. This may be the issue upon which the environment movement founders. To accept the probability of a world population of 10 billion or more people is to accept a future of massive ecological attrition and social regimentation. To stop and in some places reverse, present trends where population growth is detrimental, is technically possible. But as Garrett Hardin (1980) has well said, the population issue is not a technical problem. Were there international agreements that the immense cost of exponential population increase exceeded the costs and risks of efforts to stop global population growth now, the effort might be undertaken. A massive governmental-non-governmental health-related effort, coordinated through the United

Nations system, could achieve positive results if undertaken with full allowance for its difficulties. Were the peoples of the world to bring their reproductive behavior under agreed-upon control, a new world-view of man-biosphere relationships would be implicit.

Second, and related to population policy, is a major effort to inculcate ecological rationality throughout the world. The task here is greatest in the 'developing' societies, and least necessary among many traditional or so-called primitive people. Ecological literacy is now diffused in the industrial world, but knowing does not necessarily result in believing, or in behaving consistently with what one knows. Worldwide environmental education efforts are already underway. These efforts could be greatly augmented and accelerated with television via satellite transmission. To be effective, the effort would need to be supported by an associated effort to discover, develop, and promote technologies (and hence economies) appropriate to the circumstances under which people are most likely to achieve their socio-ecological and sustainable economic potential. If people are to behave with ecological rationality, policies should be implemented to enable them to do so. People should not be faced with the choice of destroying their future in order to survive in the present.

Third, economy, fully conceived in its proper scope, is the basis for the existence of society, and a determinant of its quality and its future. Economic policy serves society best when it addresses the substantive problems of society, rather than when employed as the *primary* criterion by which other policies are evaluated. This in no way implies that economic analysis is not an essential tool for the evaluation of policy alternatives; but the theories and fashions prevalent in the academic discipline of economics ought not to be confused with its subject matter. Economic theories have been notoriously culture-bound. Their presuppositions have been based more often upon philosophical abstractions than upon scientific information. In the world today, the interrelations between science, technology, the economy, and the environment are numerous and complex. The economic interests of society are not necessarily identical or consistent with the economic interest of particular groups or individuals. Economic policies inappropriate to the real needs of people have induced acculturation, dependency on cash-crop mono-culture, ecologically harmful land conversion – especially through deforestation – and costly public works with limited life-expectancy (among other adverse consequences). Concern with appropriate technology, the economy, and the environment should be understood as one concern – not three. Separate sectoral problems may be attacked as aspects of the more inclusive issue, which is the quality and productivity of the environment in which humans live and work. But the encompassing biospheric context should always be kept in mind.

Fourth, land and natural resources policies are fundamentally inseparable and so should the policies affecting their use be. What happens on the land affects air and water and what happens to these two media affects land. In our archaic modernity these basic elements of the natural environment have been treated categorically, with insufficient regard to their interrelationships. Policies for agriculture, forestry, energy, minerals, urbanization, and nature protection customarily have been developed with little, if any, recognition of their contextual interrelationships. The elements impacted by these policies – air, land and water – may be considered as common properties of the biosphere – but not in the economic sense exclusively common property of mankind. All other life depends upon them.

The most difficult non-human element for policymaking is land. The sense in which land may be owned as a commodity is not uniform throughout the world. But because human life and prosperity are largely derived from use of the land, its governance is everywhere a sensitive issue. Land value in modern society has been almost wholly measured in economic rather than ecological terms. Thus, we are told how much it costs in money to preserve 'old growth' forests from timbering, but we have no monetary measure to evaluate adequately the loss of species and ecosystems were the forests to be cut. Were the tropical rainforests and the high plains of East Africa, with their spectacular and unique wildlife, to be sacrificed to make room for burgeoning human populations, would the world be richer, or people happier? In the long run, the economic well-being of people might be better served by the preservation of these ecosystems than by their conversion to fill the seemingly endless demand by humans for materials and space.

Modern industrial technology has greatly augmented annual yields of agricultural products, but these advantages have exacted costs that in the long run could offset their benefits. 'Our policies' observes K. Farrell (1985) 'have been strong incentives for producers to employ technologies that sometimes have adverse environmental effects.' The uses of heavy soil-compacting machinery, of herbicides, pesticides, artificial fertilizers and of excessive irrigation have resulted in build-up of biocidal residues in soil and water. Elimination of fence rows has opened land to wind erosion and loss of wildlife habitat. Moreover, this industrialized agriculture *has* been exported, especially from the United States to developing countries, frequently to grow crops for export, at risk to sustainable economies in those countries when food production and agricultural labor are displaced.

Most tragic of all because it is unnecessary and irretrievable is the destruction of wild nature and extinction of species. A great number of smaller island ecosystems have been utterly destroyed and the larger ones such as Borneo and Madagascar are dangerously threatened. Present generations may not be regarded kindly by people in the future who may heap regret and contempt upon their forebears who lavished money on armaments and obsessed with economic competition allowed the course of events to destroy the beauty and wonder of the Earth.

The foregoing assertions are supportable by evidence and argument developed in other published work. I do not argue that conserving and remedial action *must* be followed and it would be of little consequence if I did so. To minds locked into the conventional modern paradigm, collective policies would seem utopian, impractical, and unrealistic. It remains to be seen how they will be viewed a century hence. If our behavior cannot be guided by what our best science can teach us we are indeed poor learners. Forecasts of human behavior and of scientific discovery are soundest when they allow for the unforeseen and the unexpected. My 'musts', 'shoulds', and 'oughts' are conditional, not dogmatic. If on the basis of what we now know, the world enters the twenty-first century having made policy choices consistent with what we have learnt regarding the conditions of life on Earth, it may be possible to attain in fact what we can presently conjecture in theory – a truly sustainable world economy that facilitates the optimization of higher human potentials. But I do not underestimate the immense social change that would be required, nor its apparent improbability.

In so far as humans influence the future of the Earth and their world, their choices, however expressed, are their policies. The collective impact of human behavior on earth is mediated through explicit policies – public and private. Collectively they form the governance of human behavior in the biosphere within the limits inherent in nature. The fundamental question of policy today is whether the realities of this earth, as science reveals them, can be translated into behaviors appropriate to the continuation of life on earth. The significance of the general adoption of a cosmic environmental paradigm extends far beyond ordinary limited understanding of man-environment relationships. It implies reorientation of attitudes toward life and death, war and peace, human rights and responsibilities, the meaning of and limits to growth, and the ethical basis of mankind's relationships with the rest of nature.

Can the foregoing philosophical interpretation of an attainable future be translated into the language of everyday practical politics? Generally not – but the pressure of events may cause politicians and educators to act toward the attainment of preferred popular environmental goals that are corrective, protective, and enhancing. The declaration by the political heads of the seven leading industrial democracies meeting in Paris in July 1989 indicates that circumstances alter political agendas and that the environmental movement is now a global force.[2] In the world of practical affairs explanations and rationales often come after action has been taken.

It should not be surprising if during the decade of the 1990s there emerges a coherent doctrine of international environmental responsibility which all literate people can readily understand and accept.

The history of humanity gives reason to believe that for all of the tragedies and errors of human behavior, mankind has an innate capacity to learn and to evaluate experience. If this is so it should be possible for humanity to move to a new and higher level of comprehension and existence. But this capacity may be insufficiently shared to avert disaster, or may be overriden by stronger inclinations. Survival may require a price that human society for whatever reason is unable to unwilling to pay. We have no assurance that humanity can surmount its environmental crisis; yet in the face of this uncertainty we have the option of acting as if it *could*. Here we go beyond science to a moral imperative, never better expressed than in this paraphrase by Miguel d'Unamuno:

> Man is perishable; but let us perish resisting,
> And if it is nothingness that awaits us,
> let us so act that it may be an unjust fate[3].

NOTES

1. Gail Ward Stewart (1987). The leading question: *In Situ* structures of thought? *Hydrobiologia* **149**: 145.
2. James M. Markham (1989). Paris Group urges 'Decisive Action for Environment', and Key Sections of the Paris Communique by the Group of Seven. *New York Times*, July 17.
3. *The Tragic sense of Life in Men and in Peoples* (1913). Trans. from Spanish by J. E. Crawford Flitch, London: Macmillan, 192b, p. 263. The original reads 'El hombre es perecedero. Puede ser; mas perezcamos resistiendo, y si es la nada lo que nos está reservado, hagamos que sea una injusticia esto.' *Ensayos*. Tomo II. *Del Sentimento Tragico de la Vida XI*. Madrid: Aguilar, 965. The paraphrase was from Sénancour's *Obermann*.

Between two worlds

This postscript has been added to focus again on the realm of time and circumstance in which the question addressed in this book should be understood. The question is whether humans acting through their institutions are capable of choosing and implementing decisions that will advance the prospect of a sustainable future at a high level of environmental quality. The conditional answer to this question has been: *perhaps*. Throughout this book the environment has been defined to include – directly or indirectly – nearly all of those interactive relationships that determine, for better or worse, the quality of life. Environmental quality is not a sectoral value to be enumerated among such categories as health, justice, peace, poverty, or security. The environment embraces all of them and others – it is the continuing but ever-changing context in which human affairs and all life occur.

The question of mankind's future in the biosphere would seem to be of compelling importance to thoughtful people, although in relation to practical affairs it may be regarded by some as imponderable. Then why is it that questions of policy choice involving science and the environmental movement have become critical in the world today? The reason appears to be that modern society has reached a point in time and circumstance when its customary behaviors can no longer be continued. New ways of relating to the Earth have become necessary, and so the world is passing through a historical discontinuity, the outcome of which will depend heavily upon what choices are made. I say 'passing through', because the transformation is progressive, carrying with it much of the legacy of the past. It is a radical reconfiguration of the legacy, and a reorientation of previous goals and values that justify our designating these changes as a discontinuity. It is hardly paradoxical to say that change has been a constant in human history. Yet there is broad consensus that fundamental radical change has periodically separated one era of history from another, and that the present is one of those exceptional transformations. The synergistic effects of merging forces – scientific, technical, economic and demographic – result in new circumstances for which social and political accommodation becomes necessary (Corning, 1983).

Advances in science and technology continue to generate catalytic innovations which, among intended effects, also induce unforeseen circumstances. And so, while our ability to project and predict is advancing, the incidence of the unpredicted is also increasing. Natural forces of change are likewise at work – the cosmos is not passive – and no one can be certain that a mutant virus or a change in solar radiation might not remove nine-tenths (or all) of the human species before science could discover a counteractive response.

During the latter years of this century, we see modern times moving toward a troubled close. The interval of five centuries between 1492 and 1992 may be regarded as a rough approximation of the era that we call 'modern'. Its distinctive characteristics need not be recounted here, but they include the preemption of the earth and its resources by the human species, the unprecedented expansion and concentration of human population and energy, the advent of empirical and applied science, and large scale organization of communication and of economic and political affairs. The paradoxical and often contradictory effects of science and science-based technology have permitted the modern world to become what it is – and to make inevitable its transformation into another kind of world, tentatively identified as post-modern.

In retrospect the most significant impact of science on humanity has been to increase an informed self-awareness, and to initiate a growth in understanding of mankind's changing relationships to the biosphere, within which humanity itself evolved and upon which its survival depends. The environmental movement is a social expression of this growth of understanding. Contrary to earlier uncomprehending predictions, the movement is not transitory. This heightened awareness of the human situation, and the beliefs and values associated with it will become dominant in the coming century *if* humanity copes effectively with its economic and ecological predicaments. There is no assurance that it will cope effectively. The future world may be a better place for humans – but it could be worse – perhaps more easily worse because our growing technological options have enlarged our opportunities for error.

Intimations of large events are expressed more freely and often more prophetically by the intuitive poet than by the scientist whose predictions must submit to the discipline and limitations of empirical methodologies. In his 'Stanzas from the Grande Chartreuse,' Matthew Arnold wrote of 'wandering between two worlds, one dead, the other powerless to be born.'[1] For him, the world of traditional religious faith was dead and without successor. He could not know that he was seeing only part of a larger transition, of which the fate of traditional religion was symptomatic. Could he have enlarged his context he might have written of wandering between two worlds – one dying, the other struggling to be born. Arnold sensed the discontinuity without an apparent understanding of why it had occurred. Without this understanding he could not foresee the birth of a new world.

Now, more than a century later, the paraphrase of Arnold's two worlds metaphor is even more apt. The old authority of traditional religion and status has given way before the advances of science, technology, and populism. Toward the end of the twentieth century the breakdown of the assumptions, values, and standards of the old industrial and agrarian orders has left society with few common norms or purposes. The old world has been visibly dying in the sense of transformation into another state – but what that state will be has not been, nor is it now, visible.

Rapid and far-reaching changes in science and society have stimulated new lines of scientific inquiry and have drawn forth theoretical propositions of extraordinary heuristic power. One of these, the Gaia hypothesis (Lovelock, 1979), has been identified in chapter 3 as a contribution to a more fundamental understanding of the relationships between animate and inanimate matter and the development of life on Earth. The implications of Gaia, even in its modified form, are strongly reinforcing to the more philosophic expressions of the environmental movement and deep ecology. Gaia must thus be regarded as an influence on mankind's future biospheric paradigm.

Are we in the midst of a behavioral transition that, beneath its surface manifestations, is moved by fundamental physical 'laws'? Intriguing but perhaps 'far out' suggestions as to the 'mechanics' of the present process of behavioral change may be found in two theoretical propositions growing out of physical science and mathematics. They are catastrophy theory and chaos theory, but it should be made immediately clear that their influence on social theory is suggestive and not a direct, illegitimate extrapolation.

Catastrophy theory (Zeeman, 1976) undertakes to explain the sequential changes that lead to a more radical reconfiguration event – a sudden change of state – a catastrophy. Social scientists and historians have studied the anatomy of social revolutions in search of prognostic indicators of an approaching transformation of social systems (Brinton, 1938). If one understood the incremental steps toward radical change, could that progression be guided toward a constructive non-disruptive outcome so that the new state of affairs would not be accompanied by social disaster?

Catastrophy theory, in principle, has many lesser heuristic applications to environmental policy, some of which might help governments plan more effectively for coping with sudden, violent environmental events where premonitory indicators may be detected.

Chaos theory has a similar heuristic value in searching for the presence of order and probability in seeming incomprehensible disorder (Prigogine & Stengers, 1984; Gleick, 1987). Are there discernible patterns in the presently paradoxical and disorderly state of society? This book has suggested their presence in the environmental movement. Chaos theory did not lead to this conclusion, but its sophisticated analysis of relationships between apparent order and disorder pushes social theory toward a search for more adequate explanations for behavioral anomalies and the phenomena of change. Chaos may also be leading to new ways of thinking about ecology (Pool, 1989).

Another theoretical proposition of suggestive value is R. L. Carneiro's (1970) hypothesis that political states arose as a consequence of geo-ecologic circumstances leading to the forcible integration of communities circumscribed by geophysical or social boundaries from which there was no feasible escape. The logic of circumscription theory would be world polity in some form when the planet itself became the bounding circumstance within which human societies were confined to work out their destinies in conflict or cooperation. Nation-states and empires are historical examples of the expansive tendencies described by circum-scription theory. For the planet, however, a new and different form of polity seems necessary. Barring space colonization, the planet is the final circumscribing boundary and the choice for civilized survival may ultimately be between a cooperative international planetary polity or some form of world empire.

Common to these theories and hypotheses is the assumption of an ultimate consistency in nature which science must simulate if the larger issues of evolution and cosmology are to be more fully comprehended. A reunification of science at the highest philosophical levels has been urged by Stephen Toulmin in *The Return to Cosmology: Postmodern Science and the Theology of Nature* (1982), and by Gerard Radnitzky and others in *Centripetal Forces In The Sciences* (1987). Environmental theory in its most profound sense is no less than man's relationship to the cosmos and from this relationship the foundations for both ethical and higher political principles may be discovered. Prigogine and Stengers (1984) conclude:

...that we are at a moment both of profound change in the scientific concept of nature and of the structure of human society as a result of the demographic explosion. As a result, there is a need for new relations between man and nature and between man and man. We can no longer accept the old a priori distinction between scientific and ethical values.[2]

The foregoing views seem consistent with the thesis advanced by Richard H. Schlagel in *Contextual Realism: A Metaphysical Framework for Modern Science* (1986). He writes 'that all experience and knowledge are relative to various contexts, whether physical, historical, cultural, or linguistic, and as the contexts change, so do the perspectives one has on these problems.'[3] Modern science being the major force in transforming its own cultural context is now being transformed by that context. Whatever the weaknesses of interdisciplinary and environmental science, they represent a move toward synthesis that will be inevitable if the sciences are not to find their advancement blocked in the box canyons of specialization. Albert Einstein saw in the fragmented state of the science establishment its inability to help in solving current societal problems, a role, he believed, in which science 'could exert an important and salutary moral influence upon the management of politics.'[4] To realize this idealistic hope the ethos of professional science would surely require change, and the gaps between the social, behavioral, and physical sciences would have to be narrowed.

As the twentieth century draws to a close, people sensitive to the times are wandering between past and future, but seldom understanding their feeling of anomaly. In this condition of societal aimlessness, the environmental movement is conspicuous for its sense of purpose, however limited. In a general sense, environmentalism has an agenda for the future that would change national priorities, international relations, and basic assumptions regarding man's place in nature. Dedicated environmentalists are seldom immobilized by doubt or indecision. They see a viable and sustainable relationship with nature as a necessary condition for the advancement and perhaps the survival of human life on Earth. Old-order advocates of salvation through growth, paradoxically, view environmentalism as negative and recessive, as sacrificing progress to stagnation. Environmentalists, on the other hand, see their goals as positive and indeed necessary for a sustainable high-level quality of life. Meanwhile, within the larger society, there is pervasive confusion over purposes and priorities, and there appears to be no positive consensus as to a preferred state of the environment in the future.

Is there a pattern or trend discernible in this chaotic present if examined in the light of environmental science and social psychology? Through a scattering of opinion studies we have intimations of a changing environmental paradigm, but the evidence is yet too sketchy to be conclusive.

Since modern science began in the century of Francis Bacon many observers of human behavior, especially technological optimists, have believed 'that humanity can and must produce a deliberate design for its own future.'[5] The ecological imperatives of the present transition have changed the rationale for this admonition. The need for designing a future is no longer to achieve dominion over all nature, but to achieve a sustainable and productive relationship with the natural world that will require the self-governance and restraint of human nature.

Frequently noted among the characteristics of our end-of-the-century society is a widespread state of anomie, especially evident in advanced industrial countries. Anomie is a social condition 'in which the normative standards of conduct and belief have weakened or disappeared.' In individuals it is characterized by personal disorientation, anxiety, and social isolation – and appears in the idiosyncrasy and obscurantism found by many people in personal lifestyles, literature, and the fine arts. Art – even when public – frequently expresses the inner private world of the artist, but in a state of anomie it offers no prospect beyond a rejected present. In the absence of anything to say to the world in substance, technical achievement has become the goal of artistic creativity for many painters, poets, dramatists and composers.

The decline of the old authorities is evident almost everywhere. Ours is a libertarian age in which freedom, liberation, self-expression, and rights of all kinds are vigorously asserted and defended. Freedom, undefined, appears to be the most widespread generalized goal of our time – and the personal freedom most sought for appears to be freedom to realize one's own individual identity. Very often, however, this freedom is expressed in self-centered behavior that appears to deny meaningful relationships with the larger humanity and with nature. In effect this introverted effort primarily seeks freedom from responsibility. This freedom does not comport well with the attitudes expressed through environmentalism or the requisites for survival discovered through science. Claims to unspecified freedoms have been asserted time and again during the demolishing phases of social revolutions: the United States of America, France, and Russia provide examples. But invariably the libertarian phase of social change has been followed by new authoritative controls – often more pervasive than the old. Will such a sequence characterize what Max Nicholson (1970) has called *The Environmental Revolution*? I believe that, in certain respects, it may, and that an environmental regimen may be more easily borne but less easily resisted than the regimen of the old industrialism. It may be less easily resisted because it is planetary imperative, not human fiat, that is the authority.

One interpretation of the two worlds metaphor is the replacement of a social system based on the authority of status, by one governed to a far greater extent by the authority of knowledge (e.g. the imperatives of nature). The libertarian explosion, in this interpretation, occupies an interlude between the dying (i.e. transformation) of the old world and the birth of the new. This does not necessarily imply a transition from less freedom to more freedom to less freedom – nonetheless some traditional freedoms may disappear and some new freedoms arise; especially freedom from many of the behaviors and conditions that have diminished or destroyed the quality of life for people, past and present.

What the future of man on Earth will be (cosmos permitting) depends upon the yet to be tested capabilities of the human mind. A critical part of this testing will occur in the growth and evaluation of knowledge, much of which will be gained through the processes that we call science. If history is a reliable indicator, the science of the future will have characteristics in content, scope, and method beyond those now present, with the place of interscience and synthesis in scientific interpretation becoming more important.

Insofar as mankind can safeguard its own survival, understanding its own behavior in relation to its environment is critical. This critical knowledge must link behavior and environment in scientific inquiry as they are inextricably linked in the biosphere. The role of science in this task is to enlarge understanding which, internalized beyond mere knowing, leads to social choices and action. Science does not apply this knowledge – society does – and makes its choices in the light of understanding that is derived in part from science but is also influenced by moral and emotive values beyond the realm of science. The development of knowledge in coping with problems of behavior and environment thus brings humans into direct confrontation with a fundamental question of political choice: what weights should be given to the freedom of the individual and to the welfare of society in a post-modern age?

For most people, if the choices are understood, more freedoms may seem to be protected or extended than lost. Environmental dangers and deterioration affect the welfare, health, and quality of life of all people. Yet a critical situation might arise if many people perceive a serious environmental threat but many more do not. Such circumstances might lead to a reinterpretation of democratic governance. The option to choose between individual and societal freedoms may be more apparent than real; not choice but necessity may govern.

Similarly, to choose between national and international or global governance need not imply a general loss of national self-determination. No national government has ever successfully controlled all aspects of society even though some have tried. A world polity would be workable only if restricted to those adversities that required worldwide protective action and had a similar or significant effect upon everyone everywhere. Even the greatest states are unable unilaterally to protect their people from a growing number of environmental threats. Freedom *from* may be as important to people as freedom *for*. Thus it may be shortsighted to regard as utopian and hence impractical unprecedented developments that people may accept in response to unprecedented dangers, such as depletion of the ozone layer or worldwide climate change.

Environmentalists may well be the vanguard of a post-modern age in which environmentalism itself will disappear because it will have become the pervasive and prevailing way of life. This possibility should not be taken as a utopian forecast of a problem-free world, nor one necessarily at peace with itself. Mutual coercion, mutually agreed upon, may be required to the extent that humans do not, or cannot, muster the restraint needed to keep themselves and others from involuntary risk and irreversible hazard. Should a new ecologically-based social order emerge as a consequence of a world disaster of catastrophic proportions, the authority of knowledge might require implementation through iron government until such time as sustainable conditions were restored. Catastrophic change is indeed already in progress today, but its disastrous consequences might possibly be blunted by timely action to arrest the destructive behaviors that are plainly evident throughout the world.

Today we can believe in the possibility of a world that may be better – but not in its certainty. Whether humans in sufficient numbers and in time will make the choices required for a sustainable and sanative future remains to be seen. The odds are unknown, but a reason for hope lies in the demonstrated capacity of humans to learn and, when necessary, to learn quickly. The world's resources of information and communication are sufficient to the task of conceptual transformation. It is only the purposeful consensus and the will to action that are lacking.

The crisis of our times grows out of our perverse reluctance to accept the judgment of history on the modern world, and to take up the difficult task of making the changes in attitudes, behaviors, and institutions required for the transition to an enduring and endurable future. It is a crisis of will and rationality – and its outcome remains uncertain.

QUOTATIONS

1. M. Arnold (1903). *The Works of Matthew Arnold: Fifteen Volumes* I. London: Macmillan, p. 289.
2. I. Prigogine & I. Stengers (1984). *Order Out of Chaos: Man's New Dialogue with Nature.* Boulder, Colorado: New Science Library, p. 312.
3. R. H. Schlagel (1986). *Contextual Realism: A Meta-physical Framework for Modern Science.* New York: Paragon House, pp. xxxi–iv.
4. R. Maheu, et al. (1965). *Science and Synthesis: An International Colloquium organized by UNESCO on the Tenth Anniversary of the Death of Albert Einstein and Teilhard de Chardin.* New York: Springer-Verlag.
5. R. Moss & R. Brownstein (1977). *Environment and Utopia: A Synthesis.* New York: Plenum, p. 267.

References

Between Two Worlds is an analysis and interpretation of concepts and trends – not a report on scientific research. Publications relevant to the range of subjects touched upon in this book greatly exceed the references cited here, which include items relating to some specific point made in the text and selected materials of more general character. References to quoted passages previously cited in the text are not necessarily repeated. This is not a bibliography of the subject-matter of the book and does not list many of the 'classics' with which there is widespread familiarity. A comprehensive coverage of published work pertaining to its subject matter could easily have required another book. Many of the citations, including some by this author, direct the reader to fuller treatment of points of fact or interpretation, and many of these works contain extensive bibliographies. To some extent the selection has been arbitrary because it does not list all of the publications from which the author has benefited. To have included them all would not have been feasible and so I have tried to limit the number to those that seemed to me would be most likely to help the reader of this book.

Adede, A. O. (1987). *The IAEA Notification and Assistance Conventions in Case of a Nuclear Accident: Landmarks in the History of the Multilateral Treaty-Making Process.* London: Graham & Trotman.

Adler, C. A. (1973). *Ecological Fantasies: Death from Falling Watermelons, A Defense of Innovations, Science and Rational Approaches to Environmental Problems.* New York: Dell.

Ahmed, I. (1988). The Bio-revolution in agriculture: key to poverty alleviation in the Third World? *International Labor Review* 127 (No. 1): 52–72.

Allaby, M. (1976). *Inventing Tomorrow.* London: Hodder and Stoughton.

Allen, R. (1980). *How To Save the World: Strategy for World Conservation.* Totowa, New Jersey: Barnes & Noble.

Amy, D. J. (1987). *The Politics of Environmental Mediation.* New York: Columbia University Press.

Anderson, W. T. (1987). *To Govern Evolution: Further Adventures of the Political Animal.* Boston: Harcourt Brace Jovanovich.

Anglemyer, M. & Seagraves, E. R. (1984). *The Natural Environment: An Annotated Bibliography on Attitudes and Values.* Washington DC: Smithsonian Institution Press.

Ashby, E. (1978). *Reconciling Man with the Environment.* Stanford, California: Stanford University Press.

Bailes, K. E. (1981). Science, philosophy, and politics in Soviet history: the case of Vladimir Vernadskii. *Russian Review* 40: 278–99.

Bakberis, J. (1987). *International Groundwater Resources Law.* (FAO, Legislative Studies, No. 40). Rome: FAO.

Barbier, E. B. (1987). The concept of sustainable economic development, *Environmental Conservation* (No. 2, Summer): 14.

Barker, R. G. (1968). *Ecological Psychology: Concepts and Methods for Studying the Environment of Human Behavior.* Stanford, California: Stanford University Press.

Barnard, C. J. (1983). *Animal Behavior: Ecology and Evaluation.* New York: John Wiley.

Barney, G. O. (ed.) (1980). Analysis of the projection tools: other global models, *The Global 2000 Report to the President* Vol. 2, Technical Report. Washington, DC: US Government Printing Office.

Barrett, R. N. (ed.) (1982). *International Dimensions of the Environmental Crisis.* Boulder, Colorado: Westview Press.

Bartlett, R. V. (1986). Ecological Rationality: Reason and environmental policy. *Environmental Ethics* 8 (Fall): 221–39.

Batisse, M. (1980). The relevance of MAB. *Environmental Conservation* 7 (Winter): 179–84.

Batisse, M. (1982). The future of MAB. *Environmental Conservation* 9 (Spring): 71–2.

Beckerman, W. (1972). Economic development and the environment: a false dilemma. *Environment and Development.* Ed. P. Rambach. New York: Carnegie Endowment for International Peace International Conciliation No. 586, 51–71.

Beckerman, W. (1974). *In Defense of Economic Growth.* London: Johnathon Cape.

Bernard, C. (1957). *An Introduction to the Study of Experimental Medicine.* Trans. from French by H. C. Greene. New York: Dover. (First published in 1865).

Bilder, R. B. (1980). International law and natural resources policies. *Natural Resources Journal* 20 (No. 3, July 1980): 451–86.

Blum, H. F. (1962). *Time's Arrow and Evolution.* New York: Harper & Brothers.

Boardman, R. (1981). *International Organization and the Conservation of Nature.* Bloomington, Indiana: Indiana University Press.

Bolin, B. et al. (eds.) (1986). *The Greenhouse Effect, Climate Change and Ecosystems* (SCOPE 29). New York: John Wiley.

Bolin, B. & Cook (eds.) (1983). *The Major Biogeochemical Cycles and Their Interactions* (SCOPE 21). New York: John Wiley.

Boulding, K. E. (1985). *The World as a Total System.* Beverly Hills, California: Sage.

Boulding, K. E. (1981). *Ecodynamics: A New Theory of Societal Evolution.* Beverly Hills, California: Sage.

Bowen, R. (1986). *Groundwater.* New York: Elsevier.

Brady, N. D. (ed.) (1967). *Agriculture and the Quality of Our Environment: A Symposium Presented at the 133rd Meeting of the American Association for the Advancement of Science.* Washington DC: American Association for the Advancement of Science.

Bremer, S. A. (ed.) (1987). *The Globus Model.* Boulder, Colorado: Westview Press.

Brinton, C. (1938). *The Anatomy of Revolution.* New York: W. W. Norton.

Brower, K. (1980). Environmental vigilante. *Atlantic Monthly* **246** (November): 65–8.

Brown, H. (1986). *The Wisdom of Science: Its Relevance to Culture & Religion*. Cambridge: Cambridge University Press.

Brown, L. (1981). *Building a Sustainable Society*. New York: W. W. Norton.

Bryson, R. A. (1971). Climatic modification by air pollution. *The Environmental Future: Proceedings of the First International Conference on Environmental Future*. Held in Finland from 27 June to 3 July 1971. Ed. N. Polunin. New York: Barnes & Nobel, pp. 133–55.

Brzezinski, Z. (1970). *Between Two Ages: America's Role in the Technetronic Era*. New York: Viking. (Reprinted 1982).

Buckminster Fuller, R. (1969). *Operating Manual for Spaceship Earth*. Carbondale, Illinois: Southern Illinois University Press. (Reprinted by Simon & Schuster, New York, 1969).

Burhenne, W. E. & Irwin, W. A. (1983). *The World Charter for Nature: A Background Paper*. Berlin: Erich Schmidt, (2nd ed. 1986).

Burton, I. & Kates, R. W. (1986). The great climacteric, 1798–2048: the transition to a just and sustainable environment. *Geography, Resources and Environment: Vol. II, Themes from the Work of Gilbert White*. Chicago: University of Chicago Press, pp. 339–60.

Burton, I., Kates, R. W. & White, G. F. (1978). *The Environment as Hazard*. New York: Oxford University Press.

Buttell, F. H. & Larson, O. L., III. (1980). Whither environmentalism? The future political path of the environmental movement. *Natural Resources Journal* **20** (No. 2, April 1980): 323–44.

Caldwell, L. K. (1984). Environmental studies: discipline or metadiscipline? *Environmental Professional* **5** (Nos. 3–4): 247–59.

Caldwell, L. K. (1984). *International Environmental Policy: Emergence and Dimensions*. Durham, North Carolina: Duke University Press. (Contains extensive annotation and references).

Caldwell, L. K. (1982). *Science and the National Environmental Policy Act: Redirecting Policy Through Procedural Reform*. Alabama: University of Alabama Press. See Bibliographical Note, pp. 168–71.

Caldwell, L. K. (1972). An Ecological Approach to International Development: Problems of Policy and Administration. *The Careless Technology: Ecology and International Development*. M. T. Farvar & J. P. Milton (ed). Garden City, New York: Natural History Press, pp. 927–47.

Caldwell, L. K. (1972). *In Defense of Earth: International Protection of the Biosphere*. Bloomington, Indiana: Indiana University Press.

Calhoun, J. B. (1963). *The Ecology and Sociology of the Norway Rat*. Bethesda, Maryland: National Institute of Mental Health.

Canada Law Reform Commission (1985). *Crimes Against the Environment*. Working Paper 44. Ottawa: The Commission.

Canadian Environmental Advisory Council (1987). *Canada and Sustainable Development*. Ottawa: Minister of Supply & Services.

Cano, G. J. (1975). *A Legal and Institutional Framework for Natural Resources Management*. (FAO Legislative Studies No. 9). Rome: Food and Agriculture Organization.

Cano, G. J. (1980). Frontier underground waters. *Water International.* (Official Journal of the International Water Resources Association) 5 (No. 2, June): 7–9.

Caponera, D. A. (1980). *The Law of International Water Resources: Some General Conventions, Declarations and Resolutions adopted by Governments, International Legal Institutions and International Organizations, on the Management of International Water Resources.* (FAO, Legislative Studies No. 23) Rome: Food and Agriculture Organisation.

Capra, F. (1984). *The Turning Point: Science, Society, and the Rising Culture.* New York: Simon & Schuster.

Capra, F. & Spretnak, C. (1984/1986). *Green Politics.* (Rev. ed.) Santa Fe, New Mexico: Bear (1986); New York: Dutton (1984).

Carneiro, R. L. (1970). A theory of the origin of the state…a new ecological hypothesis. *Science* 169 (21 August 1976): 733–38.

Carpenter, R. A. (1983). Ecology in court, and other disappointments of environmental science and environmental law. *Natural Resources Lawyer* 15 (No. 3, 1983): 573–95. See also Commentary: Law, Science and NEPA, 597–618.

Carpenter, R. A. (ed.) (1983). *Natural Systems for Development: What Planners Need to Know.* New York: Macmillan.

Carpenter, R. A. (1976). The Scientific Basis of NEPA – Is it Adequate? *Environmental Law Reporter* 6: 500–14.

Carroll, J. E. (ed.) (1988). *International Environmental Diplomacy.* Cambridge: Cambridge University Press.

Carter, V. G. & Dale, T. (1974). *Topsoil and Civilization.* (Rev. ed.) Norman, Oklahoma: University of Oklahoma Press.

Catton, W. R. Jr. (1980). *Overshoot: The Ecological Basis of Revolutionary Change.* Urbana, Illinois: University of Illinois Press.

Chen, Kan, Lagler, K. F., et. al. (1974). *Growth Policy: Population, Environment and Beyond.* Ann Arbor: University of Michigan Press.

Child, J. (1987). Antarctica: Issues and Options. *Marine Policy Reports* 10 (No. 1, September): 1–5.

Chorley, R. J. (comp.) (1969). *Water, Earth & Man: A Synthesis of Hydrology, Geomorphology and Socio-economic Geography.* London: Methuen.

Claus, G. & Bolander, K. (1977). *Ecological Sanity: A Critical Examination of Bad Science, Good Intentions and Premature Doomsday Announcements of the Ecology Lobby.* New York: David McKay.

Cormick, G. W. & Knastor, A. (1986). Mediation and scientific issues: oil and fishing industries negotiate. *Environment* 28 (No. 10, December): 6–15, 30.

Cotgrove, S. (1982). *Catastrophe or Cornucopia: Environment, Politics and the Future.* New York: John Wiley.

Clark, W. C., et. al. (1989). Managing Planet Earth, *Scientific American* 261 (No. 3, September): whole issue.

Clark, W. C. and Munn, R. E. (eds.) (1986). *Sustainable Development of the Biosphere.* Cambridge: Cambridge University Press for the International Institute for Applied Systems Analysis.

Clarke, Robin (1985). *Science and Technology in World Development.* Oxford: Oxford University Press/UNESCO.

Cole, L. C. (1958). The ecosphere. *Scientific American* **198** (April): 83–92.

Cole, S. D., Freeman, C., Johoda, M. & Pavitt, K. L. R. (eds.) (1973). *Models of Doom, A Critique of The Limits of Growth.* Universe Books.

Corning, P. (1983). *The Synergism Hypothesis.* New York: McGraw-Hill.

Cowen, R. C. (1988). The rise of eco-diplomacy. *Technology Review* **91** (No. 4, May–June): 18.

Crosson, P. (1986). Agricultural development – looking to the future. Clark & Munn *op. cit.*, pp. 104–36.

Curtis, R. K. (1982). *Evolution or Extinction, The Choice Before Us.* New York: Pergamon Press.

Cutrera, A. (ed.) (1987). *European Environmental Yearbook 1987.* London: DocTer International.

d'Arge, R. C. & Kneese, A. V. (1980). State liability for international environmental degradation: an economic perspective. *National Resources Journal* **20** (No. 3, July 1980): 427–50.

Dahlberg, K. A. (1979). *Beyond the Green Revolution: the Ecology and Politics of Global Agricultural Development.* New York: Plenum.

Dahlberg, K. A. & Bennett, J. W. (eds.) (1986). *Natural Resources and People.* Boulder, Colorado: Westview Press.

Dahlberg, K. A., Feraru, A. T. & Soroos, M. S. (eds.) (1983). *Environment and the Global Arena: Actors, Values, Policies, Futures.* New York: Holt, Rinehart & Winston.

Daly, H. (1977). *Steady State Economics: The Economics of Biophysical Equilibrium and Moral Growth.* San Francisco: W. H. Freeman.

Dasmann, R. F., Milton, J. P. & Freeman, P. H. (1973). *Ecological Principles for Economic Development.* New York: John Wiley for the International Union for Conservation of Nature and Natural Resources (IUCN) and the Conservation Foundation.

Davis, T. J. & Schirmer, I. (eds.) (1987). Sustainability, policies, natural resources and institutions. *Report of the World Bank Workshop on Sustainability Issues in Agriculture.* Proceedings of the Seventh Agriculture Sector Symposium. Washington DC: World Bank. Note paper by W. D. Hopper, pp. 5–16.

Deutsch, K. W. (ed.) (1977). *Ecosocial Systems and Ecopolitics: A Reader on Human and Social Implications of Environmental Management in Developing Countries.* Paris: UNESCO.

Devall, B. & Sessions, G. (1985). *Deep Ecology.* Salt Lake City, Utah: G. M. Smith.

di Castri, F., Hadley, M. & Damlamian, J. (1981). MAB: The man and the biosphere program as an evolving system. In *Ambio* **10** (Nos. 2–3): pp. 52–7.

Dinwoode, D. H. (1972). The politics of international pollution control: the Trail Smelter Case. *International Journal* **27** (Spring 1972): 219–35.

Dorfman, R. (1987). *Protecting the Global Environment: An Immodest Proposal.* Cambridge, Massachusetts: Harvard University, Harvard Institute of Economic Research (Discussion Paper 1357).

Dorst, J. (1970). *Before Nature Dies.* Boston: Houghton Mifflin.

Douglass, G. (ed.) (1984). *Agricultural Sustainability in a Changing World Order.* Boulder, Colorado: Westview Press.

Draggan, S., Cohrssen, J. & Morrison, R. E. (ed.) (1987). *Preserving Ecological Systems.* Praeger.

Dror, Y. (1971). *Crazy States: A Counterconventional Strategic Problem.* Lexington, Massachusetts: Heath Lexington.

Dryzek, J. S. (1987). *Ecology: Environment and Political Economy.* Oxford: Basil Blackwell.

Dubos, R. (1980). *The Wooing of the Earth.* New York: Scribner.

Dubos, R. (1969). *A Theology of the Earth.* (Lecture delivered on 2 October 1969 under sponsorship of the Smithsonian Office of Environmental Sciences). Washington: Smithsonian Institution.

Dubos, R. (1965). *Man Adapting.* New Haven, Connecticut: Yale University Press.

Dunlap, R. E. (1987). Polls, pollution and politics revisited – public opinion on the environment in the Reagan era. *Environment* 29 (July–August), 6–11, 32–7.

Dunlap, R. E. & Van Liere, K. D. (1978). The environmental-paradigm. *Journal of Environmental Education* 9 (No. 4, Summer), 10–19.

Dwivedi, O. P. (1986). Political science and the environment. *International Social Science Journal* 38 (No. 3, September 1986), 377–90. Note other articles in this issue relating to environmental awareness.

Dworkin, D. M. (1974). *Environment and Development: Collected Papers, Summary Reports and Recommendations.* SCOPE/UNEP Symposium on Environmental Sciences in Developing Countries, Nairobi, February 11–23, 1974. Indianapolis, Indiana: SCOPE Miscellaneous Publication.

Ehrenfeld, D. W. (1978). *The Arrogance of Humanism.* New York: Oxford University Press.

Ehrlich, P. (1986). *The Machinery of Nature.* New York: Simon & Schuster.

Ehrlich, P. & Ehrlich, A. (1981). *Extinction: The Causes and Consequences of the Disappearance of Species.* New York: Random House.

El-Hinnawe, E. & Hashmi, M. H. (eds.) (1982). *Global Environmental Issues.* Dublin: Tycooly International, published for United Nations Environment Programme.

Elkins, P. (ed.) (1986). *The Living Economy: A New Economics in the Making.* London: Routledge Kegan Paul.

Ellul, J. (1964). *The Technological Society.* Trans. from French by J. Wilkinson. New York: A. A. Knopf.

Engles, F. (1940). *Dialectics of Nature.* Trans. & ed. by C. Dutt. New York: International Publishers (First published in German in 1898).

Esser, A. H. (ed.) (1971). *Behavior and Environment: The Use of Space by Animals or Men.* New York: Plenum Press.

Etzioni, A. (1970). The wrong top priority (editorial). *Science* 168 (22 May 1970), 921.

Falk, R. (1971). *This Endangered Planet: Prospects and Proposals for Human Survival.* New York: Random House.

Falk, R. (1989). *Revitalizing International Law.* Ames, Iowa: Iowa State University Press.

Farrell, K. (1985). Our policies have been strong incentives for producers to employ technologies that sometimes have adverse environmental effects. *Ceres* 18 (No. 6, November–December), 44. An interview by Peter Hendry.

Farvar, M. T. & Milton, J. P. (eds.) (1972). *The Careless Technology: Ecology and International Development.* Garden City, New York: Natural History Press.

Federov, E. K. (1963). Science and technology for development. *Report of the United*

Nations Conference on the Application of Science and Technology for the Benefit of the Less-Developed Areas. Vol. 8. Plenary Proceedings. New York: United Nations, p. 70.

Feld, W. (1972). *Nongovernmental Forces and World Politics: A Study of Business, Labor, and Political Groups.* New York: Praeger Publishers (Praeger Special Studies in International Politics and Public Affairs).

Flinterman, C., Kwiatkowska & Lammers, J. (eds.) (1986). *Transboundary Air Pollution: International Legal Aspects of the Cooperation of States.* Dordrecht, Netherlands: Martinus Nijhoff.

Forrester, J. W. (1971). *World Dynamics.* Cambridge, Massachusetts: Wright-Allen. (2nd ed. 1973).

Friedwald, E. M. (1948). *Man's Last Chance: A Survey of Political Creeds and Scientific Realities.* New York: Viking.

Furtado, J. I. (1986). *The future of tropical forests. Ecosystem Theory and Application.* Ed. N. Polunin. New York: John Wiley.

Gabor, D. (1972). *The Mature Society.* New York: Praeger.

Garvey, G. (1972). *Energy, Ecology, Economy.* New York: W. W. Norton.

George, F. H.(1970). *Science and the Crisis in Society.* London: Wiley-Interscience.

Georgescu-Roegen, N. (1971). *The Entropy Law and the Economic Process.* Cambridge, Massachusetts: Harvard University Press.

Glantz, M. H. (ed.) (1988). An Essay on the Interactions Between Climate and Society. *Paper prepared for the Conference on Human Demography and Natural Resources.* Hoover Institution, Stanford, California, 1–3 February 1989.

Gleick, J. (1987). *Chaos, Making A New Science.* New York: Viking.

Golley, F. B. (1987). Deep ecology from the perspective of environmental science. *Environmental Ethics* 9 (No. 1), 45–55.

Goldsmith, et. al. (eds.) (1972). *Blueprint for Survival: By Editors of The Ecologist.* Boston: Houghton Mifflin.

Goleman, D. (1987). Failing to recognize bias in science. *Technology Review* 27 (26 November–December), 26–7.

Grayson, M. J. & Shepard, T. R. (1973). *The Disaster Lobby; Prophets of Ecological Doom and Other Absurdities.* Chicago: Follett.

Gregory, W., (ed.) (1938). *International Congresses and Conferences 1840–1937: A Union List of their Publications available in the United States and Canada.* New York: H. W. Wilson. Reprinted 1980.

Grinevald, J. (1985). *The Forgotten Sources of the Concept of the Biosphere* (Some historical notes for the study of origins of a holistic concept). Geneva, Switzerland: Institute Universitaire d'Etudes due Developpement.

Haas, P. M. (1990). *Saving the Mediterranean: The Politics of International Environmental Cooperation.* New York: Columbia University Press.

Hardin, G. (1980). Limited world, limited rights, *Society* 17 (No. 4, May–June 1980), 5–8.

Hardin, G. (1969). Not peace but ecology. *Brookhaven Symposia In Biology* 22, pp. 151–61.

Hardin, G. (1970). To trouble a star: the case of intervention in nature. *Bulletin of the Atomic Scientists* 26 (January 1970), 17–20.

Hare, K. F. (1985). *Climate Variations, Drought and Desertification* (WMO-No. 653). Geneva: World Meteorological Organization.

Hart, S. L. (1980). The environmental movement: fulfillment of the Renaissance prophecy? *Natural Resources Journal* **20** (No. 3, July): 501–22.

Hayden, S. S. (1942). *International Protection of Wildlife*. New York: Columbia University Press.

Hayton, R. D. (1982). The law of international aquifers. *Natural Resources Journal* **22** (No. 1, January): 71–93.

Heilbronner, R. L. (1980). *An Inquiry into the Human Prospect: Updated and Reconsidered for the 1980s*. New York: W. W. Norton.

Henderson, L. J. (1913). *The Fitness of The Environment: An Inquiry Into the Biological Significance of the Properties of Matter*. New York: Macmillan.

Henrikson, A. K. (ed.) (1986). *Negotiating World Order: The Artisanship and Architecture of Global Diplomacy*. Wilmington. Delaware: Scholarly Resources Inc.

Hirsch, F. (1976). *Social Limits to Growth*. Cambridge, Massachusetts: Harvard University Press.

Holdgate, M. W. (1986). The reality of environmental policy. *Journal of the Royal Society of Arts* **135** (No. 5368, March), 310–23.

Holdgate, M. W., Kassas, M. & White, G. F. (eds.) (1987). *The World Environment 1972–1982: A Report by the United Nations Environment Programme*. Dublin: Tycooly International for the United Nations Environment Programme.

Horn, B. R. (1980). Environmental communication and education needs. *Science and Public Policy* **7** (No. 3), 175–85.

Horn, B. R. (1978). A general systems approach to transnational environmental communication (TEC) networks. In R. F. Ericson (ed.) (1978), *Avoiding Social Catastrophies and Maximizing Social Opportunities: The General Systems Challenge*. Washington, DC: Society for General Systems Research (pp. 502–11). Reprinted (1979) in *Approtech: Journal of the International Association for the Advancement of Appropriate Technology for Developing Countries* **2** (No. 2), 3–8.

Hughes, J. D. (1975). *Ecology in Ancient Civilizations*. Alburquerque, New Mexico: University of New Mexico Press.

Huntington, E. (1945). *Mainsprings of Civilization*. New York: John Wiley.

Hutchinson, G. E. (1970). The biosphere. *Scientific American* **223** (No. 3, September): 45–53.

Iltis, H. H., Loucks, O. & Andrews, P. (1970). Criteria for a optimum environment. *Bulletin of the Atomic Scientists* **26** (January), 2–26.

Inglehart, R. (1989). *Culture Shift in Advanced Industrial Society*. Princeton, New Jersey: Princeton University Press.

Inglehart, R. (1987). Value change in industrial societies. *American Political Science Review* **81** (no. 4, December), 1289–1303.

International Commission on Large Dams, United States Committee on Environmental Effects (1978). *Environmental Effects of Large Dams*. New York: American Society of Civil Engineers, 225 pp.

International Council of Scientific Unions; Scientific Committee on Problems of the Environment (1985–6). *Environmental Consequences of Nuclear War* 2 vols. Vol. I *Physical and Atmospheric Effects*. Prepared by A. B. Pittock (1986) 359 pp. Vol. II *Ecological and Agricultural Effects*. Prepared by M. A. Harwell & T. E. Hutchinson (1985) 523 pp.

International Geosphere-Biosphere Programme (IGBP) (1988). *A Plan of Action*.

Report prepared by the Special Committee for the IGBP, Stockholm, Sweden, 24–28 October 1988, Stockholm: IGBP Secretariat, Royal Swedish Academy of Sciences.

International Law Association (1985). Lammers, J. G., rapporteur. *Committee on Legal Aspects of Long Distance Air Pollution.* First (preliminary) report of the Committee. Report of the Sixty-first Conference, held at Paris, August 26th to September 1st, 1984. London: International Law Association.

International Law Association (1983). Rauschning, D., rapporteur. *Legal aspects of the conservation of the environment.* Report of the Committee. Report of the Sixtieth Conference, held at Montreal, August 29th to September 4th, 1982, London: International Law Association, pp. 157–182.

International Law Association (1983). *International water resources law.* Report of the Committee. Report of the Sixtieth Conference, held at Montreal, August 29th, 1982 to September 4, 1982. London: International Law Association, pp. 531–52.

International Law Association (1980). *International Water Resources Law; Committee report: Regulation of the flow of water courses.* Report of the Fifty Eighth Conference, held at Manila, August 27th, 1978 to September 2nd, 1978. London: International Law Association, pp. 221–37.

James, P. E. & Martin, G. J. (1972). *All Possible Worlds: A History of Geographical Ideas.* New York: J. Wiley & Sons. (2nd ed. 1981).

Jancar, B. (1987). *Environmental Management in the Soviet Union and Yugoslavia.* Durham, North Carolina: Duke University Press.

Johnson S. P. and Corcelle G. (1989). *The Environmental Policy of the European Communities,* London: Graham and Trotman.

Johnson, U. A. & Hardesty, W. A. (1971). *Economic Growth vs. the Environment.* Belmont, California: Wadsworth.

Johnston, T. D. & Pietrewicz, A. T. (1985). *Issues in the Ecological Study of Learning.* Hillsdale: Erlbaum Association. Note Chapter 11, Wolfgang M. Schleidt, 'Learning another description of the environment' and Chapter 12, Lincoln Groy, 'The environmental dimension that influences behavior.'

Joyner, C. C. (1987). The antarctic minerals negotiating process. *American Journal of International Law* **81** (No. 4, October 1987), 888–906.

Kahn, H. (1960). *On Thermonuclear War.* Princeton, New Jersey: Princeton University Press.

Kahn, H. & Simon, J. (eds.) (1984). *The Resourceful Earth: A Response to Global 2000.* New York: Basil Blackwell.

Kane, J. (1987). Mother Nature's Army: Guerrilla warfare comes to the American forest. *Esquire* (February 1987), 98–106.

Kassas, M. (1987). The three systems and mankind. *Environmental Policy and Law* **17** (Nos. 3/4, 1987), 119–22.

Kates, R. W., Ausubel, J. E. & Berberian, M. (1985). *Climate Impact Assessment: Studies on the Interaction of Climate and Society.* (SCOPE 27). New York: John Wiley for the Scientific Committee on Problems of the Environment, International Council of Scientific Unions.

Kay, D. A. & Jacobson, H. K. (eds.) (1983). *Environmental Protection: The International Dimension.* Totowa, New Jersey: Allanheld, Osman.

Kellert, S. R. (1986). Public understanding and appreciation of the biosphere reserve concept. *Environmental Conservation* **13** (No. 2, Summer), 101–5.

Kennedy, W. V. (1988). Environmental impact assessment in North America, Western Europe – what has worked where, how, and why? *International Environment Reporter* **11** (No. 4, 13 April 1988), 257–62.

Kerr, R. A. (1988). No longer willful, Gaia becomes respectable. *Science* **240** (22 April), 393–5.

Keys, D. (1982). *Earth at Omega: Passage to Planetization.* Boston: Branden Press.

Kiss, A. C., (ed.) (1982). *Selected Multilateral Treaties in the Field of the Environment.* United Nations Environment Programme, UNEP Reference Series 3.

Klopfer, P. H. & Hailman (1974). *An Introduction to Animal behavior: Ethology's First Century.* 2nd ed. Englewood Cliffs, New Jersey: Prentice-Hall.

Kloppenburg, J. R. (ed.) (1988). *Seeds and Sovereignty: The Use and Control of Genetic Plant Resources.* Durham, North Carolina: Duke University Press.

Klopsteg, P. E. (1966). Environmental Science (editorial) *Science* **152**, (29 April 1966).

Kovda, V. A. & Rozanov, B. C. (1987). XIII Congress of the International Society of Soil Science, Held in the Hamburg Center for International Congresses, Hamburg, Federal Republic of Germany, during 13–20 August, 1986. *Environmental Conservation* **14**, (No. 2, Summer), 182–3.

Kuwabara, S. (1984). *The Legal Regime of the Protection of the Mediterranean Against Pollution from Land-Based Sources.* Tycooly International.

Laszlo, E. & Bierman, J. (eds.) (1972). *Goals in a Global Community, Volume 2 – International Values and Goals Studies.* New York: Pergamon Press.

Laszlo, E. (1972). *The Systems View of the World.* New York: George Braziller.

Laszlo, E. (1989). Global Survival and the Responsibilities of Science. *Environmental Conservation* IIe (no. 2): 103–6.

Lea, H. (1942). *The Valor of Ignorance.* New York: Harper. (Original manuscript dated 1909).

Leventhal, H. J. (1974). Environmental decision-making and the role of the courts. *University of Pennsylvania Law Review* **122** (January 1974), 509–55.

Lewis, F. (1988). Foreign affairs: the next big crisis. *New York Times* (27 July 1988), 227.

Lewis, J. P. & Kallab, V. (eds.) (1986). *Development Strategy Reconsidered.* New Brunswick, New Jersey: Transaction Books.

Lewthwaite, G. R. (1966). Environmentalism and determinism: a search for clarification, *Annals of the Association of American Geographers* **56** (March), 1–23.

Likens, G. E. (1982). *Some Perceptions of the Major Biogeochemical Cycles.* (SCOPE 17). New York: John Wiley for the Scientific Committee on Problems of the Human Environment of the International Council of Scientific Unions.

Lockland, G. T. (1973). *Grow or Die: The Unifying Principle of Transformation.* New York: Random House. (Reprinted as authored by Ainsworth-Land by Wiley, New York 1986).

Lovejoy, A. O. (1936). *The Great Chain of Being: A Study of the History of an Idea.* Cambridge, Massachusetts: Harvard University Press.

Lovelock, J. E. (1979). *Gaia, A New Look at Life on Earth*. Oxford: Oxford University Press.

Lovins, A. B. (1975). *World Energy Strategies: Facts, Issues and Options*. Cambridge, Massachusetts: Ballinger.

Lowe, P. & Goyder, J. (1983). *Environmental Groups in Politics*. London: George Allen & Unwin.

Lundqvist, L. (1974). Do political structures matter in environmental politics? The case of air pollution control in Canada, Sweden, and the United States. *American Behavioral Scientist* **17** (May–June), 731–50.

Lundqvist, L. (19). Environmental quality and politics: some notes on political development in 'developed' countries. *Social Science Information* **12** (No. 2), 43–65.

Lynch, K. (1960/70). *The Image of the City*. Cambridge, Massachusetts: MIT Press.

Lyster,. S. (1985). *International Wildlife Law: An Analysis of Treaties Concerned with the Conservation of Wildlife*. Cambridge, Cambridgeshire: Grotius.

Maddox, J. (1972). *The Doomsday Syndrome*. New York: McGraw-Hill Book Company.

Malone, T. F. (1987). Mission to Planet Earth; Integrating Studies of Global Change. *Environment* **28** (No. 8). 6–11, 39–42.

Malone, T. F. & Roederer, J. G. (eds.) (1985). *Global Change*. Proceedings of International Council of Scientific Unions (ICSU), 20th General Assembly, Ottawa, Canada. Cambridge: Cambridge University Press for ICSU.

Marsh, G. P. (1864). *Man and Nature: or Physical Geography as Modified by Human Action*. New York: Scribner (Reprinted in 1965 by Harvard University Press with introduction by D. Lowenthal).

Martin, P. S. & Wright, H. E., Jr. (eds.) (1967). *Pleistocene Extinctions: The Search for a Cause*. New Haven, Connecticut: Yale University Press.

Martinez, V. H. (1987). Hacia la creación del sistema interamericano para la conservación de la naturaleza. Ambiente y Recursos Naturales 4 (No. 2 abril–junio), 12–34.

Matthews, O. P. (1984). *Water Resources, Geography & Law*. Washington DC: American Association of Geographers.

Maybury, R. (ed.) (1986). *Violent Forces of Nature*. Mt. Airy, Maryland: Lomond.

McConnell, G. (1985). The environmental movement: ambiguities and meanings. *Natural Resources Journal* 11 427–36.

McCormick, J. (1989). *Reclaiming Paradise: The Global Environment Movement*. Bloomington, Indiana: Indiana University Press.

McCuen, G. E. & Bender, D. L. (eds.) (1970). *The Ecology Controversy*. St. Paul, Minnesota: Greenhaven Press.

McKibben, W. (1989). *The End of Nature*. New York: Random House.

McLouglin, J. & Forster, M. J. (eds.) (1982). *The Law and Practice Relating to Pollution Control in the Member States of the European Communities*. Graham & Trotman for Commission of the European Communities.

McLuhan, M. (1963). *Understanding Media: The Extension of Man*. New York: McGraw-Hill.

McMillan, T. (1987). *Canada's Perspective on Global Environmental and Development*. Address before the UN General Assembly 19 October 1987. Ottawa: Environmental Canada.

McNeely, J. A. & Pitt, D. (eds.) (1985). *Culture and Conservation: The Human Dimension in Environmental Planning*. Beckenham, Kent: Croom Helm.

Meadows, D. H., et al. (1982). *Groping in the Dark: The First Decade of Global Modelling*. New York: Wiley.

Meadows, D. H. & Robinson, J. M. (1985). *The Electronic Oracle: Computer Models and Social Decisions*. New York: Wiley.

Meadows, D. H., et al. (1972). *The Limits to Growth*. New York: Universe Books.

Michael, D. N. (1968). *The Unprepared Society*. New York: Harper.

Milbrath, L. W. (1984). *Environmentalists: Vanguard for a New Society*. Albany, New York: New York State University Press.

Miller, D. C., Barfoot, J. L. Jr., & Planchon, P. (1970). *Power and Decision Making in Megalopolis, with Special Reference to Environmental Quality Problems*. Washington, DC: Resources for the Future.

Miller, J. P. (1963). The New Science. *New York Herald Tribune*. (Monday, September 2), p. 1.

Mishan, E. J. (1967). *The Cost of Economic Growth: The Price We Pay*. New York: Praeger.

Mitchell, B. (1988). Undermining Antarctica *Technology Review* 90 (No. 2, February-March), 50–7.

Mitchell, R. C. (1984). Public opinion and environmental politics in the 1970s and 1980s. *Environmental Policy in the 1980s: Reagan's New Agenda*. Washington: Congressional Quarterly Press, pp. 51–74.

Mooney, H. A. & Gordon, M. (eds) (1983). *Disturbance and Ecosystems: Components of Response. Ecological Studies* 44. Note especially pp. 201– and 99–116.

Moos, R. & Brownstein (1977). *Environment and Utopia: A Synthesis*. New York: Plenum.

Morone, J. G. & Woodhouse, E. J. (1986). *Averting Catastrophe: Strategies for Regulating Risky Technologies*. Berkeley, California: University of California Press.

Morrison, D. E. & Dunlap, R. E. (1986). Environmentalism and elitism: a conceptual and empirical analysis. *Environmental Management* 10 (No. 5, 1986): 581–9.

Muller, R. (1982). *New Genesis: Shaping a Global Spirituality*. New York: Doubleday.

Munro, R. D. & Lammers J. G. (eds.). (1987). *Environmental Protection and Sustainable Development: Legal Principles and Recommendations*. London: Graham & Trotman.

Murphy, E. G. (1967). *Governing Nature*. Chicago: Quadrangle.

Murphy, R. (1951). The decline of North Africa since the Roman occupation: climatic or human? *Annals of the Association of American Geographers* 41 (June), 116–32.

Myers, N. (ed.) (1985). *Gaia: An Atlas of Planetary Management*. New York: Doubleday Anchor.

Naess, A. (1973). The shallow and the deep, long-range ecology movement. *Inquiry* 16 (No. 1, Spring 1973), 95–100.

Nanda, V. P. (ed.) (1983). *World Climate Change: The Role of International Law and Institutions*. Boulder, Colorado: Westview.

National Aeronautics and Space Administration (NASA) (1988). *Earth System Science: A Program for Global Change*. Washington, DC: NASA.

National Coal Policy Project. (1978). *Where we Agree: Report of the National Coal Policy Project. Summary and Synthesis.* Washington DC: Georgetown University, Center for Strategic and International Studies.

National Research Council; Committee on the Applications of Ecological Theory to Environmental Problems (1986). *Ecological Knowledge and Environmental Problem-Solving.* Washington, DC: National Academy Press.

National Science Board (1971). *Environmental Science: Challenge for the Seventies.* Washington: National Science Foundation.

Neuhaus, R. (1971). *In Defense of People.* New York: Macmillan.

Nicholson, E. M. (1970). *The Environmental Revolution.* London: Hodder & Stoughton and New York: McGraw-Hill.

Nicholson, E. M. (1987). *The New Environmental Age.* Cambridge: Cambridge University Press.

Nicholson, J. M. (1984). Converging worlds: The implications of environmental events for the free market and foreign policy developments. *The Environmentalist* 4 (No. 2), 139–42.

Nisbet, R. (1982). *Prejudices: A Philosophical Dictionary.* Cambridge, Massachusetts: Harvard University Press.

North American Association for Environmental Education (1984). *International Perspective on Environmental Education, 1984 Conference.* Madison, Wisconsin: 1986.

Norton, Bryan G. (ed.) (1986). *The Preservation of Species: The Value of Ecological Diversity.* Princeton, New Jersey: Princeton University Press.

Nyhart, J. D. (1977). *Science, Technology and Judicial Decision-Making: An Exploratory Discussion.* Proceedings of a Conference on the Subject held in September 1977. Cambridge, Massachusetts: Sloan School of Management, Massachusetts Institute of Technology.

Office of Technology Assessment (OTA) (1982). *Global Models, World Futures and Public Policy: A Critique.* OTA-R-165 (Y3.T22/2:2G51) Washington DC: OTA.

Ophuls, W. (1977). *Ecology and the Politics of Scarcity: Prologue to a Political Theory of the Steady State.* San Francisco, California: W. H. Freeman.

Organization for Economic Cooperation and Development (1979). *Interfutures: Facing the Future, Mastering the Probable and Managing the Unpredictable.* Paris: OECD.

Organization for Economic Organization and Development (1986). *OECD and the Environment.* Paris: OECD.

O'Riordan, T. (1981). *Environmentalism.* London: Pion.

Orr, D. W. & Soroos, M. S. (eds). (1974). *The Global Predicament and World Order.* Chapel Hill, North Carolina: University of North Carolina Press.

O'Sullivan, P. (1986). *Geopolitics.* New York: St. Martin's Press.

Paehlke, R. C. (1989). *Environmentalism and the Future of Progressive Politics.* New Haven, Connecticut: Yale University Press.

Park, C. C. (ed.) (1986). *Environmental Policies, An International Review.* Beckenham, Kent: Croom Helm.

Parker, G. (1985). *Western Geopolitical Thought in the Twentieth Century.* London: Croom Helm.

Partridge, E. (ed.) (1981). *Responsibility to Future Generations: Environmental Ethics.* Buffalo, New York: Prometheus.

Passmore, J. (1980). *Man's Responsibility for Nature.* London: Duckworth.

Pavlovsky, E. N. (1966). *Natural Nidality of Transmissible Diseases: With Special Reference to the Landscape Epidemiology of Zooanthropnoses.* Trans. from Russian by F. K. Plaus Jr., ed. by N. D. Levin. Urbana, Illinois: University of Illinois Press.

Pepper, D. (1984). *The Social Roots of Modern Environmentalism.* Beckenham, Kent: Croom Helm.

Perry, J. S. (1986). Managing the World Environment and International Institutions. *Environment* **28** (No. 1, January–February), 10–15, 37–40.

Petulla, J. (1980). *American Environmentalism: Values, Tactics, Priorities.* College Station, Texas: Texas A & M Press.

Pewe, T. L. (ed.) (1981). *Desert Dust: Origin, Characteristics, and Effect on Man.* Boulder, Colorado: Geological Society of America.

Pirages, D. O. (1989). *Global Technopolitics: The International Politics of Technology and Resources.* Pacific Grove, California: Brooks-Cole.

Pirages, D. O. (1978). *The New Context for International Relations; Global Ecopolitics.* North Scituate, Massachusetts: Duxbury.

Platt, R. S. (1948). Environmentalism versus geography. *American Journal of Sociology* **536.** (No. 5, March): 351–8.

Polunin, N. (ed.) (1986). *Ecosystem Theory and application.* New York: John Wiley.

Polunin, N. (ed.) (1972). *The Environmental Future: Proceedings of the First International Conference on the Environmental Future.* Helsinki and Jyvaskyla, Finland, June 27–July 3, 1971. London: Macmillan; New York: Barnes & Noble.

Polunin, N. (ed.). (1980). *Growth Without Ecodisasters.* 2nd International Conference on Environmental Future. Reykjavik, Iceland 5–11 June, 1977. New York: John Wiley.

Pool, R. (1989). Ecologists flirt with Chaos. *Science* **243** (20 January), 310–13.

Powledge, F. W (1982). *Water: The Nature, Use & Future of Our Most Precious and Abused Resource.* New York: Farrar, Straus, Giroux.

Prigogine, I. & Stengers, I. (1984). *Order Out of Chaos, Man's New Dialogue with Nature.* Boulder, Colorado: New Science Library (distributed by Random House).

Radnitzky, G. (ed.) (1987). *Centripetal Forces in the Sciences: Approaches to the Unity of the Sciences.* New York: Paragon House.

Raghunath, H. M. (1987). *Groundwater.* 2nd ed. New York: John Wiley.

Ramphal, S. S. (1987). The environment and sustainable development. *Journal of the Royal Society of Arts* **135,** (No. 5376, November 1987), 879–909.

Raspail, J. (1975). *The Camp of the Saints.* Trans. from French by N. Shapiro. New York: Scribner.

Regan, T. (ed.) (1984). *Earthbound.* Philadelphia: Temple University Press.

Rehbinder, E. & Stewart, R. (1988). *Environmental Protection Policy: Legal Imperatives in the United States and the European Community.* New York: Walter De Gruyter.

Repetto, R. (ed.) (1985). *The Global Possible.* New Haven, Connecticut: Yale University Press.

Repetto, R. (1986). *World Enough and Time, Successful Strategies for Resource Management.* New Haven, Connecticut: Yale University Press.

Revel, J. F. (1971). *Without Marx or Jesus: The New American Revolution Has Begun.* Trans. from French by S. F. Bernard. New York: Doubleday.

Rheem, D. L. (1987). Environmental action: a movement comes of age. *Christian Science Monitor* (Tuesday 13 January 1987), 16–17.

Rhoades, S. E. (1985). *The Economists' View of the World: Government, Markets, and Public Policy.* Cambridge: Cambridge University Press.

Ricklefs, R. (1976). *The Economy of Nature.* Portland, Oregon: Chiron.

Riddell, R. (1981). *Ecodevelopment, Economics, Ecology and Development.* New York: St. Martin's Press.

Rüster, B., Simma, B. & Bock, M. (eds.) (1975–83). *International Protection of the Environment: Treaties and Related Documents.* 30 vols. Dobbs Ferry, New York: Oceana.

Rubin, S. J. & Graham, T. R. (1982). *Environment and Trade: The Relation of International Trade and Environmental Policy.* London: Frances Pinter.

Sagoff, M. (1988). *The Economy of The Earth: Philosophy, Law, and the Environment.* Cambridge: Cambridge University Press.

Sagoff, M. (1985). Fact and value in ecological science. *Environmental Ethics* 7 (Summer), 99–116.

Saltzman, A. (ed.) (1977). *Energy Technology and Global Policy.* Conference in Energy Policy and the International system. Santa Barbara, California: Clia Press.

Sandbach, F. (1980). *Environment: Ideology and Policy.* Oxford: Basil Blackwell.

Sandbrook, R. (1980). NGOs and the UNEP Council – governments no longer listen. *IUCN Bulletin* 11 (No. 6 June).

Sasson, A. (1988). *Biotechnologies and Development.* Paris: UNESCO.

Schindler, D. W. (1976). The impact statement boondoggle (editorial). *Science* 192 (7 May), 509.

Schlagel, R. H. (1986). *Contextual Realism: A Metaphysical Framework for Modern Science.* New York: Paragon House.

Schmookler, A. B. (1984). *The Parable of the Tribes: The Problem of Power in Social Evolution.* Berkeley, California: University of California Press.

Schneider, J. (1979). *World Public Order of the Environment: Toward an International Ecological Law and Organization.* Toronto: University of Toronto Press.

Schrader-Frechette, K. S. (1981). *Environmental Ethics.* Pacific Grove, California: Boxwood Press.

Serafin, R. (1988). Noosphere, Gaia, and science of the biosphere. *Environmental Ethics* 10, (No. 2): 121–37.

Sessions, G. (1987). The Deep Ecology Movement: A Review. *Environmental Review* II (No. 2, Summer), 105–25.

Shapley, D. (1985). *The Seventh Continent, Antarctica in a Resource Age.* Washington, DC: Resources for the Future.

Shepard, P. & McKinley, D. (comp.) (1969). *The Subversive Science: Essays Toward An Ecology of Man.* Boston: Houghton Mifflin.

Simon, J. L. (1981). *The Ultimate Resource.* Princeton, New Jersey: Princeton University Press.

Springer, A. L. (1983). *The International Law of Pollution, Protecting the Global*

Environment in a World of Sovereign States. Westport, Connecticut: Greenwood, Quorum Books.

Sprout, H. & Sprout, M. (1974). *Multiple Vulnerabilities: The Control of Environmental Repair and Protection*. Princeton, New Jersey: Princeton University, Center for International Studies 66. (Research Monograph No. 40).

Sprout, H. & Sprout, M. (1971). *Toward a Politics of the Planet Earth*. New York: Van Nostrand Reinhart.

Sprout, H. & Sprout, M. (1965). *Ecological Perspective on Human Affairs: With Special Reference to International Politics*. Princeton, New Jersey: Princeton University Press.

Stavrianos, L. S. (1976). *The Promise of the Coming Dark Age*. San Francisco: W. H. Freeman.

Storer, J. H. (1953). *The Web of Life: A First Book of Ecology*. New York Devin-Adair.

Stone, C. D. (1987). *Earth and Other Ethics: The Case for Moral Pluralism*. New York: Harper & Row.

Stone, C. D. (1975). *Should Trees Have Standing: Toward Legal Rights for Natural Objects*. New York: Avon.

Swaminathan, M. S. (1987). The emerging global agricultural scenario. *Journal of the Royal Society of Arts* **135**, (No. 5376, November 1987): 891–909.

Talbot, L. (1980). The world's conservation strategy. *Environmental Conservation* **7** (Winter): 259–68.

Talbott, R. E. (1978). Science court: a possible way to obtain scientific certainty for decisions based on scientific fact? *Environmental Law* **8** (Spring 1978): 827–50.

Taylor, P. W. (1986). *Respect for Nature: A Theory of Environmental Ethics*. Princeton, New Jersey: Princeton University Press.

Teclaff, L. A. & Utton, A. E. (eds.) (1981). *International Groundwater Law*. New York: Oceana.

Teilhard de Chardin, P. (1956). *The Phenomenon of Man*. Trans. from French by B. Wall, 94–5. London: Collins.

Thacher, P. S. (1987). International mechanisms and global changes. *Environmental Conservation* **14** (No. 3 Autumn): 191–3.

Theobald, R. & Mills, S. (eds.) (1973). *The Failure of Success: Ecological Values vs. Economic Myths*. Indianapolis, Indiana: Bobs-Merrill. Note Part I, Economists vs. ecologists and Part II, What do we mean by development?

Thomas, W. L., Jr. (ed.) (1956). *Man's Role in Changing the Face of the Earth*. Chicago: University of Chicago Press.

Tisdell, C. A. (1985). World conservation strategy, economic policies and sustainable resources in developing countries. *Environmental Professional* **7** (no. 2): 102–7.

Tisdell, C. A. (1989). Environmental Conservation: Economic, Ecology, and Ethics. *Environmental Conservation* **16** (no. 2): 107–12.

Tolba, M. K. (1987). *Sustainable Development, Constraints and Opportunities*. United Nations Environment Programme, London: Butterworth Scientific Publishers.

Tolba, M. K. (January 1986). Desertification. *WMO Bulletin* **35**: 17–22.

Tolba, M. K. (1982). *Development Without Destruction*. Dublin: Tycooly International.

Toth, F., Hizsnyik, E. & Clark, W. C., (eds.) (1989). *Scenarios of Socioeconomic*

Development for Studies of Global Environmental Change: A Critical Review. Laxenburg, Austria: International Institute for Applied Systems Analysis.

Toulmin, S. (1982). *The Return to Cosmology, Postmodern Science and The Theory of Nature.* Berkeley, California: University of California Press.

Trail Smelter Arbitral Tribunal. (1935). Decision: Reported on April 16, 1938, to the Government of the United States of America and to the Dominion of Canada under the Convention Signed April 15, 1935. *American Journal of International Law* 33 (No. 1, January 1939): 182–212.

Trigge, G. D. (1987). *The Antarctic Treaty Regime.* Cambridge: Cambridge University Press.

Tucker, W. (1982). *Progress and Privilege: America in the Age of Environmentalism.* Garden City, New York: Doubleday.

Turnbull, C. (1972). *The Mountain People.* New York: Simon & Schuster.

UNESCO (1969). *Final Report of the Inter-governmental Conference of Experts on the Scientific Basis for Rational Use and Conservation of the Biosphere.* 9 January 1969, Paris: UNESCO, p. 9.

United Nations (1977). *Report of the United Nations Water Conference.* Mar del Plata, 14–25 March 1977. New York: United Nations.

United Nations (1977). *Report of the United Nations Conference on Desertification.* Nairobi, 29 August–9 September, 1977, New York: United Nations.

United Nations Environment Programme (1984). *Activities of the United Nations Environment Program in the Combat Against Desertification.* Kenya, Nairobi: UNEP.

United Nations General Assembly (1974). United Nations Environment Programme – The Cocoyoc Declaration, 8–12 October, 1974. A/C.2/292, 1 November 1974.

United States Congress, Senate (1988). Hearing before the Committee on Energy and Natural Resources on *The Greenhouse Effect and Global Climate Change.* 9–10 November 1987, Part 1; 23 June 1988, Part 2. Note testimony of G. M. Woodwell on report of the Villach and Bellagio meetings, pp. 95–8.

United States, Department of State, Agency for International Development (AID), et al. (1981). *Proceedings of the US Strategy Conference on Biological Diversity.* November 16–18, 1981. Washington DC: AID.

United States, National Astronautic and Space Administration (NASA), Advisory Council (1986). *Earth System Science, Overview: A Program for Global Change.* Washington: NASA.

Urquhart, B. (1986). *The United Nations and International Law.* Cambridge: Cambridge University Press.

Utton, A. E. (1973). International environmental law and consultation mechanisms. *Columbia Journal of Transnation Law* 12 (No. 1): 56–72.

Vaihinger, H. (1924). *The Philosophy of As If: A System of the Theoretical Practical and Religious Fictions of Mankind.* Trans. from Germany by C. K. Ogden. New York: Harcourt, Brace.

Van Der Leeden (ed.) (1987). *Geraghty & Miller's Groundwater Bibliography,* 4th ed. Plainfield, New York: Water Information Center.

Van Lier, I. H. (1980). *Acid Rain and International Law.* Toronto: Bunsel Environmental Consultants.

Vayda, A. P. (ed.) (1969). *Environment and Cultural Behaviour: Ecological Studies in Cultural Anthropology.* Garden City, New York: Natural History Press.

Vernadsky, W. [V.] I. (1929). *La Biosphere.* Paris: Librarie Felix Alcan.

Vernadsky, W. [V.] I. (1945). The Biosphere and the Noönsphere. *American Scientist* 33 (January): 1-12.

Vickers, G. (1980). *Responsibility–Its Sources and Limits.* Seaside, California: Intersystems Publications.

Vickers, G. (1965). *The Art of Judgement: A Study of Policy Making.* London: Chapman & Hall.

Vicuña, F. O. (1988). Antarctic Mineral Exploration: *The Emerging Legal Framework.* Cambridge: Cambridge University Press.

Wandersman, A. and Hess, R. (eds.) (1985). *Beyond the Individual: Environmental Approaches and Prevention.* New York: Haworth.

Ward, B. & Dubos, R. (1972). *Only One Earth, The Care and Maintenance of a Small Planet.* Commissioned by Secretary-General of the United Nations Conference on Human Environment. New York: W. W. Norton.

Wattenberg, B. J. (1987). *The Birth Dearth.* New York: Pharos (Ballentine Books).

Wazeka, R. (1979). A world conservation strategy is launched. *Unasylva* 31 (No. 126): 39-41.

Weber, J. A. (1977). *Grow or Die!* New Rochelle, New York: Arlington House.

Wedderspoon, A. (1981). *Grow or Die: Essays on Church Growth to Mark the 900th Anniversary of Winchester Cathedral.* London: Society for Promoting Christian Knowledge.

Westing, A. H. (1989), (ed.) *Comprehensive Security for the Baltic: An Environmental Approach.* Oslo and Nairobi: International Peace Research and United Nations Environment Programme.

Westing, A. H. (1988). The Military Sector *vis-a-vis* the Environment. *Journal of Peace Research* 25 (No. 3, September): 257-64.

Westing, A. H. (1986). *Global Resources and International Conflict.* Oxford: Oxford University Press.

Westing, A. H. (1984). *Environmental Warfare: A Technical, Legal & Policy Appraisal.* London: Taylor & Francis.

Westing, A. H. (1980). *Warfare in a Fragile World: Military Impact on the Human Environment.* London: Taylor and Francis.

Westing, A. H. (1979). *Threat of Modern Welfare to Man and His Environment: An Annotated Bibliography.* Paris, UNESCO.

White, G. (1980). Environment. *Science* 209 (4 July 1980): 183-90.

White, L. Jr (1967). The historical roots of our ecological crisis. *Science* 155 (10 March) : 1203-7.

Wilkinson, R. G. (1973). *Poverty and Progress: An Ecological Perspective on Economic Development.* New York: Praeger.

Wilson, E. O. (ed.) (1988). *Biodiversity.* Washington, DC: National Academy Press.

Wolf, E. C. (1986). *Beyond the Green Revolution: New Approaches for Third World Agriculture.* Washington DC: World Watch Institute.

World Commission on Environment and Development (1987). *Our Common Future: Report of the Commission....* Oxford: Oxford University Press.

World Meterological Organization (WMO) (1988). *Developing Policies for Responding to Climate Change.* World Climate Programme Impact Studies: based on discussions and recommendations of workshops held in Villach (28 September–3 October 1987) and Billagio (9–13 November 1987). Genoa: WMO T.D.–No. 225.

World Meterological Organization (WMO) (1986). Possible climatic consequences of a large-scale nuclear war. *WMO Bulletin* **35** (No. 2 April): 134–8.

World Meterological Organization (WMO) (1986). Villach Conference Statement of UNEP/WMO/ICSU. The Role of Carbon Dioxide and Other Greenhouse Gasses in Climate Variations and Associated Impacts. *WMO Bulletin* **35** (April 1986): 130–4.

World Wildlife Fund (1986/87). *The New Road: Bulletin of the WWF Network on Conservation and Religion.* Gland, Switzerland: WWF International. Note also *The Assisi Declarations: Messages on Man & Nature from Buddhism, Christianity, Hinduism, Islam and Judaism,* and subsequent issues of *The New Road.*

Worster, D. (1987). The Vulnerable Earth: Toward a Planetary History. *Environmental Review* **11** (No. 2, Summer).

Wright, P. (1986). Poison catastrophe has lesson for every nation – devastating pollution of Rhine releases wave of recrimination across Western Europe. *The Times* (London), Overseas News (14 November 1986): 12.

Zeeman, E. C. (1976). Catastrophe Theory. *Scientific American* **234** (No. 4, April): 65–83.

Ziman, J. (1984). *An Introduction to Science Studies: The Philosophical and Social Aspects of Science and Technology.* Cambridge: Cambridge University Press.

Index

Index